SHAKESPEARE AND THE HUNT

Shakespeare and the Hunt is the first book-length study of Shakespeare's works in relation to the culture of the hunt in Elizabethan and Jacobean society. The book explores topics generally unfamiliar to Shakespeareans, such as the variety of kinds of hunting in the period, the formal rituals of the hunt, the roles of Queen Elizabeth and King James as hunters, the practice of organized poaching, and the arguments both for and against hunting. Situating Shakespeare's works in this rich cultural context, Berry illuminates the plays from fresh angles. He explores, for example, the role of poaching in *The Merry Wives of Windsor*; the paradox of pastoral hunting in *As You Like It*; the intertwining of hunting and politics in *The Tempest*; and the gendered language of falconry in *The Taming of the Shrew*.

EDWARD BERRY is Professor of English at the University of Victoria, British Columbia. His books include *Patterns of Decay: Shakespeare's Early Histories* (1975), *Shakespeare's Comic Rites* (Cambridge University Press, 1984) and *The Making of Sir Philip Sidney* (1998). He also co-edited *True Rites and Maimed Rites: Ritual and Anti-Ritual in Shakespeare and His Age* (1992).

D1581833

SHAKESPEARE AND THE HUNT

A Cultural and Social Study

EDWARD BERRY

CAMBRIDGE
UNIVERSITY PRESS

CAMBRIDGE UNIVERSITY PRESS
Cambridge, New York, Melbourne, Madrid, Cape Town, Singapore, São Paulo

Cambridge University Press
The Edinburgh Building, Cambridge CB2 2RU, UK

Published in the United States of America by Cambridge University Press, New York

www.cambridge.org
Information on this title: www.cambridge.org/9780521800709

First published 2001
This digitally printed first paperback version 2006

A catalogue record for this publication is available from the British Library

Library of Congress Cataloguing in Publication data
Berry, Edward I.
Shakespeare and the hunt: a cultural and social study/Edward Berry
p.   cm.
Includes bibliographical references and index
ISBN 0 521 80070 6 (hardback)
1. Shakespeare, William, 1564–1616 – Knowledge – Hunting. 2.
Hunting – England – History – 16th century. 3. Hunting – England – History – 17th century
4. Hunting in literature. I. Title
PR3069.H85 B47 2001
822.3′3 – dc21   00–063063

ISBN-13 978-0-521-80070-9 hardback
ISBN-10 0-521-80070-6 hardback

ISBN-13 978-0-521-03058-8 paperback
ISBN-10 0-521-03058-7 paperback

To Margaret

Contents

List of illustrations		*page* viii
Preface		ix
Glossary		xii

1　Introduction: the culture of the hunt and Shakespeare　1

2　Huntresses in *Venus and Adonis* and *Love's Labor's Lost*　38

3　"Solemn" hunting in *Titus Andronicus* and *Julius Caesar*　70

4　The "manning" of Katherine: falconry in *The Taming of the Shrew*　95

5　The "rascal" Falstaff in Windsor　133

6　Pastoral hunting in *As You Like It*　159

7　Political hunting: Prospero and James I　190

8　Conclusion: Shakespeare on the culture of the hunt　209

Notes　226
Index　251

Illustrations

1   Robert Peake, "Henry Frederick, Prince of Wales and   *page* 2
    Sir John Harington"(1603). Reproduced by permission of
    the Metropolitan Museum of Art

2   Queen Elizabeth at a hunt assembly. From [George
    Gascoigne], *The Noble Arte of Venerie or Hunting* (1575).
    Reproduced by permission of the Huntington Library   5

3   Queen Elizabeth taking the assay. From [George Gascoigne],
    The Noble Arte of Venerie or Hunting (1575). Reproduced by
    permission of the Huntington Library   6

4   Robert Peake, "Elizabeth of Bohemia"(1603). Reproduced
    by permission of the National Maritime Museum   7

5   Paul van Somer, "Anne of Denmark"(1617). Reproduced
    by permission of the Trustees of Lamport Hall   8

6   James I taking the assay. From [George Gascoigne], *The
    Noble Arte of Venerie or Hunting* (1611). Reproduced by
    permission of the Huntington Library   9

7   County map of Warwickshire (detail). From John Speed,
    The Theatre of the Empire of Great Britain (1611). Reproduced
    by permission of the Huntington Library   16

8   Devonshire Hunting Tapestry, 1435–50 (detail). Reproduced
    by permission of the Victoria and Albert Museum   33

9   Memorial brass of John Selwyn, underkeeper of the Royal
    Park of Oatlands, Surrey (*c.* 1587)   43

10 *Les Chasses de Maximilien: Décembre* (mid sixteenth-century).
    Reproduced by permission of the Louvre   46

Preface

The current controversies surrounding the sport of hunting in Britain and North America make it likely that a book on Shakespeare and the hunt will be greeted with suspicion by both proponents and opponents. To readers engaged in the controversies, I should say that, while I have never hunted and have no desire to do so, I am not a vegetarian or a principled opponent of the sport. To readers not engaged in the controversies, and for whom the problems of urban society might make such controversies seem marginal and trivial, I can only appeal to the prominence of the hunt in Elizabethan and Jacobean culture, to the extent of Shakespeare's imaginative involvement in it, and to the continuing significance of the issues – ethical, social, ecological – that surround the killing of animals for sport.

Although the subtitle represents this book as a "cultural and social study," I tend to include social structures within the broad concept of culture throughout. Hence I refer often to a culture of the hunt. Though inexact, the phrase allows me to imagine Elizabethan and Jacobean culture as in some sense a hunting culture, presided over by monarchs who spent much time in the field and for whom hunting was a ritualistic expression of socially pervasive royal power. It is also a notion that allows me to imagine the hunting "fraternity" as a sub-culture within the broad society as a whole – a sub-culture which might itself be divided into such overlapping but sometimes antagonistic groups as hunters and poachers. Finally, the word "culture" allows me to think of the hunt in a broad sense: as a social practice, a symbol, a ritual, a discourse, an ideology. My context for understanding Shakespeare's relationship to the hunt therefore includes the practice of the sport itself, handbooks of hunting, poems and plays, mythology, theology, politics, painting – in short, the entire apparatus of what we usually understand as culture. As with most subjects in the early modern period, the evidence that survives favors high culture over low.

Research into the early modern culture of the hunt poses special challenges. Eye-witness accounts of the sport are rare and sketchy.
Descriptions in the handbooks are not only incomplete but also inconsistent. The terminology of the sport, though wonderfully pedantic, is
imprecise. And there is little in the way of modern research into either
the practice of the hunt or its cultural significance. Hence I owe a special
debt of gratitude to previous scholarship in the field – in particular, to
D. H. Madden's odd but useful book, *The Diary of Master William Silence*
(London: Longmans, Green, 1907); to Richard Marienstras's *New
Perspectives on the Shakespearean World*, trans. Janet Lloyd (Cambridge:
Cambridge University Press, 1985); and, most significantly, to Roger B.
Manning's *Hunters and Poachers* (Oxford: Clarendon Press, 1993).

The book contains eight chapters and touches on nearly every major
Shakespearean allusion to hunting. Chapter 1 surveys the theory and
practice of the hunt in the period, introduces the major issues surrounding the sport, and suggests, in general, Shakespeare's relationship
to it. Chapter 2 examines hunting in *Venus and Adonis* and *Love's Labor's
Lost*, with particular attention to the paradoxes of female hunting
embodied in the figures of Venus and the Princess of France. Chapter 3
treats the ritual of the hunt as a context for tragedy in *Titus Andronicus*
and *Julius Caesar*. Chapter 4 offers a new interpretation of *The Taming of
the Shrew* by focusing on the implications of Petruchio's speech on taming
Katherine as a falcon and the prominence of the hunting lord in the
Induction. Chapter 5 surveys the comic career of Falstaff as both stag
and poacher from *1 Henry IV* to *The Merry Wives of Windsor*. Chapter 6
explores the paradox of pastoral hunting in *As You Like It*. Chapter 7
juxtaposes Prospero's hunt of Caliban in *The Tempest* with James I's
career as a hunter and the crisis brought on by his assertions of his royal
prerogative at the time in which the play was being written. Chapter 8
concludes the study with a brief overview of Shakespeare's conception
of hunting.

Throughout the study I quote Shakespeare from G. Blakemore Evans,
ed., *The Riverside Shakespeare*, 2nd edn. (Boston: Houghton Mifflin, 1997).
In quoting from old texts, I have normalized *u, v, i,* and *j* to conform with
modern practice. I deliberately use the gendered word "man" to represent "human-kind" throughout the work since replacing it with such
terms as "people" would tend to erase the patriarchal bias of the period.

I owe thanks to a great many people for their assistance, some of
whom I must mention by name. The "onlie begetter" of this project, for
which he is in no way to blame, is François Laroque, who prompted my

invitation to address the Société Shakespeare Française on the topic of the Shakespearean "green world" and thereby precipitated my frantic search for something new to say on the topic and my discovery of hunting; an early version of the section on *Love's Labor's Lost* was published in the proceedings of this conference (*Shakespeare: Le Monde Vert: Rites et Renouveau* [Paris: Les Belles Lettres, 1995]). I owe thanks as well to the many students who were persuaded to share my esoteric interests; to my colleagues in the 1997 Shakespeare Association Seminar on *As You Like It*, so ably chaired by Christy Desmet; to Patrick Grant, who read part of the study; to Terry Sherwood and Roger B. Manning, who, heroically, read it all; to the University of Victoria for support in the way of research grants and study leave; to my efficient and gracious editor at Cambridge, Sarah Stanton; to my wonderfully supportive but too distant children; and, finally, to Margaret, to whom this book is dedicated.

Glossary

(The definitions below attempt to capture the most common meanings in early modern handbooks of hunting and falconry, but the terminology is imprecise and often inconsistent)

bow and stable hunting the most popular kind of hunting in parks, in which deer were driven towards bow-hunters, waiting in stands
buck a male fallow deer, often one of five years
coursing pursuing hares or other game with greyhounds, guided by sight
doe a female fallow deer
falcon the female of all long-winged hawks
fallow deer a medium-sized deer, most commonly kept and hunted in parks
hart a male red deer, usually one after its fifth year or possessing antlers with ten tines; the noblest animal hunted in Elizabethan England
haggard a mature hawk captured in the wild, usually considered a superior hunter
hind the female of the red deer
par force de chiens the noblest kind of hunting, in which a hart or stag was pursued in open forest by hounds guided by scent, and hunters
rascal a young, lean, or otherwise inferior deer of a herd
red deer the largest animal hunted in England, and prized for *par force* hunting
stag a male red deer, usually one five years old (not always clearly distinguished from the hart)

CHAPTER ONE

Introduction: the culture of the hunt and Shakespeare

In the British Museum, a magnificent Assyrian frieze depicts a royal lion hunt. The climactic moment of the hunt features the king Ashurbanipal killing a wounded lion. The roaring beast, an arrow lodged in its forehead, lunges at the king, who extends his left arm to ward off the attack, and with his right arm plunges a sword through its chest. The faces of king and lion are level with each other, only a foot apart, and they stare directly into each other's eyes. The rigid and almost hieratic pose of the combatants suggests primal conflict: this is the most powerful of the beasts against the most powerful of men. Despite the closeness of the two in magnificence and stature, however, the power of Ashurbanipal is triumphant. He stands erect, utterly unmoved by the assault. His face betrays no emotion, unless it be the slight suggestion of a smile. His extended arms, massive yet calm in their strength, literally stop the lion dead. The frieze, like the hunt it depicts, serves to define and glorify the power of the king.

An Assyrian frieze from the seventh century BC may seem a peculiar starting point for an exploration of the Elizabethan and Jacobean culture of the hunt. Yet its central image, which evokes with such elemental force the dominance of the king over nature, foreshadows one of the most powerful Jacobean representations of the hunt, that of *Henry Frederick, Prince of Wales and Sir John Harington*. In this painting (fig. 1), the stern young prince, with a huntsman, horse, and greyhound just behind him, sheathes his sword after executing a symbolic *coup de grâce* to a fallen deer, its antlers held by the young Lord Harington, who rests on one knee.[1] At the time of the painting, Prince Henry was nine years old.

Despite the two thousand years that separate them, the Assyrian and Jacobean images have much in common: both use the hunt to celebrate royal power and, more specifically, royal power over wild nature. In the painting of Prince Henry, the elemental conflict depicted in the Assyrian frieze has been elaborated and invested with distinctively Jacobean

I

1 Robert Peake, "Henry Frederick, Prince of Wales and Sir John Harington" (1603). The nine-year-old prince sheathes his sword after symbolically decapitating a dead deer.

significance. The beast hunted is no longer the lion but the deer, the noblest of animals routinely pursued as game in a land unhappily deprived of lions, wolves, or, for the most part, boar. The supreme hunter is not the king himself but the prince, whose youth makes the action seem a rite of initiation. The solitary conflict between ruler and animal is replaced by the image of the ruler surrounded by helpful and obedient human and animal companions: friend, huntsman, horse, and dog. The climactic action, moreover, is no longer a stab through the chest but a ceremonial assault upon an animal already dead. Despite these differences, the essential import of the two images remains very much the same: the painting, like the frieze, demonstrates and celebrates royal power. In the portrait of Prince Henry, that power extends to humans, both aristocratic and common, to domesticated animals, to wildlife, to the forested landscape in the background, and, one might add, to the viewer, whose gaze is returned head-on by the stern eyes of the young warrior-prince. In Peake's painting, one might say, the viewer plays the role of the lion in the Assyrian frieze, stopped dead not by the out-thrust arm but by the penetrating gaze of the prince.

From the Middle Ages to the end of the seventeenth century in England, hunting was one of the most significant royal activities and manifestations of royal power. "To read the history of kings," observed the democrat Tom Paine in the eighteenth century, "a man would be almost inclined to suppose that government consisted of stag hunting."[2] During the sixteenth and seventeenth centuries, every English monarch except Edward VI and Queen Mary hunted throughout his or her reign, either regularly or obsessively. As a young king, Henry VIII hunted so often and so hard that one member of the court complained to Wolsey that he spared "no pains to convert the sport of hunting into a martyrdom."[3] Queen Elizabeth was still hunting at the age of sixty-seven, as is shown by a letter from Rowland Whyte to Sir Robert Sidney on 12 September 1600. Whyte, writing from the palace at Oatlands, informs Sidney that "her majesty is well and excellently disposed to hunting, for every second day she is on horseback and continues the sport long."[4] James I so immersed himself in hunting when king of England that his recreation occasioned serious religious, political, and popular protest. Hunting was also an important recreation for Charles I, who was introduced to the sport by his father at the age of four.[5] Charles II remained true to his father and grandfather in his devotion to the sport, continuing to hunt at least until three years before his death at the age of fifty-five.[6] Among the tasks facing Charles during the Restoration was the re-establishment of the royal parks, forests, and herds, many of which had been damaged or destroyed as symbols of royal and aristocratic privilege during the Civil Wars.[7]

Throughout the reigns of the Tudors and Stuarts, then, hunting was an important part of the life of the court, and of the aristocratic households connected with it. It existed in a variety of modes and served a variety of purposes. It provided a regular source of exercise and recreation. It served as entertainment for foreign visitors. It amused the monarch on progress, both as a diversion en route and as a subject for pageantry provided by the owners of estates. It served social purposes as simple as informal recreation (if any action involving a monarch can be called informal), or as complex as court ceremonial. Images of the hunt surrounded the monarchy and nobility of the period, appearing in their plate, their tapestries, their paintings, their statuary, their poems, and their masques. Stirling Castle, the birthplace of James I, still features a statue of the goddess Diana on its exterior wall and a clear view from its interior down to what in James's time was a hunting park below. Queen Elizabeth's palace of Nonsuch included a grove of Diana with a fountain depicting Actaeon turned into a stag.[8]

Although the pictorial tradition of the hunt is rather thin in Tudor and Stuart England, a number of images confirm the importance of the sport as an emblem of monarchical power. Queen Elizabeth was apparently never painted as a huntress, despite her association with Diana, goddess of the hunt, but she appears prominently in three woodcuts in George Gascoigne's 1575 edition of *The Noble Arte of Venerie or Hunting* (two are reproduced as figs. 2 and 3). In the Jacobean court the hunt took on dynastic significance, providing memorable images of many members of the royal family. A 1603 painting of the Princess Elizabeth by Robert Peake shows a hunting scene in the background (fig. 4). Peake's hunting portrait of Prince Henry, previously mentioned, was produced in two versions. A 1617 painting by Paul van Somer features Anne of Denmark in royal hunting attire, standing beside her horse and holding her dogs by a leash (fig. 5). Although James himself seems not to have been painted as a huntsman, his image in the role was kept alive in the 1611 edition of the most important hunting manual in the period, George Gascoigne's *The Noble Arte of Venerie*; in that edition two of the three images of Queen Elizabeth and her ladies-in-waiting that had appeared in the 1575 edition were cut out and replaced with images of James and his pages (one is reproduced as fig. 6).[9]

The continuing popularity of the hunt among the monarchs of

2 Queen Elizabeth at a hunt assembly. From [George Gascoigne], *The Noble Arte of Venerie or Hunting* (1575).

England cannot be explained merely as personal inclination or even as family tradition. The easy substitution of James for Elizabeth in the images of *The Arte of Venerie* highlights the fact that the monarch's role was more important than any personal views he or she might have towards hunting. Because of its legal status, the hunt was deeply inter-twined in conceptions of the royal prerogative itself. The very definition

3 Queen Elizabeth taking the assay. From [George Gascoigne], *The Noble Arte of Venerie or Hunting* (1575).

of a forest provided by John Manwood in his *Treatise of the Lawes of the Forest* (1615) suggests the convergence of real and symbolic power in the role of the monarch as hunter: "A forest is a certaine Territorie of wooddy grounds and fruitful pastures, priviledged for wilde beasts and foules of Forest, Chase and Warren, to rest and abide in, in the safe protection of the King, for his princely delight and pleasure . . ."[10] The law

4 Robert Peake, "Elizabeth of Bohemia" (1603). Hunting (right background) is
juxtaposed with intimate conversation (left background).

5 Paul van Somer, "Anne of Denmark" (1617).

of the forests, which originated with the Norman kings and was separate from the common law, gave the monarch sole authority over every forest in the kingdom and all of the so-called beasts of forest, chase, and warren within them. According to this definition, forests were essentially wildlife preserves for the royal hunt. The right to hunt in a forest could

6 James I taking the assay. From [George Gascoigne], *The Noble Arte of Venerie or Hunting* (1611).

only be conferred by the monarch, and even the right to hunt in the boundaries of the forest, the so-called purlieus, was restricted to those of superior wealth and rank. Even the establishment of a private game park required a warrant from the monarch.[11]

Hunting was restricted not only by the forest law but by the innumerable game laws that were enacted throughout the period. Whereas the forest law privileged the monarch over all others, even his greatest peers,

the game laws aligned the monarch with the privileged elite whose property and interests they were designed to protect. The game laws, as
Roger B. Manning notes, "made crimes of hunting without a sufficient
estate, hunting at night or in disguise, breaking into a park, or being in
possession of hunting weapons, nets, or hunting dogs."[12] Under James
I, in particular, who vigorously asserted his royal prerogative in relation
to the hunt, these laws became highly controversial. Throughout the
entire period hunting served as a considerable source of social tension,
involving in various ways the complex and sometimes conflicting hierarchies of wealth, rank, and ownership of land. Since all hunting was
ultimately within the warrant of the monarch, the monarchy was necessarily at the symbolic and legal center of such social conflict.[13] Not until
the Game Act of 1671 did the squirearchy begin to dominate the sport
as it did throughout the eighteenth century, giving rise to Blackstone's
quip that "the forest laws established only one mighty hunter throughout the land, [but] the game laws have raised a little Nimrod in every
manor."[14]

The social tensions within the culture of the hunt are apparent even
in works that one might expect to represent a stable and coherent point
of view. Gascoigne's *The Noble Arte of Venerie* is for the most part a straightforward translation of a French hunting manual, giving directions on the
care of dogs, the blowing of horns, and the methods used to hunt fifteen
different animals. The dominant tone of the work is celebratory. The
1575 edition features three original woodcuts of Elizabeth as a huntress
and a preface, also original with Gascoigne, that justifies hunting in
highly conventional terms. In his emphasis upon the nobility of hunting,
however, Gascoigne situates himself in a way that reveals the ambiguity
of his own relationship to the sport. At the end of a prefatory poem that
celebrates hunting, his praise of the nobility of the sport is fraught with
ironic tension. Hunting, he concludes, is

> A sport for Noble peeres, a sport for gentle bloods,
> The paine I leave for servants such, as beate the bushie woods,
>   To make their masters sport. Then let the Lords rejoyce,
> Let gentlemen beholde the glee, and take thereof the choyce.
>   For my part (being one) I must needes say my minde,
> That Hunting was ordeyned first, for Men of Noble kinde.
>   And unto them therefore, I recommend the same,
> As exercise that best becommes, their worthy noble name.[15]

Gascoigne reveals in this passage the ironies within his own social position. As a gentleman, he is at one remove from both the servants, who

find nothing but pain in the sport, and the nobles, who find only pleasure. The choice he makes, and with self-mocking glee, is to align himself with the nobles.

The ironic self-awareness in this choice suggests the complexity of Gascoigne's own experience, which included an early life of privilege and recklessness, ruinous lawsuits that culminated in debtor's prison, and a disillusioning tour of several years in the military that he drew upon in his satiric poem on war, "Dulce Bellum Inexpertis."[16] Gascoigne returned to England from the Dutch wars in 1574; in 1575 he published *The Noble Arte of Venerie*, presumably as one part of his strategy to secure patronage and to re-establish himself within the Elizabethan court. In this sense, he himself was a kind of "beater" for the nobles he celebrates, and his self-mocking assertion of his position as a gentleman betrays the anxiety brought on by his equivocal social position. As we shall see later, the social and ideological tensions within the *Arte of Venerie* reveal much about the culture of the hunt in the period.

Gascoigne was not the only Elizabethan of equivocal social status attempting to secure privilege through the hunt. Throughout the period, but especially in the reign of James, a knowledge of hunting separated the elite from the would-be elite, and books like the *Arte of Venerie* were popular in part because they gave outsiders access to an esoteric lore from which they were otherwise excluded. Following his French original, Gascoigne is scrupulously careful to use the precise terms of the art, and he expresses some anxiety about the difficulty of getting them right. At the end of the work he lists the terms of venery, including the proper words for such things as the companies, ages, footing, excrements, and noises of beasts. The demands of this arcane language are awesome. One cannot speak of a "fayre Deare," for example, unless it is a roe deer; all others must be referred to as a "great Deare."[17] For the uninitiated, verbal pitfalls were everywhere. Shakespeare both delights in and mocks this wonderful zest for jargon in the conversations of Dull, Nathaniel, and Costard about the deer killed by the Princess in *Love's Labor's Lost*. Ben Jonson, more conventionally satirical, gives us the country gull, Master Stephen, in *Every Man In His Humour:* "why you know, an' a man have not skill in the hawking and hunting languages nowadays, I'll not give a rush for him. They are more studied than the Greek or the Latin. He is for no gallant's company without 'em."[18] Hunting was thus not merely a physical but a verbal sport, and one in which the mastery of words implied both power over nature and society.

In his depiction of hunters, Shakespeare stays realistically within the social boundaries of the Elizabethan and Jacobean hunt. Throughout the plays, as in Elizabethan society, the language, symbolism, and activity of the hunt center upon a social elite. With the exception of a few foresters or keepers, those who hunt in Shakespeare are invariably royalty, aristocracy, or privileged gentry. The only commoners who become significantly involved in the sport are Nathaniel, Holofernes, and Dull in *Love's Labor's Lost,* and their participation is restricted to accounts of a hunt that display endearingly their ignorance and ineptitude. Shakespeare also maintains the social hierarchy in the use of hunting language and allusions to the hunt. Commoners tend not to use hunting metaphors, for example, whereas they flow naturally from the lips of the higher orders. As we shall see later, the class tensions that often characterize the Elizabethan hunt find expression in the plays, but usually indirectly. Shakespeare's monarchs and nobility are never forced to defend the activity as the prerogative of a social elite. Instead, they assume their rightfulness as hunters; the forests and parks are their terrain, and they never feel the need to justify their privilege with appeals to the laws of the forests or the monarch's power. The only exception to this rule, as we shall see in chapter 2, is that of the Princess in *Love's Labor's Lost,* who questions the validity of the sport even as she engages in it.

The elevated status of the hunt in Elizabethan England makes it somewhat difficult to understand Shakespeare's obvious familiarity with and interest in the sport. Shakespeare grew up in the town of Stratford, so it is reasonable to assume that most of his early activities were those of town life; his father, John, was a glover and active in political affairs. The family must have spent some time in the country, however, for, through his wife, John owned a considerable estate at Wilmcote. Stratford, moreover, was surrounded by countryside. Warwickshire and Gloucestershire included numerous parks, among them that of Kenilworth, and the woodlands of the Forest of Arden ranged north of the Avon. At the very least, the young Shakespeare would have had opportunities to be an onlooker at hunts and to participate with other local youths as a beater.

Whether John Shakespeare would have been entitled to hunt is uncertain. Under Queen Elizabeth, the requirement consisted of ownership of land worth 40 shillings a year.[19] Although the annual income of the estate at Wilmcote is not known, the property seems to have been large enough to meet that test; in 1578, when pressed for ready cash, John was able to mortgage the house and 56 acres and, in addition, to convey another 86 acres. At the peak of his prosperity (probably 1565–71), John Shakespeare was a substantial citizen. A note appended to the 1596 application for a coat of arms asserts that during this period he was "a justice of the peace and bailiff, and a Queen's officer; that he had 'Landes and tenementes of good wealth.& Substance,' worth £500; and that he had taken for his wife the daughter of a gentleman of worship."[20] Given the dramatic decline in John's fortunes in the early 1570s, it is possible that young William was reaching puberty at the very time at which his father was losing the privilege of hunting. If so, his position would have been not unlike that of the small gentry, landless gentlemen, and yeomen who, according to Manning, "were the cause of a disproportionate amount of the riotous hunting in early modern England."[21] Perhaps the combination of youth and social resentment made young William a poacher.

As a playwright, Shakespeare would certainly have been exposed to the culture of the hunt, especially because both hunting and theater played important roles at court and at aristocratic festivities. Many members of his audiences would have been avid hunters. Once he became prosperous as a shareholder in his acting company, Shakespeare himself would have probably met the economic requirements for hunting; in May of 1602, he paid £320 for about 120 acres of arable land in Old Stratford. In 1610 this "freehold" was described as "consisting of 107 acres of land, and 20 of pasture." If, as Schoenbaum suggests, the recorded price for properties was habitually understated by a wide margin, then it is likely that such an investment would have yielded a return of at least 40 shillings a year.[22] In view of the essentially urban nature of his existence, however, it is highly unlikely that Shakespeare would have availed himself often of the privilege of hunting, even if he had it.

If Shakespeare achieved the right to hunt in 1602, a Parliamentary act of 1603 would almost certainly have taken the privilege away. And not coincidentally. In order to exclude social climbers like Shakespeare, to keep the sport within the higher gentry and aristocracy, James I initiated changes to the game laws in 1603–4, 1605–6, and 1609–10 that made them much more severely restrictive. Each act provided three categories within which Shakespeare could have been permitted to hunt. The 1603 act required freehold ownership of land worth £10 a year (increased to £40 a year in 1605); copyhold ownership of land worth £30 a year (increased to £80 in 1609); or possession of goods and chattels to the value of £200 (increased to £400 in 1609).[23] If Shakespeare fit within any of these categories, which seems unlikely, it was probably the latter; the recorded purchase price of New Place was only £60 in 1597, however, and that of the London house in the exclusive Blackfriars district only £140 in 1613. As a playwright and shareholder, then, it is unlikely that Shakespeare participated directly in the culture of the hunt. Nonetheless, his company's increasing ties with the world of the court would have given him many opportunities to indulge himself vicariously in its pleasures.

Although frustrating, the uncertainty about whether Shakespeare hunted or was entitled to hunt leads to an interesting conclusion: throughout his life Shakespeare was situated – economically, socially, and geographically – on the margins of the culture of the hunt. He grew up a town boy but had easy access to the country. He prospered in the popular London theater as an actor and shareholder but also cultivated courtly audiences, including James I himself, devoted to the hunt. He sealed his success at his craft by securing a coat of arms for his family and by buying land in and around Stratford, suggesting an affinity with the upwardly mobile in society who, like Master Stephen in *Every Man In His Humour*, struggled to learn the "hawking and hunting languages" because they were "more studied than the Greek or the Latin" and provided access to the company of gallants. If excluded from the privilege of hunting, Shakespeare was never hopelessly removed from that world. If included, he was never placed securely within it, as were the country gentry and aristocracy. He could thus combine a direct or indirect knowledge of the sport with critical detachment.

Whatever his exact social relationship to the hunt, Shakespeare's exploitation of its imagery is unique among dramatists of the period. One poem and eight of the plays include hunting scenes or episodes, and hunting imagery recurs throughout the canon. Shakespeare's plays are exceptional not only in the frequency of their allusions to the hunt but in the impression of technical mastery and experiential knowledge that these allusions convey. Ben Jonson, Shakespeare's closest competitor in numbers of allusions to the hunt, conveys in contrast only a bookish knowledge and is drawn to the subject primarily for topical satire or for courtly celebration of the monarch. Shakespeare's easy mastery of the sport has led some writers, such as D. H. Madden, to assume that he was himself an avid hunter. Madden, whose *Diary of Master William Silence* demonstrates in overwhelming detail Shakespeare's technical knowledge of the hunt, concludes that he was "beyond doubt a sportsman, with the rare skill in the mysteries of woodcraft, loving to recall the very names of the hounds with which he was wont to hunt . . ."[24] Others, however, equally impressed by Shakespeare's easy familiarity with the sport, have come to the opposite conclusion: both Caroline Spurgeon and Matt Cartmill, for example, argue that Shakespeare disliked hunting.[25] We shall examine the question of Shakespeare's "attitude" towards hunting in chapter 8, where I shall attempt to widen the arguments of Spurgeon and Cartmill. To a great extent, this study situates Shakespeare within the anti-hunting discourses of the Elizabethan and Jacobean periods.

The power of the culture of the hunt in Shakespeare's day can be seen at a glance in the county maps of John Speed, where forests are represented by clusters of trees, and parks by circles of fences (fig. 7). Most hunting, it seems, took place in parks, which are prominent features in the landscape of almost all counties; Derbyshire alone had thirty-six.[26] Susan Lasdun counts eight hundred and seventeen parks identified in the county maps made by Christopher Saxton between 1575 and 1580.[27] William Harrison, who lamented the economic and social consequences of such a wasteful use of land, scoffed also at the self-indulgent and frivolous kind of hunting the parks encouraged. Harrison estimates that "the twentieth part of the realm is employed upon deer and conies."[28] When the Duke of Stettin visited England in 1602, he noted that "'there is scarcely any royal residence, or even a nobleman's house, which has not at least one deer park – sometimes two, or even three, may be found.'"[29] Shakespeare's *Love's Labor's Lost*, as we shall see, is set in such a park, and the play evokes the ethos of sophisticated and frivolous cruelty that social critics like Harrison treat with considerably less urbanity than Shakespeare.

The number of parks throughout England testifies to the paramount status of deer hunting throughout the period. Other kinds of hunting were routinely indulged in. Coursing of hare was popular, occasionally being considered even superior to hunting deer.[30] The hunting manuals, moreover, usually provide instruction for hunting other animals, such as conies, badger, fox, and otter, although it is clear that such hunting enjoyed neither the status nor the ceremonial appeal of the deer hunt. Fox hunting, which has come to dominate the mythology of the hunt in modern England, did not begin to achieve its present status until the late seventeenth century, after the massive depletion of deer stocks during the Civil Wars. For most hunters of the sixteenth century, foxes were vermin, to be hunted without ennobling ceremony – as in King Lear's image of Cordelia and himself being "fire[d]" out of a hole "like foxes"

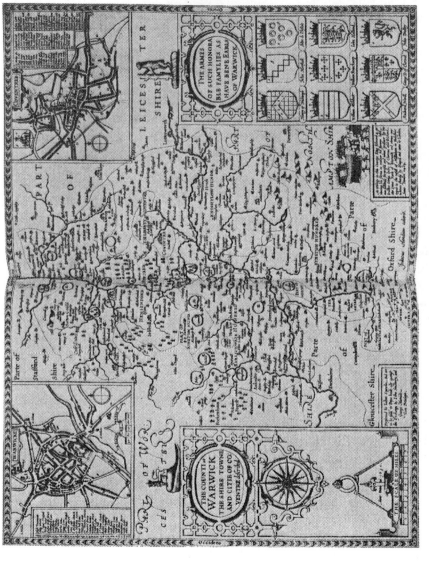

7 County map of Warwickshire (detail). From John Speed, *The Theatre of the Empire of Great Britain* (1611). Parks are shown as fenced enclosures.

(5.3.23). Because of its social importance during the Tudor and Stuart period, its long-standing artistic and literary significance, and its centrality in Shakespeare, the deer hunt will be our focal point throughout this study.

As objects of the chase, deer were arranged into a shifting but more or less hierarchical order, according to size, appearance, age, and gender. The largest and noblest were the red deer. A male red deer, the largest animal hunted in England, was usually called a "hart" after it had reached six years, although sometimes the term was restricted to an animal with at least ten tines. A male red deer of five years was called a "stag." The hunting handbooks, however, do not always distinguish the two categories. The female of the red deer was a "hind." Harts and stags were prized for their size, their magnificent antlers, their power, and their stamina in the hunt. Slightly lower in the hierarchy were the fallow deer, divided into buck and doe. These were the most common deer to be found in parks. Smaller and less impressive physically than the stag, the buck was nonetheless prized for its meat, which some judged superior. Finally, the smallest and least significant were the roe deer, also divided into buck (or roebuck) and doe. Shakespeare's allusions to deer are invariably attuned to their social and cultural connotations. The association of the stag with kingship, for example, affects our perception of both Henry VI and Edward IV in *3 Henry VI*, and of Julius Caesar in the play of the same name. When Falstaff dons horns in *Merry Wives*, the rich comic symbolism evoked by the gesture includes mock-usurpation, since he imagines himself a "Windsor stag" (5.5.12–13).

Three kinds of deer hunting dominated the sport in the period: *par force de chiens*, bow and stable, and coursing with greyhounds.[31] The former was the most physically demanding and, conventionally, the noblest and most masculine kind of hunt. In its royal or ceremonial form, which was highly ritualized, this hunt took place in field and forest and was roughly divided into five stages: the entry of the hunters into the forest; the consumption of an elaborate breakfast in a forest clearing, featuring reports of the huntsmen and the planning of the hunt; the chase of a single deer located earlier by the huntsmen; the baying, death, and dismemberment of the deer, and the rewarding of the dogs; and finally, the return of the hunting party to the court, climaxed with another feast. As its name implies, this kind of hunting depended upon the ability of the dogs to pursue the deer by its scent and to run it to its death. In his book of advice to the young Prince Henry, *Basilicon Doron*, James I praises this kind of hunting, "with running hounds," as "the most honourable and noblest sorte thereof." James dismisses shooting with guns and bows as a "theevish forme" of hunting, and notes that "greyhound hunting," or coursing, "is not so martiall a game."[32]

Although disapproved of by James, bow and stable hunting and coursing, both more appropriate to parks or chases than forests, were also very popular in the period. Shakespeare depicts bow and stable hunting in the Princess's hunt in *Love's Labor's Lost*. In the most common form of such a hunt, deer were driven before stationary hunters armed with cross-bows, who were positioned in ambushes or specially constructed stands. Greyhounds, which hunted by sight rather than scent, were often used in such hunts, both to chase the deer to the waiting hunters and to run down those that had been wounded. Whereas bow and stable hunting required at least the effort of shooting an arrow, coursing in parks was essentially a spectator sport, with observers stationed on stands en route or even in rooms with views of the chase. A description of coursing deer appears in the account of the Queen's visit to Cowdray in 1591: on one evening she watched from a turret while sixteen bucks were pulled down by greyhounds in the clearing below.[33] That morning she had used a cross-bow to kill about three or four of thirty deer enclosed in a paddock; the account does not specify whether she shot at random or whether the deer were driven before her in a rather constricted version of the bow and stable hunt.

Descriptions of hunting in parks suggest that, unlike *par force* hunting, this sport was not considered an end in itself, an action invested with the significance of ritual, but an adjunct to courtly pageantry.[34] The principal objection to the sport, as we have seen in the case of King James, was its easiness. In *The Governor*, Thomas Elyot dismisses bow and stable hunting as serving "well for the pot (as is the common saying)" but as containing "no commendable solace or exercise, in comparison to the other forms of hunting."[35] Theodore Roosevelt, commenting on descriptions in Edward, Duke of York's *The Master of Game*, found such easy kinds of hunting to be "debased," "contemptible," and guilty of "luxurious and effeminate artificiality" – "dismal [parodies] upon the stern hunting life in which the man trusts to his own keen eye, stout thews, and heart of steel for success and safety in the wild warfare waged against wild nature."[36] In their attitudes towards hunting, Roosevelt, Elyot, and James I had much in common.

Accounts of hunting in the period show that, despite its affinities with ritual, the sport could be conducted in a great variety of ways, and much of the evidence is so fragmentary that it is often difficult to discover what kind of hunting is envisaged. At times, the methods must have been very casual indeed, as when Henry VIII indulged in impromptu hunts while traveling on progress around the countryside. A letter from the French ambassador to Francis I in 1541, for example, records that King Henry's "fashion of proceeding in this progress is, wherever there are deer numerous, to enclose 200 or 300 and then send in many greyhounds to kill them, that he may share them among the gentlemen of the country and of his Court . . . "[37] It is difficult to imagine that such impromptu slaughter was accompanied with elaborate ceremony. The ritual attached to the hunt must have varied greatly, depending upon the animal hunted, the rank of the participants, and the occasion of the hunt.

As Roger B. Manning has shown, illegal hunting was also extremely common in the period and extremely disruptive. "Of all the species of disorder in England," Manning observes, "probably only the Civil Wars of the seventeenth century were more injurious to royal government and aristocratic privilege than the phenomenon of large-scale, organized poaching."[38] Illegal hunting of this kind could also take many different forms. The stereotypical image of the poacher that developed in eighteenth and nineteenth-century novels, however, that of a poor tenant setting snares for rabbits in the lord's woods, is of relatively little importance in the period. Such poaching no doubt took place, but the kind that most captured the public eye, and most obsessed the gentry, aristocracy, and, above all, King James, was far more serious and destructive. In such acts of poaching, the ceremonial of the hunt was flagrantly undermined, with riotous bands of hunters storming through a park at night, terrorizing the keepers, massacring deer, and leaving them to rot as an insult to their owner. Manning argues that such riotous hunting was a symbolic substitute for war, a method by which socially rebellious gentry and their followers could vent aggression and pursue their own vendettas.

Poaching of this kind, as we shall see especially when considering *Merry Wives*, substituted for the noble ceremonial of the hunt an inverted mock-ceremonial, of the sort customary in rituals of inversion, such as the charivari. When a gang of hunters went after the deer of Sir Thomas More's father, for example, they "impaled the head of a buck upon a staff with a stick in its mouth facing towards the manor house."[39] Manning suggests that this ritual insult may have been prompted by More's illegal enclosure of land for a park.

Deer could be killed, in sum, by a wide variety of methods and in a wide variety of modes, ranging from the highly ritualized – what Shakespeare calls in *Titus Andronicus* a "solemn hunting" (2.1.112) – through various stages of decreasing formality to casual slaughter or to the grotesque and inverted ritualism of poaching.

Shakespeare, as we have seen, may have been a likely candidate for poaching as an adolescent in Stratford. By far the most popular of the stories of Shakespeare's youth is that in which his very origin as a poet and dramatist is attributed to misadventures in this illicit sport. The story appears in print for the first time in Nicholas Rowe's 1709 edition of the works of Shakespeare. According to Rowe, as a youth Shakespeare fell into the company of some local youths prone to deer-stealing. He was severely prosecuted for that offense by Sir Thomas Lucy of Charlecote, near Stratford, and revenged himself by writing a satirical ballad upon him. This had the unfortunate effect of increasing Sir Thomas's desire to prosecute him, to the extent that he was forced to leave Stratford for London. Another version, by the Reverend William Fulman, written independently of Rowe and several decades earlier, adds the rather garbled information that Shakespeare's revenge extended to depicting Sir Thomas as his "'Justice Clodpate and calls him a great man and that in allusion to his name bore three louses rampant for his arms.'"[40] Fulman refers unmistakably to the pompous Justice Shallow in *Merry Wives*, whose coat of arms, according to Slender, includes a "dozen white luces" (a species of pike), provoking Evans to make the inevitable but unconscious pun: "the dozen white louses do become an old coat well" (1.1.16–20). In *Shakespeare's Lives*, Schoenbaum notes that "on a Lucy tomb at Warwick the three luces on the coat are repeated four times – thus providing the dozen to which Slender refers."[41] Schoenbaum discusses two other less reliable sources, Joshua Barnes and Thomas Jones, before concluding that "the deer-poaching legend has thus come down from several autonomous sources . . . all (it would seem) stemming ultimately from Stratford gossip."[42]

Although he is appropriately skeptical about the story, Schoenbaum cannot dismiss it out of hand. The evidence, though not compelling, is substantial enough to warrant serious treatment. The counter-arguments, moreover, are inconclusive. That Sir Thomas did not have a legal park but a free warren, for example, does not rule out the story, as Schoenbaum admits, because roe deer, unlike red and fallow deer, were considered beasts of warren. Although Schoenbaum finds it unlikely that Shakespeare would wait fourteen years before satirizing Lucy, he also admits the extreme difficulty of interpreting the passage in *Merry*

Wives without Fulman's gloss. He concludes, finally, that although most responsible modern scholars have rejected the episode as "traditionary romance," some have not; among the exceptions are scholars of the stature of E. K. Chambers, whose account covers the essential evidence.[43] The story, in short, is not easily dismissed. Whether true or not, however, as Roger B. Manning observes, it tells us something important about popular culture in the period: "that poaching was a usual rite of passage for the youth who wanted to assert his manhood or lay claim to genteel status."[44]

It should be clear from all of the examples above, legal or illegal, that the object of killing game in the Elizabethan and Jacobean period was neither the protection nor the sustenance of society. Society did not need to be protected from deer, especially since most of the deer lived within fences and the common farmers whose crops might have been vulnerable were not entitled to hunt in any case. Like some modern hunters, Elizabethan hunters ate what they killed, but the feasting was incidental to the joy of the chase and the status it both required and confirmed. If an Elizabethan lord desired venison, he did not need to hunt for it; a deer could be culled from a herd in his park for dinner at any time by his mere command. The venison collected at a hunt was a trophy, like the antlers, not a necessity; it was consumed in feasting or distributed as a sign of privilege among friends, dependants, and retainers. As Manning observes, "gifts of venison solidified alliances and traditional relationships."[45] In *Merry Wives*, Justice Shallow gives Master Page enough meat for a venison pasty, a gesture not unconnected to his desire to arrange a match between his nephew Silence and Mistress Anne Page. In *Titus Andronicus*, this custom is grossly parodied, with Titus serving Tamora a pasty composed of her sons.

Since hunting could not be justified in terms of social or economic necessity, two other rationales were repeatedly invoked: that of recreation, and that of war. In the *Gentleman's Recreation* (1686), Richard Blome summarizes what he takes to be the conventional encomiums for the sport, highlighting its recreational value:

To Tell you that *Hunting* is a commendable *Recreation*, and hath always been practised and highly prized by all *Degrees* and *Qualities* of *Men*, even by *Kings* and *Princes;* that it is a great preserver of *Health*, a Manly *Exercise*, and an increaser of *Activity;* that it recreates the *Mind*, strengthens the *Limbs*, and whets the *Stomach;* and that no *Musick* is more charming to the *Ears* of *Man*, than a *Pack* of *Hounds* in full *Cry* is to him that delights in *Hunting*, is to tell you that which experimentally is known, and what hath been sufficiently treated of by others . . .[46]

For Blome the hunt is not merely a recreation but a "commendable" recreation, what Nathaniel in *Love's Labor's Lost* calls a "very reverent sport" (4.2.1). As such, it does not merely preserve health, promote manliness, relax the mind, and provide the emotional and esthetic satisfaction of the cry of the hounds; it also confers the social advantage of association with kings and princes.

In law, as we have seen, a forest served only a recreational purpose, that of protecting wildlife for the "princely delight and pleasure" of the monarch. As might be expected, James I was not shy in asserting this right; in an address to Parliament on the need for laws to protect the forests, for example, he mentioned the importance of the forests for the maintenance of the navy, for fuel, and for "sports and pleasure, which is for my honor."[47] Unlike John Evelyn, who in *Sylva* (1664) tried to persuade the aristocracy that planting trees was a nobler recreation than hunting, James argued that trees were important mainly because they served the noble sport of the hunt.[48] The monarch's honor alone could thus be used to justify the hunt. More commonly, however, James defended his controversial activity on the ground of his health, as he did, for example, in a letter to his Privy Council that formalized governmental procedures during his absences in pursuit of the "open air and exercise" necessary "even in strongest bodies."[49] The hunting manuals too make much of health, citing the benefits of early rising, the open air, the avoidance of idleness, and physical exercise in general. This tendency to define hunting as a means towards some other end rather than as an end in itself typifies the mixture of moral earnestness and evasiveness found in rationales for the sport, which allowed most writers to ignore the challenging question of whether killing animals for pleasure alone was justifiable.

For those who pursued the question, the answer was generally affirmative. Implicit in any justification for hunting in the period was the conventional Christian view, outlined usefully by Keith Thomas, which sanctioned hunting as falling within the biblical injunction that nature was to be controlled by man.[50] Although this view did not sanction wanton cruelty to animals, it justified hunting, and was often cited in sermons when the issue arose, even, as we shall see, in sermons by Puritans, whose view towards the sport was generally critical.

As a mode of recreation, hunting was public, ceremonial, and often festive. It could be used as a pageant to celebrate and entertain the Queen, as at Cowdray in 1591 or at Hatfield in 1557, where the young princess was met on the way to a hunt by fifty archers wearing scarlet boots and yellow caps and armed with gilded bows, one of whom "pre-sented her a silver-headed arrow, winged with peacock's feathers."[51] It could be used to impress foreign dignitaries. It could add to the holiday atmosphere of extended festivities, such as weddings and christenings. Roger B. Manning notes that "a popular belief seems to have existed that no celebration or special occasion was complete without a bit of hunting."[52] The sport also provided an opportunity for competition and wagering, either on relatively private occasions or in public festivities, such as the Cotswold games.[53] The association of wagering and mar-riage festivities with hunting, as we shall see, underlies Shakespeare's depiction of the wager on wives at the end of *The Taming of the Shrew.*

Shakespeare's representations of the hunt often evoke this recrea-tional mode. In *3 Henry VI* kings are allowed to exercise themselves by hunting in captivity. In the *Taming of the Shrew* a noble lord hunts for his personal recreation and amusement. In *Love's Labor's Lost* the Princess is honored by a hunt of the kind that Queen Elizabeth might have arranged for a foreign ambassador. In *A Midsummer Night's Dream,* Theseus and Hippolyta hunt as part of their wedding festivities. In the comedies Shakespeare accentuates the notion of communal bonding implicit in the recreational hunt by repeatedly associating hunting with love and marriage. In the tragedies hunting is more likely to be linked with war or, as in *Titus Andronicus,* developed in such a way that the ritual of communion is grotesquely parodied and inverted. Titus invites Saturninus to a "solemn hunting" (2.1.112) in honor of his marriage, but the forest becomes a setting not for social harmony but for rape, mutila-tion, and murder.

Far more important than the recreational justification for hunting in the period was the militaristic, which promoted the sport as a training ground in the arts of war. Sir Thomas Cockaine's argument in *A Short Treatise of Hunting* (1591) is typical:

And for the first commendation of Hunting, I find (Gentlemen) by my owne experience in Hunting, that Hunters by their continuall travaile, painfull labour, often watching, and enduring of hunger, of heate, and of cold, are much enabled above others to the service of their Prince and Countrey in the warres, having their bodies for the most part by reason of their continuall exercise in much better health, than other men have, and their minds also by this honest recreation the more fit and the better disposed to all other good exercises.[54]

Machiavelli advises princes never to turn their mind "from the study of war" and to do "a great deal of hunting" in order to harden the body and master the terrain.[55] In the *Governor,* Sir Thomas Elyot carries this argument to an extreme, approving only the kind of hunting that comes closest to war itself. His model is the hunting described in Xenophon's *Cyropaedia*, which includes education in justice and temperance, vigorous exercise, exposure to extreme physical hardship, the use of bows, swords, or hatchets, fasting while hunting, and eating only what was killed. Lamenting the softness of hunting in contemporary England, Elyot recommends the use of "javelins and other weapons, in manner of war."[56] Even James I, who never tired of lecturing his people on his need to hunt for the sake of his health alone, draws upon Xenophon in his *Basilicon Doron* to support his preference for the *par force* hunt as a more "martiall" game than hunting with greyhounds.[57] Robert Peake's painting of Prince Henry demonstrating his prowess before a slain deer embodies this militaristic notion of the hunt, even to the point of implying, in the extreme youth of the prince, an initiatory function. The youth who can achieve mastery over a deer promises to be a warrior.

The military rationales for hunting in the period are invariably nostalgic and anti-technological. Elyot's idealization of Xenophon's description of the hunt in *Cyropaedia*, his attempt to promote the javelin as the most warlike of hunting weapons, James I's aversion to the use of guns as a "theevish forme of hunting" – these are all symptoms of a desire to make of hunting an elemental test of man's power. In some respects this impulse confirms Ortega y Gasset's view of hunting: "in hunting man succeeds, in effect, in annihilating all historical evolution, in separating himself from the present, and in renewing the primitive situation."[58] For Ortega y Gasset this meant strolling in the woods accompanied with no more than a dog and gun. For James I, it meant racing through the forests on horseback, sword at the side, in the midst of a throng of dogs, foresters, and fellow huntsmen.

The obvious institutional power behind the leading justifications for the hunt, which are found in the handbooks for governors, the hunting manuals, the church, and even the speeches and writings of James I himself, should not obscure the fact that hunting was a source of considerable ideological controversy and social tension throughout the period. Although the ideological opposition appears in many different quarters and guises, three main strands are dominant. The first in time and importance is that which might be called broadly the humanist opposition, led by such figures as More, Erasmus, and Agrippa. The second might be called the sentimental opposition, embodied most powerfully in Montaigne, who stands almost alone in his detailed condemnation of the cruelty of the hunt, but whose moral sensitivity resonates in other authors. The third might be called the Puritan opposition, which developed mainly during the reign of James I. Since all three provide a potential backdrop for Shakespeare's treatment of the hunt, they are worth individual attention in some detail.

As Robert P. Adams has shown, the satiric attacks on hunting by early sixteenth-century humanists such as Erasmus and More were closely related to their opposition to war.[59] Instead of celebrating the hunt for its capacity to initiate young men into the strategies and hardships of war, they attacked it for its cruelty and its tendency to brutalize. In *Utopia*, the Utopians regard hunting "as a thynge unworthye to be used of free men," relegating the activity to butchers, who are all slaves, and for whom hunting is a lower occupation than butchery, being unnecessary. The so-called pleasure of the hunt, according to Utopians, is no more than a pleasure in killing or mutilation, and it either reveals a cruel disposition or creates one, the hunter losing his humanity "by longe use of so cruell a pleasure."[60] Erasmus takes a similar view in *Praise of Folly*. [61] Throughout his plays, Shakespeare draws upon this connection between hunting and human violence.

As we shall see when we consider *Titus Andronicus* and *Julius Caesar*, some of Shakespeare's most aggressive images of the hunt probably derive not from legitimate hunting but from poaching, which, as Roger Manning has shown, constituted in the period a kind of symbolic warfare. When King Edward's brothers rescue him from captivity in *3 Henry VI*, they jestingly refer to themselves as poachers, stealing the "Bishop's deer" (4.5.17). In *Titus Andronicus* the attack on Lavinia is conceived as an episode of poaching, in which Lavinia becomes a "doe" taken in secret and "borne . . . cleanly by the keeper's nose" (2.1.93–94). In *As You Like It*, Duke Senior and his men are technically poaching, since they live as outlaws, taking deer from land that is under the authority of Duke Frederick. Justice Shallow accuses Falstaff of poaching his deer in *Merry Wives of Windsor*, and the motif of wild and disorderly hunting runs throughout the play.

The most savage humanist critique of hunting in the sixteenth century is that of Agrippa in *Of the Vanitie and Uncertaintie of Artes and Sciences* (1530). Both more scathing and more systematic than either More or Erasmus, Agrippa finds hunting a "detestable" and "cruell Arte," one that leads men to set "all humanitie apart" and "become salvage beastes." Following Augustine, Agrippa locates the origin of hunting in the act of original sin, which ended forever the peace between men and animals. When God said to the serpent, "I will set hatred betweene thee and the woman, and betweene thy seede and her seede," asserts Agrippa, "of this sentence the battail of huntinge tooke his beginning." Throughout history, then, hunting is a "battle" and a symptom of human depravity: it is linked to "wicked menne and sinners" like Nimrod and Cain in the Bible, and to wicked nations like that of the Thebans. In contemporary Europe, according to Agrippa, kings, princes, nobles, and even churchmen devote their lives exclusively to hunting, driving farmers from their farms and herdsmen from their pastures. "Huntinge," he says, "was the beginninge of Tyrannye, because it findeth no Authoure more meete then him, whiche hathe learned to dispise God, and nature, in the slaughter and boocherie of wilde beastes, and in the spillinge of bloude."[62] Agrippa's connection between hunting and tyranny also appears in the beast fable told by Philisides in Sidney's *Old Arcadia*; in this account, the final stage of man's tyranny over the animals is reached when he turns to killing them not for food but "for sport."[63] Shakespeare draws most directly upon the association of hunting with tyranny, as we shall see in chapter 7, in his treatment of Prospero's hunt of Caliban.

Agrippa's notion that hunting appears only as a consequence of original sin implies that life in Eden was vegetarian. The idea of an original and lost age of peace between humans and animals was available during the period in both biblical and classical versions, often interrelated. The account of creation in the King James version of Genesis seems to imply a vegetarian regimen (1:28–30), with meat eating sanctioned only with the establishment of the new covenant after the flood (9:2–4). The image of the New Jerusalem in Isaiah supports the many conventional depictions of Eden as a peaceable kingdom, in which "the wolf and the lamb shall feed together" (65:25). In Ovid's *Metamorphoses*, the most popular classical source for images of the Golden Age, hunting is associated with the decline of human society that takes place in the age of iron. Although the account of the four stages of civilization – Golden, Silver, Bronze, and Iron – offered in Book I does not refer specifically to the invention of hunting, the narrative implies that humans turned to killing animals in the Iron Age, an age that also marks the introduction of war. In Book XV, when Ovid gives voice to Pythagoras, the association between social decline and hunting becomes explicit. Pythagoras, who espouses both vegetarianism and the doctrine of transmigration of souls, argues that neither hunting nor fishing occurred in the Golden Age. Meat eating began only with the imitation of lions, and was the first step humans took "on the road to crime."[64] We shall return to such Edenic and Golden Age thinking when considering Prospero's hunt in *The Tempest*.

Montaigne alludes to both Pythagorean and Christian attitudes towards animals in his critique of hunting in the essay "Of Cruelty." His starting point, however, as always, is his observation of his own most intimate feelings and behavior. Noting that he hates cruelty above all other vices, he admits that he cannot bear even to see "a chickins neck pulld off" or to hear the "groane" of "a seely dew-bedabled hare . . . when she is seized upon by the howndes." In discussing the capacity of emotion to overwhelm reason, Montaigne finds the pleasure of sexual passion less compelling than the surprise of the chase: "whereby our reason being amazed, looseth the leasure to prepare her selfe against it: when as after a long questing and beating for some game, the beast doth sodainely start, or rowze up before us, and happily [perhaps] in such a place, where we least expected the same." Montaigne's account of the irresistible excitement of the hunt – the "riding, and the earnestnes of showting, jubeting and hallowing, still ringing in our eares" – captures the primitive quality of the chase that Ortega y Gasset celebrates: "Suddenly the orgiastic element shoots forth, the dionysiac, which flows and boils in the depths of all hunting."[65] Despite his susceptibility to these emotions, Montaigne recoils at the suffering imposed upon the animal: "As for me, I could never so much as endure, without remorce and griefe, to see a poore, silly, and innocent beast pursued and killed, which is harmeles and voide of defence, and of whom we receive no offence at all."

In its remarkable candor and complexity, Montaigne's view of the hunt offers us a unique glimpse into the subjective experience it provided for at least one exceptional figure in the sixteenth century. His aversion to cruelty, however, although rarely articulated in such detail or with such sensitivity to animal suffering, can be found in other writers in the period as well, such as More and Agrippa, or, much later, Margaret Cavendish, Duchess of Newcastle, whose "The Hunting of the Hare" (1653) is the most powerful anti-hunting poem of the early modern period in England.[66] Sometimes, however, the persistent metaphoric identity of animal with human suffering makes it difficult to tell whose pain is really at issue. When Jaques sits beside a stream in *As You Like It*, for example, and moralizes upon the death of the sobbing deer, his language so confuses deer behavior with human behavior that one is tempted to say that the "real" subjects of the passage are not animals at all but human beings. What seems to be sensitivity to animal suffering, in short, may actually be satiric contempt for the human condition. We shall deal with these ambiguities later in relation to *As You Like It* .

An interesting example of this interpretative problem occurs in Gascoigne's *Arte of Venerie*, a hunting manual that paradoxically gives voice to four of the victims themselves. After describing the methods of hunting the hart, hare, fox, and otter, Gascoigne provides poems for each animal, in which the animal itself laments its fate and accuses humans of cruelty, hypocrisy, and immorality. The sudden shift in perspective from technical descriptions of chasing, killing, and dismembering prey to poetic laments spoken by the animals themselves forces the reader to perceive the hunt as a moral problem. Although Matt Cartmill suggests that the device might have been intended as a joke and therefore might imply no true sympathy for the animals themselves, Gascoigne's ambiguous social position and his cynicism towards war are more likely to have made him genuinely ambivalent about the very art that he describes.[67]

Although its significance may sometimes be uncertain, an emerging sympathy for animals is certainly evident in the period, particularly among English Puritans of the middle and late seventeenth century. The theological basis for this view is to be found in the biblical doctrine of stewardship. Keith Thomas quotes John Calvin, who argues that God "will not have us abuse the beasts beyond measure . . . but to nourish them and to have care of them. . . If a man spare neither his horse nor his ox nor his ass, therein he betrayeth the wickedness of his nature. And if he say, 'Tush, I care not, for it is but a brute beast,' I answer again, 'Yea, but it is a creature of God.'"[68] While this view mitigated against cruelty to animals, both wild and domestic, it was rarely used, as in Montaigne or Cavendish, to attack hunting. Both Luther and Calvin accepted hunting as a proper recreation, if conducted in moderation. The Puritan John Downame, in *A Guide to Godlynesse* (1629), lists hunting, hawking, fishing, and fowling among lawful recreations, but courting, gambling, theater-going, and dancing as unlawful. For most Puritans, attending Shakespeare's plays was more likely to lead to sin than killing deer.

Puritans who protested against hunting were less concerned with cruelty to animals than with the social abuses attendant upon the sport – the destruction of property through the wanton pursuit of deer across farmers' fields, the waste of time, and the waste of resources that might have been used to alleviate poverty. In *The Anatomie of Abuses*, Philip Stubbes expresses the Puritan viewpoint with unusual succinctness:

If necessitie or want of other meats inforceth us to seek after their [animals']
lives, it is lawfull to use them in the feare of God, with thanks to his name: but
for our pastimes and vain pleasures sake, wee are not in any wise to spoyle or
hurt them. Is he a christian man or rather a pseudo-christian, that delighteth in
blood? . . . Is hee a Christian that buieth up the corne of the poor, turning it
into bread (as many doo) to feed dogs for his pleasure? Is hee a christian that
liveth to the hurt of his Neighbour in treading and breaking down his hedges,
in casting open his gates in trampling of his corne . . .?[69]

According to Stubbes, hunting should be conducted only in necessity,
and in fear and gratitude towards God.

Justifying hunting as a necessity, however, was exceedingly difficult.
Gascoigne's otter attacks the hypocrisy of this traditional religious
defence by reminding humans of their insatiable gluttony:

> Well yet mee thinkes, I heare him preache this Texte,
> *Howe all that is, was made for use of man:*
> So was it sure, but therewith followes next,
> This heavie place, expounde it who so can:
> *The very Scourge and Plague of God his Ban,*
> Will lyght on suche as queyntly can devise
> To eate more meate, than may their mouthes suffise.[70]

Given the fact that hunting was not necessary for food, most Puritans
defined recreation itself as a necessity, although Stubbes's position is
somewhat ambiguous. Wanton destruction and cruelty, however, are
clearly indefensible: not only sinful in themselves but leading to unchar-
itable actions towards fellow human beings. Under James I the Puritan
argument against hunting became part of a broader assault upon the
policies and practices of the monarchy, as we shall see when we consider
Shakespeare's treatment of Prospero's hunt in *The Tempest*.

The Puritan concern for the poor shows that the opposition to the
hunt was not merely ideological but also economic and social. As we
have seen, hunting was a highly visible sign of privilege, and the vast
parks and forests set aside for the pursuit of that privilege, defined as recreation, could not help but be an irritant, both literally and symbolically,
to the less privileged. Unfortunately, the views of commoners on the
hunt are rarely recorded, except indirectly, as in the diatribes of Puritan
ministers such as Philip Stubbes. Although the wholesale destruction of
hunting parks during the Civil Wars had many causes, the most important was probably popular rage against a repressive social custom. The
rage was vented not just against parks but the deer within them, symbols
of aristocratic privilege. As E. P. Thompson observes, "there was an

ancient enmity between democracy and these gentle creatures."
Thompson shows that in Windsor Forest alone the deer population
declined from 3066 in 1607 to 461 in 1697, despite efforts to replenish the
herds during the Restoration.[71]

In his *Description of England* (1587), William Harrison, whose sympa-
thies inclined strongly in the direction of the Puritan reform movement,
generalizes this kind of local resentment by placing the hunt within a
contemporary social and economic framework. For Harrison, the practice of hunting, particularly as manifested in the keeping of parks, was
dangerously destructive. The keeping of deer, he says, is of no economic
benefit to their owners, for deer cannot be sold and are merely
exchanged as gifts. The reduction of arable land necessary to the
support of parks leads owners to enclose common lands, which impov-
erishes and dislocates the common people and causes under population.
The lack of population means a lack of soldiers, and consequent military weakness for the kingdom. In his chapter entitled "Of Savage
Beasts and Vermins," Harrison notes with admiration the hunting habits
of monarchs of the past: Alexander the Great, for example, hunted tiger,
boar, and lions; Henry I "loved to hunt the lion and the boar"; and
Henry V "thought it a mere scoffery to pursue any fallow deer with
hounds or greyhounds, but supposed himself always to have done a
sufficient act when he had tired them by his own travel on foot and so
killed them with his hands in the upshot of that exercise and end of his
recreation." In contrast to these heroic pursuits, the hunting of fallow
deer and conies in parks, and even the hunting of the stag are "pastimes
more meet for ladies and gentlewomen to exercise . . . than for men of
courage to follow, whose hunting should practice their arms in tasting of
their manhood and dealing with such beasts as efstoons will turn again
and offer them the hardest [danger] rather than their horses' feet, which
many times may carry them with dishonor from the field." Harrison
wittily includes fallow deer and conies among the few remaining "per-
nicious" beasts in England because their great numbers make them as
destructive to arable land as sheep.[72]

For Harrison, then, the traditional argument in favor of hunting, that
it prepares men for war, is subverted in two senses. First, the contemporary practice of hunting, which depends primarily on vast lands
devoted to parks – more of them in England, he observes, than in all
Europe[73] – results in poverty and depopulation, reducing thereby the
potential number of recruits for military service. Second, the debased
form of hunting encouraged by parks "feminizes" men, providing none

of the discipline and hardship that they need as soldiers. Along with Elyot, whose criticism of the "softness" of contemporary hunting practices we have already considered, Harrison finds in hunting a threat to the perpetuation of a military elite; unlike Elyot, he extends his critique to the effect of hunting upon the common people and the nation as a whole.

The conventional linkage between hunting and masculinity that underlies the views of writers such as Elyot, Harrison, and James I was complicated by the fact that aristocratic women routinely hunted and had done so in Britain and on the continent for many centuries. Elizabeth's image appears prominently three times in *The Noble Arte of Venerie*. Lord Henry Berkeley's wife, Katharine, as we shall see in dealing with *The Taming of the Shrew*, acquired a reputation as a remarkable huntress. Manning even records the "unique" example of Catherine Gawen, "a recusant lady who actually led and rode with a poaching gang."[74] In pursuing the hunt throughout her reign, Queen Elizabeth was thus exceptional but not unique among women of the period. In the hunt, as in other activities, gender seems to have been less influential in determining one's social role than social status. The handbooks for women in the period seem to have had no concern with hunting, no admonitions comparable to those that appeared, say, in the Victorian magazine *The Field*, which in 1853 listed "six reasons why ladies should not hunt."[75] Despite the participation of high-ranking women in the hunt, however, the sport had powerfully masculine connotations. The gentler kinds of field sports, such as falconry or bow and stable hunting, were often recommended for women, and their participation in the more demanding kinds, such as *par force* hunting, seems to have carried with it an aura of masculinity.

Although few of Shakespeare's women hunt, those who do reflect Elizabethan customs and attitudes. They are aristocrats or royalty, for example, and their participation in the hunt is accepted by the males as natural and unworthy of comment. The pervasively masculine atmosphere of the hunt is particularly apparent in two cases, those of Hippolyta in *A Midsummer Night's Dream* and Tamora in *Titus Andronicus*. Hippolyta is quite literally an Amazon. Tamora, whose propensity for hunting is linked to her delight in rape, murder, and mutilation, is Queen of the Goths. Although the more "feminine" Lavinia also hunts in *Titus Andronicus*, she does so only to become herself the prey. The most complicated instance of the female hunter in Shakespeare, as we shall see, is that of the Princess in *Love's Labor's Lost*, who disapproves of hunting but still shoots a deer. The fact that few of Shakespeare's women hunt, and that they include an Amazon, an inciter to murder and rape, and a princess with doubts about the sport, suggests a certain "unnaturalness" in female participation in the sport. Women also rarely use the language of the hunt metaphorically in Shakespeare, with the result that their world, like the world of the lower social orders, both male and female, is for the most part insulated from the world of the hunt.

The gender tensions underlying the custom of female hunting may explain why Elizabeth's role as huntress did not become a more central part of her own political mythology or that of the courtiers around her. Elizabeth was often celebrated as Diana, of course, and occasionally the image was exploited in such a way as to highlight Diana's role as goddess of the hunt. The palace at Nonsuch, as mentioned previously, featured a grove of Diana with a fountain depicting Actaeon turned into a stag, and a hunting pageant at Cowdray in 1591 celebrated Elizabeth as Diana the huntress.[76] A widespread use of the image of Diana the huntress, however, might have evoked connotations of a virginal power too aggressive and deadly to be promoted by Elizabeth or to be happily endorsed by her courtiers. As Roy Strong has shown, moreover, the image of Elizabeth as Diana took on imperial connotations at an early stage, so that it was the moon as goddess of the seas that dominated the political mythology of the court; Ralegh's "Ocean to Cynthia," for example, ignores Diana's association with the hunt.

Hunting is of course a pervasive metaphor for the experience of love throughout Western culture, one that finds powerful expression in such works as The Song of Solomon, Virgil's *Aeneid*, Ovid's *Metamorphoses*, Petrarch's *Rime*, and *Gawain and the Green Knight*. The metaphor is capable of almost infinite variation: the male or female might play the role of hunter, for example, or either or both might fall prey to Cupid's arrow, or to their own desires, as in one popular interpretation of Actaeon, devoured by his own hounds. The most common use of the metaphor, however, in Shakespeare and in the tradition as a whole, places the male in the role of hunter and the female in the role of prey. In a hunting poem by William Cornish, for example, composed in the reign of Henry VIII, the male narrator describes, with obvious and sustained sexual innuendo, how he first struck a doe to the ground, then, weary, urged a companion to pursue her and do the same, and then finally discovered the creature with an arrow in her haunch, confirming that his companion's bow was now "well unbent, / Hys bolt may fle no more."[77]

8 Devonshire Hunting Tapestry, 1435–50 (detail). The disemboweling of a doe is
juxtaposed with a hunter's sexual advances.

Medieval and Renaissance art often represents the hunt as a site for
male sexual adventure. One conventional image, it seems, is of aristocratic male hunters fondling common women, as if the poetic convention of the love-chase were so strong it became inevitably realized in
the literal hunt. The fifteenth-century Devonshire Hunting Tapestries
show the prostrate and open carcass of a doe and, immediately and
disturbingly juxtaposed, a nobleman fondling the breast of a miller's
wife or daughter, while the miller looks on (fig. 8). A tapestry in the
Louvre – the month of May in the sixteenth-century series known as
Les Chasses de Maximilien – features, juxtaposed suggestively with preparations for a forest banquet, an aristocratic hunter fondling the breast
of a woman presumably from the village just visible in the background.

The Elizabethan pictorial tradition contains no such images, as far as
I am aware, and it is even possible that under Elizabeth, the Virgin
Queen, the connotations of male sexual aggression that surround the
hunt may have been somewhat suppressed. The images of Elizabeth
provided in Gascoigne's *Arte of Venerie* are devoid of sexuality, as is the
work itself, with the exception of a few inevitable jokes in the section on

antlers. The French original, in contrast, includes a long poem of love, "The Adolescence," which combines hunting with the pastoral in a way that is rare in the period. In this poem, the author, while hunting, comes upon a beautiful shepherd lass, seduces her, and shares her love for many years. Gascoigne excises this poem from his edition with the following comment:

And that which I have left out is nothing else but certayne unsemely verses, which bycause they are more apt for lascivious mindes, than to be enterlaced amongst the noble termes of Venerie, I thought meete to leave them at large, for such as will reade them in French.[78]

Gascoigne is an English patriot – he takes pains to include English terms and customs when they differ from the French – and he writes for a Virgin Queen.

In the opening scene of *Twelfth Night* Shakespeare provides a complex comic variation on the motif of love as a hunt. When Curio attempts to distract Orsino from his melancholy with the suggestion that he hunt the hart, Orsino responds with the inevitable pun:

> Why, so I do, the noblest that I have.
> O, when mine eyes did see Olivia first,
> Methought she purg'd the air of pestilence!
> That instant was I turn'd into a hart,
> And my desires, like fell and cruel hounds,
> E'er since pursue me.   (1.1.17–22)

The tortuous development of his thought suggests the disoriented state of Orsino's mind. The "heart" that he hunts is Olivia, whose virtues are associated with the powerful curative properties traditionally ascribed to the hart.[79] Yet in the very act of hunting he himself is turned into a hart, and, like Actaeon, who had become a traditional emblem of lust, is pursued by his own hounds. The convoluted image of Orsino hunting Olivia while his desires hunt him not only suggests the diseased nature of Orsino's imagination but anticipates the comically morbid intermingling of love and death that characterizes the chief romantic entanglements of the play.[80]

The comic treatment of sexuality in relation to the hunt often focuses on puns and wordplay that link the two activities. Jokes on "dear" and "deer" recur throughout Shakespeare's plays, as do allusions to the horns of the cuckold. Such wordplay runs riot in *Love's Labor's Lost*, especially in the dialogue between Boyet and Rosaline, which features bawdy allusions to shooting, pricks, horns, and hitting the target, much to the delight of Costard, for whom their wit "comes so smoothly off, so obscenely as it were, so fit" (4.1.143). The most blatant comic symbol of the sexuality of the hunt is the figure of Falstaff wearing the stag's horns at the end of *The Merry Wives of Windsor*. The disguise links him simultaneously and paradoxically to the sexual potency of the stag, the impotency of the cuckold, for whom he is a stand-in, and the violence of the hunter, represented by the legendary figure of Herne.

Shakespeare's most obviously tragic treatment of the hunt in relation to male sexual aggression is to be found in *Titus Andronicus*, in which the rape and mutilation of Lavinia by Tamora's sons is portrayed as a grisly parody of a hunt, even to the symbolic dismembering of the victim. In *The Rape of Lucrece*, Lucrece is compared to a frightened doe, and her rape becomes thereby a kind of hunt. *Venus and Adonis* plays out an inversion of this convention, in which the female figure becomes the aggressor and the male the passive victim; although never literally a hunter of Adonis, Venus plays the role of predatory animal. As usual, Shakespeare resists easy generalization: as soon as one begins to stereotype the male and female roles in the hunt, one encounters a reversal that calls the stereotype into question.

Both comic and tragic love occasionally evoke from Shakespeare hunting images from mythology. *Venus and Adonis*, of course, is a sustained treatment of one such myth, in which the violence and eroticism of the hunt are combined. In the Induction to *The Taming of the Shrew*, the lord and his servants offer Sly a chance to hawk, hunt, course, or view a picture of "Adonis painted by a running brook, / And Cytherea all in sedges hid" (Ind.2.50–51). Allusions to Diana are frequent throughout Shakespeare but only occasionally evoke her role as huntress. In a hunting scene in *Titus Andronicus*, Bassianus mocks Tamora as a "Dian" who has "abandoned her holy groves / To see the general hunting in this forest" (2.3.57–59). Diana's victim Actaeon appears more often than Diana herself, but almost exclusively in satiric or comic contexts as a symbol of lust or cuckoldry. Tamora replies to Bassianus's taunt by wishing she could use Diana's power and plant his head with horns like Actaeon's (2.3.61–65), an insult with prophetic overtones, since she later urges her sons to rape Lavinia, thereby transforming Bassianus into a cuckold. As a symbol of cuckoldry, the figure of Actaeon plays a major role in *The Merry Wives of Windsor*, with Ford's potential horns thrust upon Falstaff at the end of the play.

Shakespeare's use of the literary tradition of the hunt re-enforces the notion that his fascination with the sport is experiential rather than

merely bookish. The allusions to myth and classical literature are relatively infrequent, despite the powerful presence of hunting in such
authors as Ovid and Virgil; nor are there significant allusions to the rich
and evocative hunting motifs of medieval romance. To read
Shakespeare in the context of medieval hunting stories such as
Tristram's in Malory or Bercilak's in *Gawain and the Green Knight* is to
become aware of the loss of an enchanted world. Shakespeare's forests
are without unicorns, without figures like St. Eustace, who is converted
at the sight of a stag with Christ's cross between its antlers, and without
boars that represent the Devil. Such mystical images of the hunt are kept
alive to a certain extent in Spenser's imaginative universe, but not in
Shakespeare's.

The position of the hunt in both Shakespeare and in Elizabethan and
Jacobean society was thus complex. As a subject for art, it had a long and
rich tradition, capable of almost infinite elaboration. As a social practice, it embodied distinctive cultural tensions. On the one hand, and most
significantly, it was an activity that drew support from and re-enforced
the patriarchal and authoritarian tendencies within Elizabethan society.
Hunting was sanctioned by the Church. The legal position of the hunt
vested enormous power in the hands of the monarch and in those aristocrats fortunate enough to share in the privilege. The hunt itself, especially in its most ceremonial form, was a ritual celebration of the power
of the monarch. Its dominant social justification was as preparation for
war, a means of perpetuating the power of the landed elite. As such,
moreover, its most potent connotations were masculine. Hence the hunt
can be seen religiously, politically, socially, and sexually as a manifestation of various kinds and levels of patriarchal power.
    If this is the dominant paradigm, however, each of its terms was con-
tested. The hunt was a site of controversy. Christianity could be used to
oppose the hunt, as it was in the emergent attitude of sympathy for
animals, or in the Puritans' concerns for the poor. The monarch's
powers in the hunt could be, and were, challenged, as were those of the
aristocracy. The justification of the hunt as preparation for war could be
inverted and made to serve pacifist ends. The ceremony of the hunt
could be undermined ritualistically in poaching, as defiant mockery of
the authority of the aristocracy or monarch. And the notion of masculinity could be extended to include powerful women, as in the case of
Amazonian huntresses like Elizabeth, or used to challenge effete kinds
of hunting as symptoms of a decadent aristocracy.

As a social reality, then, hunting provided Shakespeare with a variable and conflicting set of practices, symbols, and attitudes. Hunting was not a source of social stability but of social tension. As both a potent social institution and traditional symbol, moreover, the hunt crystallized some of the most important tensions characteristic of the period as a whole: tensions in conceptions of the monarchy, of social status, of gender, of power over nature. Given its cultural richness and complexity, and its role as a site of social conflict, it is not surprising that Shakespeare found in the hunt a powerful source of drama.

CHAPTER TWO

Huntresses in Venus and Adonis *and* Love's Labor's Lost

The cultural conflict between the martial and sentimental views of the hunt, represented by such figures as James I and Montaigne, is invoked every time an Elizabethan or Jacobean female participates in the sport. Within this patriarchal society, the custom of female hunting involves a paradox: it liberates women to play the most virile of male roles but constrains them by denying their "essential" female nature. It is not surprising, therefore, that the most powerful anti-hunting poem of the period, Margaret Cavendish's "The Hunting of the Hare" (1653) is written by a woman who says of herself elsewhere, "according to the constitution of my *Sex*, I am as fearefull as a Hare."[1] In the activity of the hunt, tenderness, compassion, timidity – the traditionally female emotions – must be suppressed or somehow joined in tension with the traditionally male attributes of strength, fierceness, and courage. The huntress is therefore inevitably a kind of Amazon.

The paradox of the huntress is not explored in contemporary handbooks or in the dominant discourses of the hunt. Huntresses appear frequently in Shakespeare's plays, however, and we shall examine later such figures as Hippolyta in *A Midsummer Night's Dream* and Tamora in *Titus Andronicus*. In this chapter we shall consider two radically different huntresses who dominate their respective works: the goddess Venus in *Venus and Adonis* and the Princess of France in *Love's Labor's Lost*. In one sense, these figures share little in common: the one is the goddess of love, the other a mere princess; the one is at the centre of a tragic narrative, the other at the centre of a comic drama. For this reason, the figures will be treated in separate sections, in relation to their own distinctive works.

Juxtaposing the two characters, however, highlights their common involvement in the culture of the hunt. Both are huntresses, and the works in which they appear are deeply implicated in the conventional metaphor of love as a kind of hunt; the works have often been discussed, indeed, with this metaphor in mind. In both works, moreover, hunting is more than a conventional metaphor for erotic experience. The love-hunts are played out within a distinctive social ambiance. Each of the characters is defined in relation to specific kinds of hunting that have rich cultural meaning: Venus in relation to the hunting of boar, hare, and deer in parks, the Princess in relation to the latter motif alone. As huntresses, the two characters represent some deep social tensions within the bloody customs of the hunt. Caught within these tensions, both characters are forced to confront some unsettling truths about themselves and about the nature of love.

THE "BLOODING" OF VENUS IN *VENUS AND ADONIS*

At the end of November 1996, at Balmoral, Scotland, Prince William, son of Prince Charles and, after his father, heir to the British monarchy, killed his first stag. He was fourteen. In the weeks after the event the British press was filled with cries of moral indignation. A headline announcing a column of commentary in the *Observer* proclaimed, "Balmorality is Plain Obscene." The pursuit of blood sports by the royal family, the article argued, was anachronistic and immoral. In other reports moral outrage was accompanied with laments about the negative effect of hunting on the royal family. William's mother, Diana, Princess of Wales, it was said, was a strong opponent of blood sports, and her son's obvious love of hunting had driven a wedge between the two and had made it impossible for her to be selected as president of the Royal Society for the Prevention of Cruelty to Animals (*Irish Times*, 2 Dec.). In his love for the hunt, it was repeatedly implied, Prince William had been clearly influenced by his father, who accompanied him in this escapade, as did his brother, Harry, and the rather ambiguous and shadowy figure of Tiggy Legge-Bourke, who was not only a keen hunter but William's nanny.

For our purposes, the most curious feature of this event was the fascination in the press with one unknown fact: was Prince William "blooded" after he killed the stag? To think that this fourteen-year-old boy might have had his face daubed with the blood of his first stag as a mark of his initiation into the world of the hunt aroused more than a little discomfort in certain quarters. To think that it might not have happened, however, aroused equal discomfort in others. "The only shame," wrote Andrew Roberts in *The Times*, "was that the countryman prince was apparently not, possibly for reasons of political correctness, 'blooded' in the traditional Highland manner" (1 Dec.). One writer,

Adam Nicolson, was moved to describe his own "blooding" as a youth, which was accomplished in two stages, first, by a decorous stalker, who carefully used his fingers, but later, by the Dionysiac lord of the manor, who scooped up the blood with cupped hands (*Sunday Telegraph*, 1 Dec.). Despite the pressure of the reporters, the royal family never revealed whether the "blooding" actually occurred; most articles simply recorded the lack of certainty. A writer in the *Guardian* (28 Nov.), however, implied rather strongly that the deed had been done: "The prince is believed to have had blood smeared on his forehead by Sandy Masson, the head stalker, in a ritual similar to that faced by his father when he killed his first stag in the 1960s." *The Times* reported without comment that the artist Andre Durand had begun a portrait to commemorate the event, which would show Prince William "dressed in flowing red robes, his face smeared in the stag's spent blood and Balmoral Castle [nestled] sweetly in the snow-capped peaks beyond" (5 Dec.).

The tradition of "blooding" is certainly of ancient origin, although its history, not surprisingly, is obscure. It almost certainly existed in Shakespeare's time. A report from a Venetian ambassador in 1618 describes James I "blooding" his hunting companions as part of a *par force* hunt of the stag:

On his Majesty coming up with the dead game, he dismounts, cuts its throat and opens it, sating the dogs with its blood, as the reward of their exertions. With his own imbrued hands, moreover, he is wont to regale some of his nobility by touching their faces. This blood it is unlawful to remove or wash off, until it fall of its own accord, and the favoured individual thus bedaubed is considered to be dubbed a keen sportsman and chief of the hunt and to have a certificate of his sovereign's cordial good-will.[2]

As described by the Venetian observer, "blooding" was not restricted to one's first kill but was a mark of honor for heroic action, a kind of knighthood conferred to commemorate one's part in the day's victory. Erasmus's satiric description of the hunt in *Praise of Folly* does not mention "blooding," but his account of the ritual dismemberment of the deer suggests a similar initiatory significance: "the standers by, not speakyng a worde, behold it solemnly, as if it were some holy **Misterie**, havyng seen the like yet more than a hundred tymes before. Than (sir) whose happe it be to eate parte of the flesshe, marie he thynkes verily to be made therby halfe a gentilman."[3]

Although it seems to have escaped the attention of critics of the poem, a rite of "blooding" also appears in Shakespeare's *Venus and Adonis*.[4] At the very end of the work, the grief-stricken Venus looks down at the body of Adonis and, in a sudden reversal, identifies herself with the boar. It has killed Adonis out of excess love, she imagines, and she acknowledges that she herself would have done the same. The action that follows is the climax of the narrative: "With this she falleth in the place she stood / And stains her face with his congealed blood" (1121–22). The narrator's description is slightly ambiguous, but it is clear from the ensuing description of Venus's avid examination of the body that she does not fall and bloody her face involuntarily, as in a faint; instead, she drops suddenly but deliberately to the ground and daubs herself with Adonis's "congealed blood." As John Roe observes, the word "congealed" suggests that Venus applies the blood "ceremoniously like dye or paint."[5] In her case, unlike that of James's courtiers, the blood will not later fall off; it is a stain and will endure. As a rite of "blooding," Venus's action is curious indeed: she daubs her own face, making herself both the experienced hunter and the novice, and the blood she uses is that of Adonis, who becomes therefore not only the boar's prey but her own. To understand the significance of this peculiar action, which occurs at the climactic moment of the narrative, it helps to place the poem as a whole within the Elizabethan culture of the hunt.

Shakespeare's main source for *Venus and Adonis* is Ovid's account of the story in Book Ten of *The Metamorphoses*. His most striking departure from this source, as has often been observed, is in making Adonis resistant to Venus's love. Both Ovid's Adonis and Shakespeare's love to hunt, but Ovid's also makes love to Venus, and his account gives no suggestion that the two sources of pleasure are in conflict. In Ovid's version, Venus even tucks up her skirts like Diana and hunts the gentler game with him. For Ovid, Adonis's tragic death is caused not because he prefers hunting to love, but simply because he fails to heed Venus's warning against hunting the boar. In Shakespeare's version of the tale, in contrast, Adonis is an adolescent boy almost prudishly hostile to sexual love and strongly enamored of the hunt. The effect of this redefinition of Adonis's motives is to focus the tragedy on a conflict between two modes of behavior, hunting and love.

Because Venus has far more to say about love than Adonis about hunting, the significance of Adonis's preference makes itself felt mainly indirectly, by implication. In the Elizabethan context, however, especially that of the aristocratic coterie for which the poem was apparently written, Adonis's silences could be to some extent filled in by a shared cultural understanding. Shakespeare's Adonis is an adolescent boy on the verge of manhood, and it is towards his manhood that the poem as a whole seems to drive. Venus wants Adonis to act the part of a man by making love to her: "Thou art no man, though of a man's complexion, / For men will kiss even by their own direction" (215–16). Adonis wants to become a man by killing the boar: "if any love you owe me, / Measure my strangeness with my unripe years; / Before I know myself, seek not to know me" (523–25). Adonis's resistance to Venus is embodied in his resistance to the pun on "know": for him, self-knowledge precedes sexual experience; for her, self-knowledge and sexual experience occur at the same time.

Although some critics find Adonis's rejection of Venus merely prudish or narcissistic, his own formulation leaves open the prospect of sexual love, only deferring it to a later stage in his development.[6] He is not against love, it seems, but against Venus's love at this time; the difference is subtle but important.[7] Even Venus is not altogether opposed to hunting, merely the most dangerous kind of hunting, the hunting of boar. Both characters thus see Adonis's entry into manhood as a desirable end, but they define the experience in antithetical ways. For Venus, it is the act of love that initiates: Adonis will "know" himself when he "knows" her. For Adonis, self-knowledge proceeds from hunting. Although Adonis has presumably hunted before – "hunting he lov'd, but love he laugh'd to scorn" (4) – the killing of the boar thus takes on an initiatory significance. Two modes of initiation are played off against each other throughout the poem in Ovidian fashion, each metamorphosing into the other in ways that ultimately make it difficult to tell them apart.

Adonis's conception of the hunt as part of an initiatory process that culminates in manhood, as a means of knowing the self before committing the self to love, translates into Ovidian terms a conception of adolescent experience grounded in Elizabethan culture. For adolescent males of all social classes, hunting or poaching served an important initiatory and educational function. As works like Elyot's *Governor* and James I's *Basilicon Doron* make clear, boys in the period were introduced early to the hunt as a training ground for war, a test of their ability to master terrain, to endure physical hardship, to show courage, and to kill. In this, young aristocrats emulated their betters. James I, obsessed with hunting as an adult, was already alarmingly "addicted" to the sport, according to a contemporary observer, at the age of nineteen; an early portrait of James shows him as a boy of about fourteen, holding a falcon on his left hand.[8] Charles I was introduced to hunting at the age of four, and note was taken that he took great delight in seeing a buck hunted

9 Memorial brass of John Selwyn, underkeeper of the Royal Park of Oatlands, Surrey (*c.* 1587). The brass was originally affixed to a gravestone, with one of its sides invisible. Presumably, the family was unhappy with one version.

and killed.[9] His young son, later Charles II, provoked admiration when, at the age of eleven, he leapt from his horse, waded through some ditches and killed a hare that had been wounded by his father.[10] The epitome of this adolescent bravado, in its "adult" manifestation, is the monumental brass depicting John Selwyn, underkeeper of the Royal Park of Oatlands, stabbing a stag in the throat while riding it; the brass commemorates a deed said to have been performed before Elizabeth (fig. 9).

Venus and Adonis is dedicated to Henry Wriothesley, Earl of Southampton, who was only nineteen in 1593 when the poem was published.[11] Whether Shakespeare's portrayal of Adonis alludes to the Earl's resistance to a marriage arranged by Lord Burghley is uncertain, but the atmosphere of adolescent male camaraderie in which such young men grew up pervades the poem. "The younger sort," according to Gabriel Harvey, "takes much delight in Shakespeare's Venus and Adonis."[12] From the age of eight to his maturity Southampton was one of Burghley's wards. In his early years, he lived and studied with the other young wards in Burghley's household. At twelve he entered the entirely masculine world of St. John's College, Cambridge; at fifteen he was admitted to the equally masculine and more fashionable world of Gray's Inn. He became close friends with two of Burghley's other wards, the young Earls of Rutland and Essex.

Throughout his life Southampton was closely associated with the world of the hunt. In 1589, when he was sixteen, his steward brought suit on his behalf against one Richard Pitts and his companions for stealing deer and beating the keepers one night at Whiteley Park.[13] Southampton's friend Rutland shared with him his own avidity for the sport. In a letter of 14 July 1590 to Burghley, Rutland included commendations to Southampton, who was sixteen at the time, with the regretful note that he doubted whether he would even kill one buck that summer. In another letter, Burghley had to urge Rutland not to forget his books: "'you will, whan you ar weary of huntyng, recontinew some exercise of huntyng in your book.'"[14] Burghley himself kept parks stocked with game, loved his horses and dogs, and was a skilled rider and archer.[15] Southampton went on to a military career – he was knighted by Essex for his role in the Azores expedition – but was imprisoned by Elizabeth for his role in the Essex rebellion. He was released and restored to favor by James I in 1603, when he was made "Master of the Queen's Game with direction over all Her Majesty's forests and chases." He hunted often with the King and Queen thereafter, and in 1607 was appointed Keeper of the New Forest.[16]

As is well known, Elizabethans conceived of adolescence as a distinct period, with a wide range of stereotyped behaviors and attitudes.[17] For most young male aristocrats, the potential period of adolescence covered roughly the ages of 12 to 26, and was marked at one end by departure from the family home and at the other by marriage and full adult status. The higher the social standing, the more pressure there was to marry early; Burghley attempted to force Southampton to marry his granddaughter, Lady Elizabeth Vere, at the age of sixteen. In most cases young male aristocrats had a period of ten to fourteen years in which to serve as pages in others' households, attend university and the inns of court, travel abroad, fall in and out of love, and hunt. Hunting, of course, continued after marriage, and love often preceded it. The relatively late age of marriage, however, tended to make of the wedding ceremony, with its dominant symbol of sexual consummation, an initiation rite in which mature heterosexual experience and the acquisition of adult social status converged.

Unlike marriage, hunting involved initiation into an essentially masculine society, and at a very early age. John Smyth's history of the Berkeley family links hunting to the period of life he calls "the age of puberty" and the "age of adolescency." Smyth notes the great delight that the young Sir Thomas Berkeley took in hunting in the reign of Edward I, an adolescent enthusiasm that seems to have been passed down to his descendant Henry, Lord Berkeley, who, as a young man in the reign of Edward VI, lived with his mother in London and hunted daily in the fields of Gray's Inn.[18] Adonis's conception of the hunt as an initiatory experience, a way of knowing the self that precedes and, in effect, prepares one for adult heterosexual love, is recognizable within this social context. Hunting was a form of education, a training ground for war, and a means of bonding adolescent males to each other and to the adult fraternity of the chase.

Suggestive evidence for the importance of hunting as an initiatory experience for adolescent males appears in two hunting portraits of the period: one, a painting by Robert Peake that we have considered in chapter 1, shows the nine-year-old Prince Henry sheathing his sword after ritualistically cutting the neck of a deer (fig. 1); the other, the "December" tapestry from the hunting series in the Louvre entitled *Les Chasses de Maximilien*, features a young man, whose beardless face contrasts markedly with the faces of the hunters coming to his aid, killing a boar (fig. 10).[19] In each case the drama of the moment of the kill is heightened by the obvious youthfulness of the protagonist. The portrait of Prince Henry is the less exciting of the two, since the animal is already dead, but an aura of power is evoked by the Prince's imposing sword and intimidating stare. There is no adolescent awkwardness or hesitation in the pose. The attack upon the boar in the "December" tapestry is highly theatrical and highlights the notoriety of the animal as the most dangerous of prey. Compared to this image of the hunt, the tapestries in the series devoted to killing the stag – "September" and "October" – are anticlimactic: in both of them the hunting party is in the foreground, and the pursued stags are visible only in the distance.

Shakespeare's choice of the boar for Adonis's hunt was of course dictated by the myth, and his treatment of the animal, not surprisingly, is more obviously "literary" than his treatment of the hare and the horse, the descriptions of which evoke the countryside around Stratford.[20] In his survey of the medieval conception of the boar, John Cummins calls the animal an "archetype of unrelenting ferocity." In both medieval and Elizabethan hunting manuals the boar is treated as the most dangerous animal hunted. The medieval writer Gaston Phoebus claims to have seen a boar "strike a man and split him from knee to chest, so that he fell dead without a word."[21] In *The Noble Arte of Venerie*, Gascoigne is reluctant even to recommend the boar hunt, in view of its destructive effect upon dogs; the boar, he says, "is the only beast which can dispatch a hounde at one blow."[22]

Hunting the boar, then, is a supreme test of manhood, one that accords fully with the values of those who, like Thomas Elyot, William

10 The December tapestry from *Les Chasses de Maximilien* (mid sixteenth-century). The climax of a boar hunt.

Harrison, and James I, praise only the most "manly" kinds of hunting. James's praise of *par force* hunting and contempt for less "manly" kinds, such as coursing, occurs in *Basilicon Doron*, a book he published in 1599 for the instruction of his young prince Henry, then six years old. Elyot's attempt to resurrect the hunting of deer on foot, following the heroic examples of Alexander the Great and Henry V, also appears in a book devoted to the instruction of boys, *The Book Named the Governor*. Both Elyot and James, moreover, draw upon Xenophon's *Cyropaedia* for their idealization of the initiatory qualities of the hunt, a work that was taught in the grammar schools with great effect, if Sidney's admiration for it in the *Defence of Poetry* is any test. Elyot recommends the reading of the *Cyropaedia* between the ages of fourteen and seventeen.[23] Hence the most prominent rationale for the hunt in the period, that it trained young men for war, invites an initiatory approach to the hunt itself.

Adonis's quest to "know" himself through the boar hunt is thus an initiatory quest. The boy becomes a man in the conquest of death, taking on the warrior-status of the ferocious beast he kills. In this sense the boar is a symbol of Death, as many critics have observed.[24] But the boar's role as an "archetype of unrelenting ferocity" is not restricted to killing. The boar is also a conventional symbol of dangerous virility. In *The Historie of the Foure-Footed Beastes*, for example, Edward Topsell describes the "venerial rage" of the boar in a manner that makes sexuality itself a force of death:

Being inflamed with venerial rage, he so setteth upright the bristles of his neck, that you would take them to be the sharp fins of Dolphins; then champeth he with his mouth, grateth and gnasheth his teeth one against another, and breathing forth his boyling spirit, not only at his eies, but at his foaming white mouth, he desireth nothing but copulation, and if his female endure him quietly, then doth shee satisfie his lust, and kill all his anger; but if she refuse, then doth he either constraine her against her will, or else layeth hir dead upon the earth.[25]

As A. T. Hatto has shown, literary counterparts to this naturalistic tradition appear in many writers, including Boccaccio and Chaucer, both of whom describe Troilus's dream of a boar making love to Criseyde.[26] Shakespeare himself evokes the tradition in *Cymbeline*, where Posthumus expresses his jealous rage in an image of the lustful Jachimo mounting Imogen with a cry "like a full-acorn'd boar" (2.5.16). The notion that the boar kills Adonis merely because he wanted to kiss him also appears often in sixteenth-century verse.[27]

Eros is thus everywhere in this Ovidian poem, and Adonis's adolescent attempt to flee love for boar-hunting is doomed to fail. But

Shakespeare gives the story another twist. Although he is not original in ascribing amorousness to the boar, Shakespeare seems to be unique in ascribing to Adonis himself a reciprocal erotic longing. In a way that Adonis does not foresee, his tragic quest of the boar plays out the implications of the narrator's account of his motives as early as line four: "Hunting he lov'd, but love he laugh'd to scorn." Adonis scorns love but loves hunting. Like Ovid's Hippolytus, as William Keach remarks, Adonis "has committed himself to chastity and redirected all his repressed erotic energies to the hunt."[28]

As an adolescent in pursuit of manhood, barely awakening to sexuality, Adonis does not understand his own motives. "I know not love," he tells Venus, "nor will not know it, / Unless it be a boar, and then I chase it . . ." (409–10). The familiar pun on the word "know" suggests here an unconscious confusion between sexuality and killing, as does the image of the "chase," which is equivocal enough to refer to sexual pursuit or the pursuit of the hunt. The equivocation is later resolved, in Venus's description, at the moment of Adonis's death: "nousling in his flank, the loving swine / Sheath'd unaware the tusk in his soft groin" (1115–16). Although one might be tempted to read these lines dramatically, as merely a projection of Venus's own psychology, both the conventional symbolism of the boar and the development of Adonis throughout the poem serve to confirm the intuitive truth of her words. The initiatory consummation of the boar's "love" for Adonis, and Adonis's unconscious love for the boar, brings forth not only blood but a purple flower, which Venus "cradles" (1185) in her breast as if it were Adonis's child.

As Don Cameron Allen has shown, *Venus and Adonis* rests upon a long-standing metaphoric relationship between love and hunting: love itself is a kind of hunt, a "soft" hunt opposed to the heroic "hard" hunt of dangerous prey such as the boar.[29] Allen's account ignores, however, Shakespeare's Ovidian reversal of that motif, which converts hunting into a kind of love. Although the reversal may be implicit in the metaphoric equation – if love is a hunt, then hunting must be a love – there seems to be no comparable literary tradition behind it.[30] As Matt Cartmill has shown, however, the notion often surfaces in modern discussions of the motivations of hunters. Cartmill quotes William Thompson, who helped to establish the sport of bow-hunting in America, as saying of the deer he has pursued, "I have so loved them that I longed to kill them." According to Cartmill, this "pathological" motif "crops up again and again throughout the literature of hunting:

many hunters deeply and sincerely love the animals they kill, and they identify that love as one of their reasons for wanting to kill them."[31]

Although Adonis too loves his prey, Shakespeare's treatment of the motif is quite different from that described by Cartmill. Adonis is vague and uncertain about his motives, for one thing, driven by his awakening manhood to pursue drives he does not fully understand; the impulse that Cartmill finds pathological is in him innocent, although at the same time dangerous. The prey that Adonis pursues, moreover, is not the shy and seductive deer lusted after by William Thompson but a boar; Adonis's love object is hyperbolically masculine, a symbol of raging virility. The eroticism that in Cartmill's example is associated with traditional notions of male dominance over women is thus in the case of Adonis more complex. From one perspective, as we have seen, "knowing" the boar may be conceived of in heterosexual terms, as the acquisition of an aggressive adult masculinity. From another, however, it may be conceived of in homosexual terms, as an act of masculine self-sufficiency. Both potential outcomes are inimical to Venus's desires, and both are thwarted by Adonis's death.

Although it does not figure in Ovid's account of the myth, the homoeroticism in Shakespeare's treatment of Adonis is nevertheless Ovidian, as Jonathan Bate has so persuasively argued; in this regard, Ovid's stories of beautiful adolescent boys who, like Narcissus or Cyparissus, flee from heterosexual love are as relevant to Shakespeare's version of the myth as the story of Adonis himself.[32] Here too Shakespeare's imagination seems to have been prompted as much by the Elizabethan culture of the hunt as by the literary tradition. When Venus asks Adonis if he will meet her the next day, he "tells her no, to-morrow he intends / To hunt the boar with certain of his friends" (587–88). The hard hunt of the boar, as we have seen, is the most conventionally masculine kind of hunting. Adonis hunts with boys and men, and one of the traditional functions of such hunting was to bind men to one another, to create a warrior-class set apart from and superior to the "effeminate" society of the court. In this respect the early life of the Earl of Southampton, to whom Shakespeare's poem is dedicated, is a paradigm. He was brought up among boys in Burghley's household and educated among boys and men at Cambridge and the Inns of Court. Burghley's attempt to marry him off at the age of sixteen was thus an intrusion of adult heterosexuality into a dominantly masculine adolescent world.

While the Elizabethan proponents of the hard hunt saw clearly the danger represented by the love of Venus, whose softness was emasculating, they did not see the danger represented by the love of the boar, a danger that, as Shakespeare develops it, grows directly out of the initiatory impulse behind the hunt. If young boys are to become not only men but warriors through the pursuit of the boar, and if that pursuit is driven by an erotic impulse, then the very love of men that such an initiation fulfills is inevitably tied to the death of men; the animals hunted are, after all, only surrogates for the men to be hunted later in war. Although Shakespeare only hints at this dangerous and destructive eroticism in *Venus and Adonis*, it underlies his later representation of the warriors Coriolanus and Aufidius in *Coriolanus*. The fascination that draws these two characters to each other seems that of a deadly eroticism, and one that is expressed in the language of hunting. "He is a lion," Coriolanus says of Aufidius as he prepares for battle, "That I am proud to hunt" (1.1.235–36). "Let me twine / Mine arms about that body," says Aufidius, greeting Coriolanus, "where against / My grained ash an hundred times hath broke, / And scarr'd the moon with splinters" (4.5.106–09). At the end of the play, Coriolanus is "entwined" by Aufidius's soldiers, who encircle and slaughter him like a beast of prey.

To speak of homoeroticism in the case of the "love" of Adonis and the boar, however, is ultimately misleading, for it implies a rigid categorizing of sexual experience that does not occur in the poem. As we have seen, the boar functions as a symbol of both homosexual and heterosexual passion. As Bruce R. Smith observes, the "temporary freedom" that such androgynous figures as Adonis "grant to sexual desire allows it to flow out in all directions, toward all the sexual objects that beckon in the romantic landscape."[33] Just how many sexual objects there are in the landscape of *Venus and Adonis* is shown in Jonathan Bate's account of Shakespeare's adaptation of his Ovidian sources, which include stories of incest (Adonis's mother is Myrrha), homosexuality, heterosexuality, narcissism, and hermaphroditism. Given such a polymorphous poetic landscape, one is tempted to add bestiality to the list; the "love" that Adonis pursues, after all, is a boar. To speak of heterosexuality or homosexuality in such a poem is thus inevitably reductive; at issue is eros itself, which drives the universe. And eros, in this poem, leads only to death.

Venus, of course, believes that eros leads to life, and throughout the poem she uses all her arts to persuade Adonis of this truth. She appeals to her beauty, threatens him with the dangers of narcissism, argues that procreation is not only delightful but a duty, berates him with the example of his virile and willing horse, maneuvers him into inviting sexual postures, holds before him the immortality to be won by propagation – yet she fails utterly to convince him. And she fails to convince the reader. If an unconscious eroticism underlies Adonis's pursuit of the hunt, an unconscious violence underlies Venus's pursuit of love. She is as much a "hunter" as Adonis or the boar. In her case the hunt is the traditional hunt of love, and her prey is Adonis. Much of the wit of the poem lies in Shakespeare's variations on this conventional theme.

The Venus of Ovid's story is not opposed to hunting, as we have seen; she tucks up her skirts and accompanies Adonis on the chase. Shakespeare's Venus, however, prefers a more passive approach. She invites Adonis to be her "deer":

> "Fondling," she saith, "since I have hemm'd thee here
> Within the circuit of this ivory pale,
> I'll be a park, and thou shalt be my deer:
> Feed where thou wilt, on mountain, or in dale;
>   Graze on my lips, and if those hills be dry,
>   Stray lower, where the pleasant fountains lie."   (229–34)

This is a wonderfully seductive vision of love, not the less so because it wittily parodies the Song of Solomon, in which the bride imagines her bridegroom a roe or young hart that feeds among the lilies (2.16–17). From a modern perspective, the image is not only erotic but comically nurturing: Adonis is invited to graze at will, to luxuriate in her bounty. An Elizabethan park, however, was by no means a nature preserve in the modern sense. Deer were coddled in parks – fed and cared for, protected from winter's harshness – but for one reason only: to be killed by arrows or run to death by greyhounds. Venus's "ivory pale" is a lovely and inviting "circuit" of death. Her very words of reassurance – "No dog shall rouse thee, though a thousand bark" (240) – are ominous, since they make the languor of sexual fulfillment seem suspiciously like the silence of the grave. Commenting on the "effeminate" custom of hunting in parks, William Harrison remarks wryly that keeping deer enclosed makes it difficult to tell "whether our buck or doe are to be reckoned in wild or tame beasts or not."[34] Parks are killing fields for pet deer.

The deadly eroticism of Venus's delightful park thus derives not merely from the literary tradition linking love with the hunt but from the social practice of hunting in Elizabethan parks. Such hunting provided a casual and relaxing form of entertainment, one that could be easily indulged in as part of the socializing one expected when entertaining the Queen on progress or a foreign visitor. Robert Peake's portrait of Princess Elizabeth in 1603 provides a suggestive image of such an occasion (fig. 4).[35] The painting itself is innocuous, but the links it forges between hunting in parks and intimate affairs of the heart have the potential to be developed in less innocent directions. In this painting the Princess, dressed elaborately in white, stands in an outdoor setting, directly facing the viewer. To our right, in the background, a small bridge across a stream leads the eye to the pales of the park, within which a hunt is in progress, represented by the figures of two horsemen, a huntsman on foot, and deer fleeing across a lawn. To our left, in the background, and juxtaposed exactly with the image on the right, a winding path leads the eye upwards to a small circle of trees enclosing a wooded bower, in which sit two women in close conversation. The absence of sexuality in the painting differentiates this park from the one envisaged by Venus: the young princess is virginal and dressed in white, set off from the landscape in which she finds herself; the conversing women are prim and decorous figures. Peake's choice of background imagery, however, is highly suggestive. For him, pursuing deer within a pale and conversing intimately within a bower are not merely part of the same landscape; they occur at the same time and are visually equivalent. Both activities occur within "circuits" reminiscent of Venus's "circuit of this ivory pale." Venus imagines her arms the pale of a park; Peake displays two "pales," the one devoted to the death of deer, the other, simultaneously, to intimate personal affairs.

Queen Elizabeth's visit to Cowdray in 1591 provides another suggestive gloss on Venus's fantasy of herself as a park. Most country estates had good views of the park, and it was often possible simply to watch a hunt from a window, as one might watch a tennis match from the gallery. At Cowdray Elizabeth watched from a turret in the evening while sixteen bucks were "pulled downe with Greyhoundes, in a laund." That morning, she had been led to a "delicate Bowre" in the park, listened to a "dittie" that celebrated her as an eroticized Diana, received the gift of a crossbow, and killed "three or four" deer that had been "put into a paddock." The erotic ambiance of this kind of hunting, which mingles the death of tame deer with sophisticated courtly compliment, are evoked in the "dittie" sung to Queen Elizabeth as the bow is presented:

> Goddesse and Monarch of (t)his happie Ile,
>   vouchsafe this bow which is an huntresse part:
> Your eies are arrows though they seeme to smile
>   which never glanst but gald the stateliest hart,
> Strike one, strike all, for none at all can flie,
> They gaze you in the face although they die.[36]

Although the Queen assumes the role of Diana in accepting the bow "which is an huntresse part," the power of her arrow-eyes kills all who behold her, deer or courtiers, with love. It is not difficult to see behind Venus's longing for her timorous deer, the nibbling Adonis, the menacing undercurrent that one detects in the ditty sung before Elizabeth. In both cases, the deer are there to die for love.

Venus's attempt to seduce Adonis by appealing to the eroticism of the hunting park is greeted only by his smile "as in disdain" (241). When she discovers that he intends to hunt the boar, she shifts the ground of her appeal from the hunting of deer in parks to the coursing of hare in open woods and fields. Unlike Ovid's Venus, who actually indulges in such hunting with her lover, Shakespeare's merely urges it upon Adonis, and only then because the hunting of "fearful creatures" (677) such as the "timorous flying hare" (674) is preferable to hunting the boar. In her fear, she thus turns to another soft kind of hunting, one that, although slightly less "effeminate" than hunting in parks with bows, aroused the contempt of such advocates of the martial hunt as Elyot, Harrison, and King James. In the *Governor*, for example, Elyot begrudgingly accepts hare-hunting as a sport for "effeminate" men, such as scholars, and for women who might otherwise be idle:

Hunting of the hare with greyhounds is a right good solace for men that be studious, of them to whom nature hath not given personage or courage apt for the wars. And also for gentlewomen, which fear neither sun nor wind for impairing their beauty. And peradventure they shall be thereat less idle than they should be at home in their chambers.[37]

In the *Basilicon Doron*, James I echoes this point of view, disparaging "greyhound hunting" as "not so martiall a game" as the running of deer with hounds.[38]

In her account of the hare hunt, as in her vision of love in a deer park, Venus projects upon the hare her own erotic fantasies; in doing so, however, her identification of herself with the hare leads her into an argumentative impasse. The hare is of course a traditional symbol of sexuality, and even the popular name that Venus uses, "Wat" (697), alludes to the female genitalia.[39] In this sense the hunt that Venus so vividly urges upon Adonis is the hunt of herself, his willing prey, and critics tend to treat her description in such erotic terms.[40] Although this kind of conventional eroticism is present in the episode, it is less pronounced than one might expect; the subtlest source of wit is less predictable and draws upon the contemporary discourse of hunting. Despite her sexual obsessiveness, Venus's description of the hunt is curiously chaste, and its effect is to dampen her ardor and disrupt her seductive train of thought. As she describes the flight of the hare in its "cranks and crosses with a thousand doubles" (682), it becomes increasingly human-ized and its plight increasingly desperate and moving. Even at the begin-ning of the description the hare is a "poor wretch" (680). By the end, it has been given a name, "poor Wat," has been shown standing patheti-cally on its "hinder-legs with list'ning ear" (697–98), and, as a "dew-bedabbled wretch" (703), has become, to Venus's own surprise, an emblem of human misery: "For misery is trodden on by many, / And being low, never reliev'd by any" (707–08). [41] She herself is shocked by her conclusion: "To make thee hate the hunting of the boar," she says, "Unlike myself thou hear'st me moralize . . ." (711–12). Distracted by the effect of her own exhortation to hunt the hare, she ends by losing her train of thought altogether: "Where did I leave?" (715).

In "moralizing" the hunt, Venus follows a familiar convention. Emblematic readings of the book of nature were customary even in the hunting manuals themselves. In *The Noble Arte of Venerie*, for example, George Gascoigne praises hunting for its capacity to "represent" other activities, noting that the "nimble Hare, by turning in hir course, / Doth plainly prove that *Pollicie*, sometime surpasseth force."[42] Within the initiatory context of the hunt, in which the danger and hardship of the sport become a test of manhood, Venus's argument in favor of hunting hare, as one might expect, is dangerously "effeminate." The comedy of the hare-hunt thus depends upon the way in which Venus's desperate argument, intended to encourage Adonis towards a harmless kind of hunting and save him from the boar, misfires. She has moralized in the wrong direction. Given the conventional associations of hare-hunting with a lack of virility, it is not surprising that Venus's eloquent descrip-tion of the hare hunt has no effect at all upon Adonis. His response to Venus's distracted question, "Where did I leave?" is wittily abrupt and dismissive: "No matter where, . . . / Leave me, and then the story aptly ends" (715–16).

More surprising is the effect of her description upon Venus herself, for she is unexpectedly moved to pity the very animal she has been recom-mending as prey. She not only advocates an "effeminate" kind of hunting; she is psychologically and morally unable to sustain even the thought of killing such a beast. She is beginning to think like Montaigne, in the essay "Of Cruelty," whose translator, Florio, seems to echo Venus's own characterization of the hare as a "dew-bedabbled wretch":

"I cannot well endure a seely dew-bedabled hare to groane, when she is seized upon by the howndes." [43] Her anthropomorphic treatment of the hare and the moral that she draws, with its sympathy for those who are "low" and "trodden on by many," are reminiscent not only of Montaigne but of the Puritans, who saw hunting both as potentially cruel and as an attack upon the poor. Her distraction at the end of this increasingly impassioned speech thus marks her confused awareness that sympathy for the hare has undermined not only the hunting she advocates but the sensual love she represents.

Behind Venus's attempt to seduce Adonis through images of hunting deer in parks and coursing hare in the fields lies a hierarchy of social values within the culture of the hunt itself. In the debate between love and hunting, she positions herself not merely on the side of love but on the side of the debased kinds of hunting that transform a heroic and martial activity, an initiation into manhood, into an ignoble and effeminizing kind of entertainment. The coursing of hares, the shooting of tame deer in parks – these are activities that blur the distinctions between martial values and courtly eroticism, that threaten to turn hunting itself into love. And this is of course exactly what Venus hopes to accomplish. She herself is an agent of metamorphosis, a force devoted to transforming one kind of venery into another. Shakespeare's poem enacts the transformative possibilities on either side of that pun.

Venus's emasculating energy, like that of the boar, manifests itself in paradoxical ways. On the one hand she desires a tame Adonis, attempting to transform him from a hunter of boar into a hunter of deer or hare, or worse, into her own pet deer, grazing on her lips and "sweet bottom grass" (233, 236). On the other hand, she wants him to act the part of a man. "Thou art no man," she complains, "though of a man's complexion, / For men will kiss even by their own direction" (215–16). When she falls upon the ground, she tries to jostle Adonis into the appropriate male position, and when his highly-sexed stallion proves his masculinity with a breeding jennet, she provides Adonis with the moral: "Thy palfrey, as he should, / Welcomes the warm approach of sweet desire" (385–86).

The powerful example of natural passion provided by Adonis's horse has led many critics to adopt Venus's point of view and to find Adonis's resistance priggish or narcissistic. As William Keach argues, however, Venus herself embodies neither in words nor actions the powerful argument for natural passion implied in the majestic and primitive sexuality of the horses.[44] The range of her sexual expression, which mingles comedy and pathos, coyness and direct assault, sophistication and simplicity, is no more "natural" than that of Cleopatra, whose character she anticipates. Underlying all of her varied appeals to love is a manipulative desire for sexual domination that belies her wish that Adonis were a man. What she most desires is a man, but a man who is child-like because under her control. As Heather Dubrow observes, "Venus connects loving Adonis with controlling him, mastering him; indeed, so deep is the connection as to make us suspect that even had he been less reluctant her impulse would have been to assert sovereignty by grasping and entrapping him."[45] Like Adonis, she cannot escape her mythological destiny. What she desires – and as Venus must desire – is another Mars, led prisoner by a "red rose chain" (110). *Venus and Adonis* is a poem about sexual domination, and shadowing the struggle between loving and hunting is the archetypal struggle for mastery between Venus and Mars.

Although fundamentally opposed, Venus and the boar therefore have much in common. Both love Adonis with a love that destroys. Venus herself is described at many points in the poem as a hunter or predatory animal whose sexual aggression is not only unattractive but murderous and devouring. She kisses Adonis's brow like "an empty eagle . . . devouring all in haste" (55–57). She holds him as one holds a hunted bird, "tangled in a net" (67). When they fall to the earth, "their lips together glued," she feeds "glutton-like" upon the "yielding prey," as if she were a vulture (546–51). Even upon Adonis's death she "crops the stalk" (1175) of the flower that has grown from his blood, aware that in doing so she destroys it but excusing herself by remarking that "it is as good / To wither in my breast as in his blood" (1181–82). In her pursuit of Adonis, Venus is in many respects identified with the boar itself. She accosts Adonis at the beginning of the poem as a "bold-fac'd suitor" (6). In her passion, she becomes so "enrag'd" that she plucks him from his horse (29–30), and so "red and hot" that she burns like "coals of glowing fire" (35). She pushes him backward, "as she would be thrust" (41). When he speaks, she "murthers" his words "with a kiss" (54). When Adonis finally yields a kiss, she exhibits symptoms comparable to those that Edward Topsell calls the "venerial rage" of the boar:

> And having felt the sweetness of the spoil,
> With blindfold fury she begins to forage;
> Her face doth reek and smoke, her blood doth boil,
> And careless lust stirs up a desperate courage . . .   (553–56)

When Venus discovers Adonis dead upon the ground, her shock is thus a shock of recognition. She sees in the deadly eroticism of the boar an image of herself:

> "Had I been tooth'd like him, I must confess,
> With kissing him I should have kill'd him first,
> But he is dead, and never did he bless
> My youth with his, the more am I accurs'd."
>   With this she falleth in the place she stood,
>   And stains her face with his congealed blood.   (1117–22)

Although a goddess and eternally young, Venus sees herself now as old, as looking back upon a "youth" that was never blessed with Adonis's love. The true initiation towards which the poem has been driving is now revealed: not Adonis but Venus achieves maturity and self-knowledge, and she does so, not through the blessing of youthful love, but through the deadly eroticism of the hunt. She knows herself, in the violence of her passion, the boar. The mark of that knowledge is the mark of the hunter: the stain of her prey, Adonis, forever upon her face. As the goddess of love, she initiates herself.

In his insightful account of Shakespeare's Ovidianism, Jonathan Bate calls Venus's prophecy, with which the poem concludes, an "etiology of love's anguish."[46] The Ovidian context certainly invites the identification of origins, and Venus herself concludes her prophecy with what seems to be a curse: "Sith in his prime, Death doth my love destroy, / They that love best, their loves shall not enjoy" (1163–64). In a deeper sense, however, the moment is not one of origin but of recognition; Shakespeare works a variation on the Ovidian theme. Venus does not cause the future but merely sees it: "Since thou art dead, lo here I prophesy, / Sorrow on love hereafter shall attend" (1135–36). The catalogue of sorrows she describes – of inconstancy, deception, madness, jealousy, war – is not called into being by Venus but called into consciousness. The sorrows of love are not new to the poem. Mars has already been led by a golden chain, and even the naive Adonis has heard that love is "a life in death, / That laughs and weeps, and all but with a breath" (413–14). The sorrows of love are part of Venus's inescapable nature: she is the goddess of love, eternal and immutable; she has always had and will always have a deep affinity with the boar. Her staining of her face, in short, has an initiatory rather than an etiological significance: the nature of reality is not altered by the act but understood and accepted. Venus now knows who she is; she knows what it means to be Venus.

The poem does not moralize its tragic theme, but merely enacts its paradoxes in a ritual of "blooding," in which the goddess of love plays the roles of initiator and initiate. Despite the long-standing efforts of critics to do so, one cannot read the poem as a cautionary tale, placing blame on either Venus or Adonis. The ultimate fate of both characters is that of Ovidian tragedy: they are doomed to enact their own mythology.

Ovidian tragedy, of course, is not mature Shakespearean tragedy. Adonis dies without insight. Venus's insight must be by definition unredemptive: she cannot be other than she is. The maternal impulse that makes her "cradle" Adonis's flower in her breast (1185), and that earlier made her pursue him to the hunt "like a milch doe, whose swelling dugs do ache" (875), might make her plight sympathetic but is nonetheless tinged by a continuing and deadly self-absorption. "To grow unto himself was his desire," she tells the flower she has torn from its stem, "And so 'tis thine, but know it is as good / To wither in my breast as in his blood" (1180–82). She has not allowed Adonis to "grow unto himself," and now she denies the same impulse to his "child," who is plucked from its source of nourishment and whose fate is to be smothered by her love: "There shall not be one minute in an hour / Wherein I will not kiss my sweet love's flow'r" (1187–88). As Heather Dubrow observes, Venus's plight at the end of the poem involves us in "a seesawing between sympathy and judgment that characterizes the whole poem."[47] To understand the significance of Venus's ritual of "blooding," then, is not to resolve the ambiguity of her character, which is by definition unresolvable, or to simplify our response to it. Attending to her ritual act, however, does illuminate the distinctive nature of her tragedy and heighten what William Keach calls the poem's "surprisingly powerful sense of erotic pathos."[48] For a goddess, insight does not and cannot produce guilt or reformation; the only mark of Venus's initiation as a hunter is the enduring stain of Adonis's blood.

Venus and Adonis is a stylish and sophisticated poem, one that captures the ambiance of the young aristocratic males for whom it was apparently written. This ambiance is on the one hand modishly literary, and much of the delight of the poem springs from the twists and turns, the paradoxes and perversities, of Ovidian themes, many of which depend upon the traditional identification of love with hunting. But the ambiance is also modishly social, deeply implicated in the values and customs of the hunt within which young aristocratic males were so deeply immersed. The zest for country life that so animates the imagery of the poem does not derive merely from Shakespeare's Stratford youth, important though that may be. Adonis's love of the heroic hunt of the boar, Venus's seductive attempts to deflect that love into the soft hunting of deer in parks or hare in the open field, the ritual of "blooding" with which the poem concludes – such episodes achieve their witty resonance in large part because they draw upon the traditions, practices, debates, and values embedded in the Elizabethan world of the hunt. The poem was dedicated to the young Earl of Southampton. It might have pleased as well another hunter, the hunting lord of *The Taming of the Shrew*, who knows and loves his hounds, who enjoys a good joke, and who has a picture of

> Adonis painted by a running brook,
> And Cytherea all in sedges hid,
> Which seem to move and wanton with her breath,
> Even as the waving sedges play with wind. (Ind.2. 50–53)

"VERY REVERENT SPORT": THE PRINCESS'S HUNT IN *LOVE'S LABOR'S LOST*

The most significant event in *Love's Labor's Lost* is one that is merely reported at the end of the play: the death of the French king. Marcade's sudden and unexpected account of this shocking occurrence stuns the Princess and her companions, disrupts their festive merriment, thwarts the amorous desires of the young suitors, and destroys the anticipated resolution of the comedy. Given the theatrical power of this event, it is not surprising that few readers or viewers remember a second death that also occurs offstage in the play – the death of a deer, killed in act 4 scene 1 by the French King's daughter, the Princess of France. This death, in contrast to that of the King, seems completely insignificant, provoking little attention among the characters of the play and even less among its critics.[49] Yet the death of the deer is in its own way shocking. It occurs not in a distant court but in the very heart of the play's ostensibly restorative green world, the park of Navarre. It results, moreover, not from natural causes – the King dies from lingering illness and old age – but from a sudden act of violence, an act that the Princess herself calls a murder (4.1.8).

The most common critical approach to the play's hunting scene has been to treat it as a metaphor for love. From this perspective the Princess, as a representative of the women, becomes a typical Petrarchan mistress, "killing" the men who worship her. Louis Adrian Montrose, for example, interprets the Princess's reflections on the killing of a deer as indirect

reflections of her own attitude towards the King's desire.[50] John Barton's
1978 production of the play, according to Miriam Gilbert, represented
the Princess's motives in this way, by making her comments on the deer
grow out of her disappointment at not seeing the King.[51] There is much
to recommend such interpretations. The convention of the love-hunt
was virtually a cliché in the period, and the play's language evokes it.
The language of hunting in the scene, as we shall see, bristles with high-
spirited sexual wordplay, and even the love-stricken men see themselves
later as prey: "the King he is hunting the deer," says Berowne, "I am
coursing myself" (4.3.1–2).

The hunting scene, however, is not merely a stage metaphor for love;
it is a representation of actual events that would have occurred frequently in the Elizabethan court. For the Elizabethan aristocracy, and
for Elizabeth herself, park-hunting was a favorite pastime, a "sport" that
was also a festive entertainment; as in Shakespeare's play, it was a
common entertainment for visiting nobles and ambassadors. By imitating such an event, the Princess's hunting scene joins the vast repertory
of "games" that define the action of *Love's Labor's Lost* – among them,
word-games (the stock-in-trade of nearly every character), practical
jokes, a masque of Russians, and a pageant of the Nine Worthies. As
many critics have noted, the play is not only based on games and entertainments but is to a great extent about them. In this sense, the play both
reflects – and reflects upon – the life of the Elizabethan court. In doing
so, as John Turner has argued, the play captures the tension within the
Elizabethan word *competitor*, which might mean either *partner* or *rival*.[52]
The various games of the play embody not only the high spirits and *camaraderie* of the court of Navarre but its tendencies towards narcissism and
aggression. Because of this tension, the play's tone sits on the knife-edge
between romantic comedy and satire.

In 1591, as we have seen earlier, Queen Elizabeth killed three or four
deer in the park at Cowdray after being presented with a crossbow and
celebrated in a song as an eroticized Diana. Addressed as the "Goddesse
and Monarch of (t)his happie Ile," she was told that her "eies" were
"arrows," attracting the fascinated gaze of the stately "harts" that they
killed. This is the social atmosphere of the hunting park that Venus
invokes in her attempt to seduce Adonis away from the dangerous hunt
of the boar. In *Love's Labor's Lost* Venus's fantasy of park hunting becomes
literalized. The Princess is taken to the park of Navarre and positioned
in a stand to await the deer to be driven before her. Although not as
heavily eroticized as the setting that Venus imagines, the park of Navarre

is at once a site of love-games and a field of death. Like the eroticized Diana who was celebrated at Cowdray, this Princess "kills" both deer and men.

In *Love's Labor's Lost*, the Princess's hunt holds a unique place among the play's festive entertainments. Although many of the games and pageants of the play are aggressive, including the love-games, the Princess's hunt is the only one that results in the literal death of the competition. While the Princess can compliment both of her two bantering ladies on "a set of wit well played" (5.2.29), no one can do the same for both her and the deer. Hunting, in short, carries the aggressive tendencies of the play's courtly games to a disturbing extreme, suggesting that behind a joke may lie a desire to kill.

An entrance into the distinctive hunting culture evoked by this play is provided by Shakespeare's endearingly pompous curate, Nathaniel. In act 4, Nathaniel, Holofernes the schoolmaster, and Dull the constable engage in a dizzying debate about the nature of the deer the Princess has just killed. While much scholarly effort has been expended on the mock pedantry and misunderstanding that characterize this disagreement, the statement that initiates it, Nathaniel's pious approval of the hunt, has for the most part escaped attention. "Very reverent sport truly," he says, "and done in the testimony of a good conscience" (4.2.1–2). Why, we might ask, does Nathaniel call the Princess's hunting a "reverent" sport, one undertaken with the warrant of a good conscience? And why is a curate's sanctimonious approval a natural way for Shakespeare to open a scene in which a few village worthies chat about the sporting activities of their social betters?

The word "reverent" in Nathaniel's phrase means "worthy of veneration." It contains two complementary ideas – one religious, the other social. The godliness of the sport is emphasized by the phrase "done in the testimony of a good conscience," a phrase that echoes Paul's words to the Corinthians: "For our rejoycing is this, the testimonie of our conscience, that in simplicitie and godlie pureness, and not in fleshlie wisdome, but by the grace of God we have had our conversation in the worlde, and moste of all to you wardes."[53] In his role as village curate, Nathaniel endorses the sport in language appropriate to his calling; as William C. Carroll observes, "virtually everything he says has a biblical or patristic allusion lurking near the surface."[54] Like his colleagues, Nathaniel is an admiring and respectful member of the commonwealth, a sympathetic supporter of the powers that be. He voices complacently the position of the established church and state on hunting. In this he is

supported by Holofernes. "Away," says the pedant, as he leads Nathaniel
and Dull from the hunt to their festive dinner, "the gentles are at their
game, and we will to our recreation" (4.2.165–67). Hunting is a "game"
for "gentles," and worthy of veneration.

As we have seen in chapter 1, the religious and social justification of
hunting as a recreation sanctioned by God, a result of man's dominion
over nature, was opposed in the period on three closely related fronts: by
humanists, for whom hunting transformed men into beasts; by Puritans,
for whom hunting provoked cruel and destructive behavior both to
animals and to the common people; and by others who, like Montaigne,
felt instinctive sympathy for animal suffering. Erasmus's satire on
hunting in *The Praise of Folly* provides an apt gloss on Nathaniel's words,
since he mocks not only the social status of the hunters, who think they
inhale exotic perfume even in "the verie stenche of the houndes
kennell," but the "reverence" implied in their ritual actions upon the
death of a deer. "Ye know your selves," says Folly, "what ceremonies they
use about the same."[55]

In *Love's Labor's Lost*, the folly of hunting is voiced by the huntress
herself. As the Princess waits, bow in hand, for the hunt to begin, she
acknowledges the cruelty of her role, that of playing "the murtherer" in
ambush (4.1.8). Her theatrical vocabulary implies that hunting of this
kind, as in Elizabeth's hunt at Cowdray, is a form of pageant. She reflects
upon the unworthiness of her motives, admitting that she hunts "for
praise alone" (34), a statement that suggests the Puritans' emphasis upon
the cruel frivolity of the sport. In lines that resonate throughout the play,
moreover, she treats the desire for praise in hunting as a symptom of the
destructive quest for fame in all human activities:[56]

> And out of question so it is sometimes:
> Glory grows guilty of detested crimes,
> When for fame's sake, for praise, an outward part,
> We bend to that the working of the heart;
> As I for praise alone now seek to spill
> The poor deer's blood, that my heart means no ill.   (4.1.30–35)

Like Erasmus and More, the Princess sees behind the hunt the desire for
glory; like the Puritan Philip Stubbes, she emphasizes the lack of charity
in her action. She adds to all of these opposing voices, moreover, a distinctive note of sympathy for the deer itself, the suffering of which tran-
scends its mere emblematic meaning. For a brief moment, she edges
towards the sentiments of Montaigne.[57]

Through the Princess's own words, then, Shakespeare embeds in his text a familiar satirical perspective on hunting, a perspective, moreover, that provides a framework for the whole of act 4. Although the development of the hunting motif in the several scenes of act 4 is complicated, its central core is the connection between hunting and human vanity, which turns every action into a kind of hunt, an irreverent sport. Behind the vanity, in most cases, lie threats of aggression, often sexual, which are sublimated into attacks of wit. Armado's letter, which Boyet reads for the Princess, concludes with his flamboyant threat to play the "Nemean lion" to Jaquenetta, his helpless prey (4.1.88–89). After the Princess leaves the stage, Boyet and Rosalind remain, and Boyet's "Who is the shooter?" (108) triggers off a verbal sparring match in which "shooters" are likened to "suitors" and hunting to the pursuit of the cuckold's horns; the contest is joined by Maria and Costard and eventually becomes so openly obscene as to elicit Maria's laughing protest, "Come, come, you talk greasily, your lips grow foul" (137). For Rosalind, Boyet, Maria, and Costard, the hunt has no reality except as an excuse for a playful competition in sexual puns, a contest that concludes with Costard awarding victory to himself and the ladies: "Lord, Lord, how the ladies and I have put him down" (141). Costard's phrase "put him down" captures tersely the mixture of sexuality and aggression that characterizes the dialogue as a whole. Sport consists of putting down. The satire of hunting is thus implicated in several respects in the "preposterous reversals" of high and low that Patricia Parker identifies in the language of the play throughout.[58]

In the next scene, which begins with Nathaniel's comment on the reverence of the sport, the hunt provides an opportunity for the learned commentators to display their knowledge of aristocratic recreations. In this contest the pedantical verbiage of curate and schoolmaster are set against the simple constable's inarticulate yet unshakable conviction. Although one risks a Holofernian pedantry in glossing the wordplay of the scene, to do so highlights further the satire submerged in Nathaniel's phrase "a very reverent sport." The point of debate among the three is the worth of the deer that the Princess has killed; the more fully mature and majestic the animal, the more "reverent" the sport. Holofernes begins by asserting that the deer was "*sanguis*, in blood" (4.2.3–4) – that is, fully mature, in the full vigor of health, and therefore, to adopt Nathaniel's terminology, capable of providing "very reverent sport" and great praise to the Princess. Nathaniel, however, objects that the deer was not fully mature but "a buck of the first head" (10) – that is, a buck about five years old, with its first fully developed antlers. Holofernes then protests with the pedantical Latin expression *"haud credo,"* (11) or, "I cannot believe it," a statement that is apparently misheard by Dull as "old grey doe" and vigorously denied; to kill such a weak specimen would be an act of shame. Dull insists that the deer was a "pricket" (12), a buck of two years – that is, a kill more "reverent" than an old grey doe but not as "reverent" as a buck of the first head.[59]

It is characteristic of the play that this debate is never resolved, and that we never discover the age or value of the Princess's deer. This in itself undermines the idea of pursuing hunting as a means of winning fame or reputation, for, as Falstaff knows, one's honor depends upon the fickleness of others' perceptions. Dull is allowed the final word in his debate with his more learned companions, but only because Holofernes deflects the conversation into another kind of self-display, that of making a poem, a contest in which he is the only competitor and therefore destined to win.

The monstrosity that results – "The preyful Princess pierc'd and prick'd a pretty pleasing pricket" (56) – reduces the question of the deer's age or worth to one of mere verbal convenience, the word "Princess" demanding the alliterative "pricket." The suffering and death of the deer, moreover, are completely trivialized, for its wounds merely provide inspiration for Holofernes' poetic vanity. The sore pricket becomes a "sore," a deer of four years, or adding a letter, a "sorel," one of three years. When the "l" is transformed into the capital "L" representing the Roman numeral fifty, and a second "L" is added to make one hundred, the number of wounds on the deer killed escalates accordingly. Holofernes' epitaph on the death of the deer thus conveys no sense of "reverence," to use Nathaniel's term, but serves merely to feed the vanity of the speaker, whose verbal pyrotechnics suggest the unfeeling violence of the sport itself. As a parody of an epitaph, Holofernes' poem pricks the bubble of reputation both for the unfortunate deer and the Princess, whose kill is lost altogether in the sweet smoke of rhetoric.

For the King of Navarre and his young companions, the hunt provides a setting for their own massacre by love. Berowne opens act 4 scene 3 with a line that frames the action that follows: "The King he is hunting the deer: I am coursing myself" (1–2). When he observes the King entering with a love-sonnet in hand, he remarks to himself, "Shot, by heaven! Proceed, sweet Cupid, thou hast thump'd him with thy bird-bolt under the left pap" (22–24). The entire scene, in which Berowne watches unobserved as each of his companions betrays his love for one of the women, might be called one of ambush, with the final victim being Berowne himself. Having forsworn themselves while hunting, the young men now transform hunting into open warfare, for which it provides the traditional training ground: "Saint Cupid, then!" shouts the King, "and, soldiers, to the field!" (363). The Princess's satiric linkage between hunting and vanity provides an apt gloss not only on the love of the young men but on their initial devotion to their little academe. In the opening line of the play, the King commits himself to the pursuit of "fame, that all hunt after in their lives" (1.1.1). Hunting after fame in books, he becomes eventually both the hunter and the hunted in love. In study and love, the metaphor of the hunt, with its overtones of narcissism and aggression, shapes the overall action of the play. The metaphor situates the literary convention of the love-hunt within the social tensions surrounding the practice of hunting in parks.

One of the play's many paradoxes is that the satirist of the hunt, the Princess, includes herself among the satirized, mocking her own vanity along with all the others. In this she is like Berowne, whose mockery is also self-reflexive. She is like Berowne, too, in the discrepancy between her emotions and her actions. Berowne knows that he will be unable to keep the oath the King asks him to swear at the beginning of the play, yet he pledges his word nonetheless. The Princess knows that she hunts with no purpose but vanity; she acknowledges her compassion for the deer; and yet she kills. She suffers a guilty conscience but participates nonetheless in a social ritual her mind and heart oppose. Her action, ironically, receives the pious blessing of Nathaniel, who finds the hunt "very reverent" and "done in the testimony of a good conscience."

Like most of the heroines of the romantic comedies, the Princess is often idealized by critics, taken to be a clear-sighted, playful, and emotionally mature center of value in the play. She is certainly as close as the play comes to such a character. The killing of the deer, however, underlined by the unconscious irony in Nathaniel's blessing, marks the Princess out as a target among all the others, only for more sophisticated satire. Like Berowne, she is ruefully conscious of her own folly at moments, but this consciousness does not guide her actions. Her satiric assaults on others, moreover, like Berowne's, betray a delight in verbal aggression rather than any desire to educate or reform. In the words of Holofernes' poem, she is a "preyful Princess." When she first meets the King of Navarre, she mocks him for welcoming her not to the court but to the fields (2.1.91). In the scene before the hunt (4.1.), she befuddles the poor forester by accusing him of not recognizing her beauty. In this scene too she orders the seal of Armado's letter broken so that she can mock the contents, despite her knowledge that the letter is addressed not to her but to Jaquenetta.

The Princess characterizes her mockeries as "sport," but her use of the word invokes notions of violence rather than reverence. When she learns that the young men are coming as wooers in the guise of Russians, she proposes the wearing of masks so that "sport by sport" will be "o'erthrown" (5.2.153) and the wooers sent "away with shame" (156). In response to Boyet's observation that having the women avert their faces when the men address them will "kill the speaker's heart," she answers, "Therefore I do it" (149–151). Later in the same scene, she urges the King to watch the pageant of worthies because "that sport best pleases that doth [least] know how" (516). This is so, she continues, because "Their form confounded makes most form in mirth, / When great things laboring perish in their birth" (519–20). Berowne takes this remark as a "right description of our sport" (521). The Princess's image of a mirth that comes from watching "great things laboring" only to "perish in their birth" conveys not only the vanity that drives the festive merriments of all the nobles, a vanity evoked in Hobbes's description of laughter as "sudden glory," but the insidiously life-denying quality of its pleasure. Comedy does not thrive on abortion.

As Louis Adrian Montrose observes, the word "sport" is used throughout the play in relation to activities that, unlike rituals, divide participants into winners and losers.[60] Play in the world of *Love's Labor's Lost* is almost invariably a form of aggression, as in the Princess's delight at the promise of watching the men make fools of themselves in disguise: "There's no such sport as sport by sport o'erthrown, / To make theirs ours and ours none but our own" (5.2.153–54). The contrast is not merely between sport and ritual but between Elizabethan and modern notions of sport. The words that link sport to fair play – "sportsman," "sportsmanship," being a "good sport" – did not enter English until the eighteenth century. In Shakespeare's usage, the word "sport" is far more likely to refer to mere diversion or entertainment than to an organized game with rules and proper decorum. The entertainment, moreover, is as likely to be cruel as innocuous, as when Longaville singles out Costard and Armado to be "our sport" (1.1.179), or when, in *Merry Wives of Windsor*, Master Ford promises his neighbors that they "shall see sport anon" when they capture his wife's lover (3.3.169). Hunting itself seems not to have been called a "sport" in the period. In the titles of handbooks, it is most commonly an art (*The Noble Arte of Venerie*) or a recreation (*The Gentleman's Recreation*). The tension between delightful wit and disturbing verbal aggression that runs throughout the play seems related to a tension within the culture in attitudes towards sport itself, of which the deadly game of hunting is a special case.

The Princess's chief targets throughout the play are the young men. Like Elizabeth at Cowdray, she is the object of male desire, but she kills. Although not an Amazon, like the huntress Hippolyta in *A Midsummer Night's Dream*, she threatens male dominance with her aggressive wit and disturbs the patriarchal order. She kills the deer with a literal arrow and the King with a metaphoric one. Before she goes off to the hunt, the Princess is questioned by Boyet about her admission that she "for praise alone" seeks "to spill / The poor deer's blood, that [her] heart means no ill" (4.1.34–35). "Do not curst wives hold that self-sovereignty / Only for praise' sake," asks Boyet, "when they strive to be / Lords o'er their lords?" (36–38). To which the Princess replies, "Only for praise – and praise we may afford / To any lady that subdues a lord" (34–40). The word "subdues" crystallizes the complex nature of the threat the Princess represents to the adolescent male ego: the mastery of this "curst" wife is at once psychological, physical, and sexual. A similar mastery is evoked in the unconscious innuendoes of Holofernes' song, with its unconventional application of familiar male terms for sexual aggression to the Princess: "The preyful Princess pierc'd and prick'd a pretty pleasing pricket."

The subversive laughter of the Princess comes to a sudden halt upon Marcade's announcement of the French King's death. Although her characterization in this final scene is not entirely clear, there are hints that her father's death shocks the Princess into a new state of mind. She speaks of her "new-sad soul" (5.2.731) and apologizes to the suitors for "the liberal opposition of our spirits" (733). When the King attempts to continue his suit, moreover, she is for once at a loss for words; her mocking wit leaves her, and she can only say "I understand you not, my griefs are double" (752). If there are signs of reform in the Princess's language, however, they are left tantalizingly vague; as David Bevington observes of all the female roles in the play, "essentially complete in themselves, the women remain a mystery."[61]

The ineffectual efforts of the King and Berowne to reform, on the other hand, are certainly clear, and both are required to endure a year's penance for their continuing folly. The King's retreat into a hermitage and Berowne's term in a hospital, "[enforcing] the pained impotent to smile" (854), are intended to produce in them "new-sad" souls that will make them worthy of marriage. Berowne's task in particular is to transform his delightful but ultimately cruel and unfeeling wit into what might be called a "reverent sport," a recreation that cures rather than kills because based on a respect for life. Whether such a transformation can be achieved remains a disturbingly open question. "To move wild laughter in the throat of death?" asks Berowne, "It cannot be, it is impossible: / Mirth cannot move a soul in agony" (855–857).

The event that shocks the aristocrats into perceiving the gap between deadly and curative sport is the death of the French King. The insight has already been embedded, however, in the scene in which the Princess, in "sport," and with no more than self-professed vanity as a goal, kills a deer. The values implied in Berowne's curious description of laughter as "wild" suggest the dangers of the enclosed, hermetic, and ultimately unnatural world of the little academe and its park of tame deer. To "move wild laughter in the throat of death," as the Princess makes clear in her reply to Berowne, is to empathize with human suffering, to use wit not as a means of assault but as a cure. Curative laughter is released by empathy. In the hunting scene, the Princess feels empathy as she prepares to "spill / The poor deer's blood, that [her] heart means no ill" (4.1.34–35). But she kills nonetheless. The play's juxtaposition of two invisible deaths, that of a king and that of a deer, implies a link between human and animal suffering, a link endorsed at the end of the play in the quest to release "wild laughter" through empathy. Although the values finally upheld by the Princess do not imply that animal and human life are of equal value, they do promote the existence of what Montaigne calls a "mutuall bond" between them.[62]

Nathaniel complacently approves of hunting as a "reverent sport." Yet the play as a whole mocks that complacency, insinuating into its language and action disturbing doubts about the prospects for reverence in any "sport," so deeply engrained are the aggressive and narcissistic impulses that characterize the various entertainments at Navarre. The full text of 2 Corinthians, to which Nathaniel's blessing of the hunt alludes, includes not only Paul's assurances to his church that his own conscience is clear, but his exhortations that they avoid the dangers of vanity, act charitably towards their neighbors, and follow the spirit of the New Law, engraved in the heart, rather than the ritualism of the Old Law, preserved in tablets of stone. The contemporary controversy over hunting touches the values of this text, as we have seen, and Shakespeare's ending probes skeptically the capacity of the aristocracy to enact them. The commoners in the play, interestingly, share the folly of their social betters but lack somewhat their aggressive edge. Unlike their superiors, they are not licensed to hunt.

As a "comedy," *Love's Labor's Lost* does not pursue Berowne's doubts about the possibility of moving "wild laughter in the throat of death." The consequences of the death of a father and the death of a deer remain uncertain. To invoke the ghost of the Princess's deer, however, is to learn something about the skeptical overtones of this curious romantic and satirical comedy. Although one cannot help but be exhilarated by the exuberance, playfulness, and *camaraderie* that many readers have emphasized in the language and action of the play, one should not underestimate its critical energy or probative force. Nor should one underestimate, as in its use of hunting as a central metaphor for the life of a contemporary court, the play's close relationship with Elizabethan social experience. In representing the courtly sport of park-hunting, Shakespeare insinuated himself into a contemporary debate with broad social ramifications, one that touched even a royal English huntress who, like the Princess of France, shot deer from ambush and killed courtiers with arrows from her eyes.

Although not explicitly invoked by Shakespeare, the image of Queen Elizabeth hunting at Cowdray, her eyes killing courtiers and her bow killing deer, seems to haunt both *Venus and Adonis* and *Love's Labor's Lost.* Elizabeth, Venus, and the Princess of France are all "preyful princesses," implicated by their Amazonian roles in the deathly eroticism of courtly hunting. The role is one Elizabeth at least seems to have found comfortable; if she experienced ambivalence in any of her numerous hunts throughout her reign, the evidence has gone unrecorded. Shakespeare's huntresses, in contrast, feel within themselves the tension of their Amazonian identity. The goddess Venus is startled to be moved by the plight of a hunted hare and shocked to discover in the death of Adonis her identity with the boar. The stain on her face marks the knowledge of her own inner contradiction. The Princess of France is also a killer, and one moved by the innocence of her prey. In her case, unlike that of Venus, the tension embodied in the role of the huntress is not resolved in tragic or comic paradox but left suspended, as irresolvable, perhaps, as the play in which it appears.

CHAPTER THREE

"Solemn" hunting in Titus Andronicus *and* Julius Caesar

As Roman tragedies, *Titus Andronicus* and *Julius Caesar* have much in common. Although set in very different periods, they share many of the familiar concerns of the Shakespearean Roman world: with tyrannical political power, with social conflict and civil war, with family values and family honor, and with the idea of Rome as a civilized society. Both of the plays begin with an image of an unstable society, a Rome threatened by internal political dissension following upon recent military triumph; both depict the unraveling of the state into savage anarchy; and both conclude with the Roman polity restored, if only in formal terms, by a powerful ruler.

The two plays share a more curious feature in common, a preoccupation with imagery of the hunt. *Titus Andronicus* includes a literal hunting scene (2.3), in which the hunted creatures are not the panther and hart to which the hunt is ostensibly devoted but Bassianus and Lavinia, who become human prey for the predatory sons of Tamora. The language of hunting spans the play as a whole. Although *Julius Caesar* does not enact a hunt, the central event of the play, the assassination of Caesar, is characterized as a hunt by both Brutus and Antony and is staged in a manner that strongly evokes the death of a stag. The civil war that ensues, moreover, is envisaged by Antony in terms that suggest the wild, anarchic hunting of an Elizabethan poaching raid.

Why should Shakespeare's representation of these two Roman worlds feature the language and imagery of hunting? The choice may have been triggered by brief allusions in his sources. Although the narrative source of *Titus Andronicus* is in dispute, the most likely candidate is *The History of Titus Andronicus*, which is recorded in an eighteenth-century chapbook. In that version of the story, Tamora, the Moor, and her two sons plot to invite the prince to hunt "in the great Forest, on the Banks of the River Tyber, and there murder him." While in the forest, the sons not only murder the prince, but, "like two ravenous Tygers," rape and mutilate Lavinia.[1] If Shakespeare used this story, he converted mere hints of a forest setting into a full-scale representation of a Romanized Elizabethan hunt. In North's translation of Plutarch's *Life of Julius Caesar*, the major source for that play, North includes a single but powerful image from the hunt in his description of the assassination: Caesar, he says, "was hacked and mangeled amonge them, as a wilde beaste taken of hunters."[2] This single image becomes a major symbol in Shakespeare's tragedy. In both plays, then, Shakespeare seems to have seized on incidental allusions to the hunt in his sources and to have amplified them into powerful poetic and theatrical symbols. Neither the specific sources nor the generalized Roman settings explain, however, why he should have done so, or why he should have based his imagery of the hunt on the most elevated and ceremonial kind in the Elizabethan period, what Aaron calls the "solemn hunting" devoted to the hart or stag (2.1.112).[3]

To explain the peculiar prominence of the hunt in both plays, and its distinctive overtones, we must attend to another feature they share in common, a preoccupation with ceremony. As many critics have observed, Shakespeare's conception of Rome is richly ceremonial. *Titus Andronicus* opens with a Roman triumph, the election of an emperor, and the ritual sacrifice of Tamora's son, Alarbus. It ends with a ritual banquet, a cannibalistic feast in which Tamora devours her own sons. As Eugene M. Waith observes, the most important ceremonies in the play are those that "order or partly conceal discordant energies."[4] *Julius Caesar* also begins with a triumph, the celebration of Caesar's victory over Pompey, a ceremony which is combined with the observances of the Feast of the Lupercal.[5] The play includes as well the taking of auguries, the celebration of the Ides of March, and Caesar's funeral. As is often the case in Shakespeare, the ceremonies represented in both plays are deeply problematic; the social ideals behind the ceremonies are never fulfilled but are perverted, travestied, or manipulated for political ends. At the core of both plays is a concern with the most disturbing and paradoxical of ceremonies, that of human sacrifice: the tragic events of *Titus Andronicus* begin with the ritual death of Alarbus, and the civil war of *Julius Caesar* follows upon Brutus's attempt to see himself and the other conspirators as "sacrificers, but not butchers" of Caesar (2.1.166).[6]

The link between hunting and ritual implied by Shakespeare's juxtaposition of the two themes in these plays becomes particularly suggestive in the light of an influential study of the origins of ritual sacrifice. In *Homo Necans*, Walter Burkert not only links hunting to sacrifice but finds in the hunt the origin of all sacrificial ritual. The introduction of hunting into human society, according to Burkert, was the crucial and defining event in the development of humanity. The age of the hunter, the Paleolithic period, is by far the longest in human history and, according to Burkert and others, has had a profound effect upon the development of the human species and human society. Both human physiology and the patriarchal order of society, with its gendered division of labor and child-rearing, owe their origins, in this view, to the needs of a hunting culture.

For Burkert, the ritualistic behavior characteristic of the hunt in hunter-gatherer societies – the purifications and abstinences before the hunt, the ceremonial of the death and dismemberment, the preservation of trophies of various kinds – answers to the shock of killing, a shock that must be overcome in order for the society to survive. The hunted animal thus becomes a sacrificial animal, and the ritual of its death enacts the paradox that life is "nourished and perpetuated by death." The ceremonies of the death purge feelings of fear and guilt both through the dynamics of group solidarity and through the symbolic restoration, in the preservation of relics or trophies, of the life that has been lost. "The shock felt in the act of killing," observes Burkert, "is answered later by consolidation; guilt is followed by reparation, destruction by reconstruction."[7]

As Burkert himself acknowledges, any argument of this kind is bound to be speculative, depending as it does on the fragmentary evidence of pre-history, sweeping generalizations about the historical practice of the hunt in very different cultures, and a functional view of ritual that is open to challenge. His conception of hunting ritual, nonetheless, provides a touchstone against which to test Elizabethan custom and Shakespeare's representations of it. Such a touchstone is particularly useful in the absence of Tudor or Jacobean attempts to explain or justify the obsessive attention to ritual detail that characterized the practice of the hunt. The hunting manuals all insist upon a meticulous observance of custom, especially in the killing of the noblest of animals, the hart, yet none of them poses the question, why.

The entirety of a hunt may be considered a ritual structure, one that corresponds in a broad sense to the tripartite rhythm that Van Gennep and others associate with seasonal rites and rites of passage.[8] Characteristically, the hunters begin in the social world of the court, proceed into the forest, and return to the court for a feast. Each part of the event has its own ceremonies. Gascoigne's *Noble Arte of Venerie*, for example, features illustrations of Queen Elizabeth presiding over the ceremonial feast in the forest before the hunt (fig. 2) and receiving the ceremonial presentation of the fumets, or excrement, of a deer from the chief huntsman as evidence of the worthiness of the animal to be hunted.[9] The climactic moments of the hunt, as made clear in the descriptions in the handbooks of the sport, are those of the death and, especially, the dismemberment of the animal, an event that features elaborate ceremonial behavior. Although the hunting manuals are generally of one accord in their descriptions of the dismemberment of the hart or stag, their accounts of the kill naturally differ. The pursuit of a wild animal to the death with dogs and horses does not lend itself to ceremonial behavior. Death is difficult to control and may come in many guises. The tendency in the manuals, and certainly in the artistic representations of the scene, is to stylize the kill, and to emphasize the role of the ruler or noblest personage, to whom by rights it belongs. This is done by focusing on the decapitation of the deer, which occurs after its death. The quintessential statement of this ritualistic assertion of royal privilege occurs, as we have seen, in Peake's painting of Henry, Prince of Wales (fig. 1).

For our purposes the most representative description of the death and dismemberment of the hart occurs in Gascoigne's *Noble Arte of Venerie*, published in 1575 and reprinted in 1611. The ritual of breaking up the hart is so important to Gascoigne that he recounts it in two versions: first, following his French source, he describes the method used in France; then, after alerting the reader to the fact that French custom differs in part from English, he describes the distinctive features of the English method.[10] In describing the event, I shall assume that unless Gascoigne indicates otherwise the French and English versions are sufficiently similar to be treated as one.

The death of the hart is first marked by the sounding of the horns and the "whooping" of what Gascoigne calls "a deade note" to call the hunters together (126). Once the hunters are assembled, the hounds are brought to the deer and permitted, for a short time, to "byte and teare him about the necke"; they are then coupled to await their reward. In England, as Gascoigne illustrates by a woodcut of Queen Elizabeth (fig. 3), the chief person takes the "assaye of the Deare with a sharpe knyfe" (133), slitting along the brisket of the deer towards the belly while the deer is held by the kneeling chief huntsman; this is done to test the "goodnesse of the flesh" (134). Next, the deer's head is cut off, usually "by the chiefe personage. For they take delight to cut off his heade with

their woodknyves, skaynes, or swordes, to trye their edge, and the goodnesse or strength of their arme" (134). The head is then "cabaged,"
which removes the antlers for a trophy and the brains and other morsels
for the hounds. At this stage too certain "deintie morsels," which include
the tongue, ears, and "doulcets" (testicles), are put in "a faire hand-
kercher altogether, for the Prince or chiefe" (134). In France these
morsels are roasted and eaten on the spot as carbonados, with much
rejoicing of the nobles, who offer rewards to the best of their hounds and
huntsmen.

The dismembering of the deer then proceeds in two stages. First, the
huntsman removes the skin in a precise order, beginning with a slit at the
throat. After this is accomplished, the huntsman must pause for a hearty
draught of wine, "for if he shoulde breake up the Deare before he
drinke, the Venison would stinke and putrifie" (128). The breaking up of
the deer is also done in a precise order, with particular parts given to the
huntsman who harbored, or roused, the deer, and to the chief personage. At this point Gasgoigne adds a substantial paragraph to his source,
describing in meticulous detail the "ceremonie" the English use "in
taking out the shoulder." The ceremony tests the skill of the huntsman:
"If . . . he touch the shoulder or any part of the legge, with any other
thing than his knyfe, untill he have taken it out, it is a forfayture, and he
is thought to be no handsome woodman" (134–35). In *Merry Wives*,
Falstaff, imagining himself a Windsor stag, sees himself the victim of
such a ceremony, divided between Mistress Ford and Mistress Page:
"Divide me like a brib'd buck, each a haunch. I will keep my sides to
myself, my shoulders for the fellow of this walk – and my horns I
bequeath your husbands" (5.5.24–27). The image suggests that even
poachers divided their "brib'd" deer with a consciousness of the customary ritual.

The ceremony of the breaking up of the hart also includes the
rewarding of the hounds. The honor of assembling them is given to the
"Prince or chiefe," who begins "to blow and to hallow." After the other
huntsmen have also blown, the hounds are set loose upon the food,
which is spread on the deer skin. When they have almost finished eating,
a huntsman holding the deer's head hallows them to the hunt again. He
shows them the head, "lifting it up and downe before them to make them
baye it: and when he hath drawne them al about him baying shall cast
downe the heade amongst them that they may take [?] their pleasure
thereon" (132). Finally, he leads them back to the skin, and prepares them
for the kennel. Although Gascoigne does not describe it, the ceremony

almost certainly concludes with a procession homeward. William Twiti's directions for the return are as follows: "Carry the head home before the Lord; and the heart, tail, and gullet should be carried home on a forked branch, and you should blow the menée at the door of the hall."[11]

The foregoing account of the ceremonial death and dismemberment of a stag provides only a rough idea of its general nature. Because Gascoigne mixes French and English custom, his account is not always clear. Nor is it necessarily complete. Since the ceremony is to a great extent customary, moreover, it was probably subject to local variation. All of this said, however, Gascoigne's description conforms so closely to others in the period and exercised such influence upon Elizabethan readers that it provides us with our closest approximation of the actual event.

What are we to make of this ritual? In the absence of either an Elizabethan or modern anthropological account, how can we explain its significance? More specifically, what is there about the ritual that might explain its presence in Shakespeare's imagination as he envisaged the Roman worlds of *Titus Andronicus* and *Julius Caesar* ? Four elements, it seems to me, are especially important: the respectful imposition of human order upon wild nature; the centrality of the chief personage; the emphasis upon hierarchical solidarity among all participants; and, in the reward of the hounds, the disciplined re-enactment of savage violence. Let us examine each of these elements in turn.

The meticulous observances that accompany the dismemberment of the deer and the rewarding of the hounds can be attributed, of course, to practical necessity: efficiency demands that an animal be butchered methodically, and the continuity of the hunt depends upon re-enforcing the instincts of the dogs. The emphasis upon the specific observances to be followed and their precise ordering, however, far exceeds what practical necessity requires. The taking of the assay; the decapitation with a sword; the use of specific knives (owned by the huntsmen themselves); the precise parts removed as specific rewards; the precise order of the cutting; the explicit acknowledgment of "some ceremony" in the cutting out of the shoulder, with punishments imposed if it is done improperly – all of these suggest a very powerful need to "civilize" the event by marking off the boundaries between art and nature. The ceremony as a whole represents the domination of man over nature, the imposition of a specifically human order upon the wildness of the animal. In this it is a microcosm of the entire ceremony of the hunt in which the death of the animal acknowledges human power.

When one considers the inherent messiness of dismemberment, the emphasis upon its artfulness is striking. Although the event is called the "breaking up" of the hart, the language of dismemberment is more like that of carving at table than that of butchery. Gascoigne's most graphic verbs, for example, are "cut" and "slit," and his most common expressions are the euphemistic "take off," "take from," or "take out" – as in "we use some ceremonie in taking out the shoulder." A hunting manual of 1614, *A Jewell for Gentrie* by T. S., actually refers to the dismemberment as "carving the hart" (G2v). Shakespeare himself uses "carving" as a synonym for "breaking up" in *Love's Labor's Lost* (4.1.57).

In many societies this imposition of human upon natural order is accompanied by ritual acknowledgment of the limitations of human power, of the dependency of civilization upon nature. Often these ritual gestures signify as well a reverence for the animal that has been killed and ritual gestures of reparation or atonement. Burkert's theory of sacrifice, as we have seen, draws heavily upon such a pattern as central to the ritual event, which assuages the guilt of the kill. Given Elizabethan attitudes towards animals, which were by no means reverential but assumed human uniqueness and rightful ascendancy, one would not expect to find in the ceremonies of the hunt a strongly reverential dimension or acknowledgment of guilt.[12] In the Elizabethan context, however, the very provision of a ceremony implies a respectful, if not reverential, acknowledgment of the worth of the animal.

The animal with the most symbolic potency in the Elizabethan hunt was the one treated with the highest degree of ritual, the hart. The hart was a potentially dangerous fighter, physically magnificent, and sexually powerful. It was, in short, the wild counterpart to a warrior prince. Hence the ritual dismemberment of the hart gathers into it some of the chivalric notions that linger on in the Elizabethan period. The dead animal is honored in death by the ceremonies that it deserves. This is not so much a question of sympathy for the animal but of respect for its status. The adversary is honored by being symbolically killed by the "chief personage" of the hunt.

The second element, the centrality of the "chief personage," follows from the first. If a specifically human order is to be imposed on wild nature, then that order must replicate the hierarchy of human society, as imagined by Elizabethans. In Gascoigne's treatise, the dominance of the Queen herself is overwhelming. She appears in a woodcut taking the assay, attired in a costume that in its artifice alone demonstrates the absolute authority of the human to the natural world. In the texts cited, the "chief personage" not only takes the assay but cuts off the head, receives the special delicacies, blows for the hounds to be rewarded, and leads the procession homeward, preceded by the trophy of the hunt. The animal is hers, as is the forest or park, hers. The ceremony of the breaking of the hart thus crystallizes the exalted conception of the monarch's power that is manifest in all the laws of the forest. In no other activity – political, religious, or social – was the Queen's authority so absolute as in the hunt.

Not only does the centrality of the "chief personage" assert the supremacy of the monarch; it imposes on all present, human and beast, a third element, that of the conventional social and biological hierarchy. Each participant has rights, responsibilities, and rewards that are established hierarchically. The nobles (in the French version) are depicted chatting gaily as they reward "theyr best favoured houndes and huntesmen before them" (128); the alliterative balance of "houndes" and "huntesmen" suggests ironically a rather more democratic than hierarchical attitude on the part of the nobility. The huntsman who breaks up the deer has the privilege of pausing for drink. The huntsmen responsible for the hounds are able to sit and drink while the varlets of the kennel reward the hounds. The bloodhound that harbored the deer has the privilege of the first reward at the hands of its master. And the list could go on, with even the knives arranged in importance according to the worth of their task. The ritual of the hunt is thus a rite of incorporation, binding the human community to itself in a hierarchy of social order that parallels the order of nature.

The fourth and final element, the disciplined re-enactment of savage violence in the rewarding of the hounds, seems to run counter to the impulses towards the imposition of civilized order we have already examined. In one sense, it does. As domesticated animals, the dogs are intermediate creatures, poised between civilized humanity and wild nature. The success of the hunt depends upon both their innate savagery and their imposed discipline. In releasing that savagery, the ritual acknowledges its importance both literally and symbolically: the hunt must be re-enacted so that the dogs will associate the action with their reward. At this point the ceremony becomes highly theatrical, with the horns sounded yet again, the hounds running, the deer's head held aloft before the yapping pack, and then thrown to the ground for them to be torn apart.

This is a richly suggestive ceremony. It seems significant in at least two ways. First, it dramatizes the wild and vicious instincts upon which the hunt depends, instincts that man controls by subjecting the dogs to his

will. From this perspective the ritual endorses the conventional
Elizabethan separation between human and animal nature. The stag is
hunted with dogs; as Gervase Markham puts it, hunting is "a curious
search or conquest of one Beast over an other, pursued by a naturall
instinct of enmitie, and accomplished by the diversities and distinction
of smells onlie . . ."[13] In this sense, the image of the savage pack, led by
the basest of senses, the smell, represents another version of wild nature
subjected to the ordering power of human civilization. Second, and
perhaps more speculatively, the rewarding of the hounds represents a
subterranean acknowledgment of the deeper human motives that
underlie the hunt: the instinct to chase and kill, which Montaigne
acknowledges so powerfully in the essay "Of Cruelty."[14] In this sense, the
theatrical re-enactment of the hunt as unbridled savagery perhaps
permits a catharsis of emotions aroused by the hunt itself. Once this
catharsis is achieved, the hunters leave the world of nature for the civilized world and the feast.

Overall, then, the ritual dismemberment of the hart may be said to
enact human domination over wild nature while at the same time
acknowledging implicitly the wildness in human nature itself. As
hunters, humans live in order to kill, and kill in order to live. In a hunter-
gatherer society, the ritual of the hunt has real meaning and is tied to a
real human need, the need for food; in Elizabethan society, however, no
one needed to hunt in order to live. In the high culture of the
Elizabethan hunt, indeed, hunting "for the pot" was considered vulgar.
In Elizabethan culture, therefore, the ritual of the hunt was extremely
artificial. It is difficult to sustain the notion of ritual sacrifice when the
hunter simply kills for sport, and when forests themselves, as John
Manwood puts it, are places for deer to "rest and abide in, in the safe
protection of the King, for his princely delight and pleasure."[15] In the
context of "princely delight" the very notion of a ceremonial, or, as
Aaron calls it, a "solemn hunting," is suspect.

The ease with which the ritual of the hunt could be debunked in the
period is suggested by Erasmus's witty travesty of the ceremony of dismemberment in the *Praise of Folly*. In this short passage Erasmus brings
together several of the motifs we have been exploring: the highly ritualistic nature of the action; the solidarity achieved through participation
in the event; the hierarchical aspiration towards nobility that underlies
this participation; and the ironic incongruity between this aspiration and
the savage impulses released by the hunt itself. I quote Folly's speech in
the Elizabethan translation, by Thomas Chaloner:

For as touchyng the death of a deare, or other wilde beast, ye know your selves, what ceremonies they use about the same. Every poore man maie cutte out an oxe, or a shepe, wheras suche venaison maie not be dismembred but of a gentilman: who bareheadded, and set on knees, with a knife prepared proprely to that use, (for every kynde of knife is not allowable) also with certaine iestures, cuttes a sunder certaine partes of the wild-beast, in a certaine order verie circumstantly. Whiche duryng, the standers by, not speakyng a worde, behold it solemnly, as if it were some holy **Misterie**, havyng seen the like yet more than a hundred tymes before. Than (sir) whose happe it be to eate parte of the flesshe, marie he thynkes verily to be made therby halfe a gentilman. So therfore, wheras these hunters through continuall chasyng and eatyng of theyr venerie, gaine nothyng, but in a manner dooe them selfes also degenerate into wilde and salvage propretees, ye maie see yet, how through this errour of mine, thei repute thyr lyves ledde in more than princely pleasure.[16]

For Erasmus, the breaking up of the deer parodies the ritual of the Mass. The huntsman becomes a priest, bareheaded and kneeling, wielding his ritual implement in the precise ritual order; the onlookers become worshippers, solemnly participating in a "holy Misterie," with some fortunate enough to partake in the ritual communion, eating of the flesh of the animal and, through grace, elevating themselves to become "halfe a gentilman." This is an unholy communion, however, a barbarous rite of incorporation, for although thinking of themselves as princes, the hunters degenerate into wild and savage beasts. Erasmus, then, breaks apart the ritual paradox, making the ritual of the hunt not a symbol of the artful and civilized domination of wild nature by humanity but of human bestiality. For Erasmus, as for other humanists, this incongruity between the ritual of the hunt and the bestial reality is not merely symbolic but causal: hunting bestializes human beings.

Titus Andronicus may be said to begin where Erasmus leaves off. As part of the festivities to mark the double wedding of Bassianus and Lavinia and Saturninus and Tamora, Titus offers to provide what Aaron later calls a "solemn hunting" (2.1.112). On the morning after the marriages, the court will hunt the panther and the hart. That Titus turns to the ceremonial hunt for courtly entertainment is not surprising: he is a warrior, for one thing, and, like Theseus and Hippolyta in *A Midsummer Night's Dream*, sees the hunt as a festive extension of his martial role. More importantly, Titus has what might be called a ritualistic or ceremonial impulse that characterizes his actions throughout the play. In the opening scene of the play he yields to his sons' insistence upon sacrificing Tamora's first-born son, despite her powerful plea for human compassion. "Religiously," he says, his sons "ask for sacrifice" — to which

Tamora replies, "O cruel, irreligious piety!" (1.1.124,130). The sacrifice that ensues, gleefully described by Titus's son Lucius, is not merely abhorrent because it constitutes a pagan ritual of dismemberment and burning but because the motives behind it are undisguisedly vicious and revengeful. "See, lord and father," exults Lucius,

> how we have perform'd
> Our Roman rites. Alarbus' limbs are lopp'd,
> And entrails feed the sacrificing fire,
> Whose smoke like incense doth perfume the sky. (1.1.142–45)

The language with which Lucius describes the dismemberment of the body has none of the delicacy of the hunting manuals: he goes out to "hew [Alarbus's] limbs" (1.1.97) and returns exulting that he has "lopp'd" them.

It is clear, then, to all but Titus, that his sons do not "religiously" ask a sacrifice; they ask vengefully for sacrifice, exploiting ritual as a cover for their own barbarous impulses. The ceremonial form becomes a travesty, even in the imagined Roman world of the play, by serving merely to disguise the desire for bloody revenge. This dichotomy between ritual action and reality, so artfully developed by Erasmus in his satire upon the hunt, escapes Titus. He sees the ritual as the reality itself and is committed to ceremony as the true external manifestation of inner belief. The human paradoxes imposed by such ritualism become evident when he must decide whether to sanction the burial of the son he himself has killed in a rage for his disobedience. At that point he becomes entangled in a ritual dilemma created by his own action: he cannot allow a proper burial for one who has dishonored the family, yet he cannot bring himself to oppose his other sons or his own paternal feelings. He allows the burial rites. He thus violates the ritual demands of his honor for the sake of his own child, although he has previously refused to violate the demands of ritual sacrifice for the sake of Tamora's child. What might be called Titus's ritual naiveté is again apparent at the end of the opening scene, as he takes optimistic solace from the double marriages intended to resolve the discord between Bassianus and Saturninus and offers his own courtly gesture to greet Saturninus the next morning with "horn and hound" (1.1.494).

Act 2 scene 2 begins with the entrance of Titus and his three sons, "*making a noise with hounds and horns*" (s.d.), a direction that implies the presence of dogs on stage. With joyful exuberance, Titus celebrates the beauty of the day, the fields, and the forest, and awakens Saturninus and the court with the noises of the hunt:

The hunt is up, the [morn] is bright and grey,
The fields are fragrant and the woods are green.
Uncouple here and let us make a bay,
And wake the Emperor and his lovely bride,
And rouse the Prince, and ring a hunter's peal,
That all the court may echo with the noise.   (2.2.1–6)

Beneath this festive show lie ironies of which Titus is unaware. He himself admits to having been "troubled in [his] sleep this night" (l.9), so his exuberance belies an inner anxiety. The description of the beauties of the day and the natural world, as we shall see later when we examine the observations of other characters, is highly subjective and suggests his own inner need for harmony.[17] The Emperor's "lovely bride," moreover, is the vengeful Tamora.

More sinister ironies are implied in the action itself, which, like the hunt in *A Midsummer Night's Dream,* joins festivity with latent aggression. Titus's noisy salute is a hunting variant of the customary *reveille* by which newlyweds were awakened the morning after their marriage. The action itself, however, the uncoupling of hounds and making a bay, pushes merriment to the edge of assault. It mimics the final stage of the hunt, when the hounds are released and the exhausted and encircled animal stands at bay to meet its death.[18] Titus's gleeful *aubade* is thus unconsciously a murderous attack, foreshadowing later events. When Titus's madness later prompts him to shoot arrows to the heavens, Marcus fulfills the sinister implications of this festive gesture by ordering the arrows to be aimed at the court itself. At the grotesque banquet with which Titus finally achieves his revenge, moreover, Saturninus's stepsons are devoured in pasties, which for festive occasions were commonly filled with venison.

The most pressing and tangible irony in the scene preparing for the hunt occurs in the final lines, when Demetrius and Chiron confirm their plan to rape Lavinia. "Chiron," says Demetrius, "we hunt not, we, with horse nor hound, / But hope to pluck a dainty doe to ground" (2.2.25–26). The scene that begins with a festive image of the hunt as a celebration of human bonding and the joys of nature ends with an image of murderous sexual violence. Chiron and Demetrius need no animal intermediaries between themselves and the wild prey they hunt; they are beasts themselves, the predators for whom sexual attack and violent death are interchangeable. In this they degrade even the imagery of Aaron, who earlier likened them to human hunters, singling out a deer to be run to death, or hunted *par force*: "Single you thither then this dainty doe, / And strike her home by force, if not by words" (2.1.117–18). The allusion to *par force* hunting, the most "solemn" or ceremonial kind, heightens the perversity of their deed. Long afterwards, Demetrius remembers the event nostalgically as a great hunt: "I would we had a thousand Roman dames / At such a bay, by turn to serve our lust" (4.2.41–42). In his crafty madness, Titus calls the sons and mother "a pair of cursed hell-hounds and their dame" (5.2.144). The "hunting" of Demetrius and Chiron, one might say, plays out the latent violence of Titus's festive call to the hunt, transforming the playful baying at newly-weds into rape, mutilation, and murder.

Although Titus's "solemn hunting" takes place in the forest, the symbolic opposition implied by such a setting – a contrast between Rome and wilderness, civilization and barbarism – is evoked only to be dissolved. As we have observed already, the Rome of the Andronici is already at the point of barbarism and includes within its civilized boundaries ritual slaughter of an enemy and the impetuous murder of a son. With an ease afforded by the bareness of the Elizabethan stage, Shakespeare turns the image of the forest inward, making its landscape a projection of the forces that lie within the characters. For Aaron, who urges Chiron and Demetrius on to rape and murder, the "woods are ruthless, dreadful, deaf, and dull" (2.1.128). For Tamora, the landscape alters with her mind: "the birds chaunt melody on every bush" (2.3.12) when she woos Aaron to take advantage of their solitude, yet when she accuses Bassianus and Lavinia of attacking her the same setting becomes a "barren detested vale" in which "nothing breeds, / Unless the nightly owl or fatal raven" (2.3.93,96–97). For Titus, the "fragrant" fields and "green" woods of his joyful *aubade* become finally the "ruthless, vast, and gloomy woods" described by Ovid as the backdrop for the rape of Philomel. "Ay, such a place there is where we did hunt," he cries, as he reads the passage marked by Lavinia,

> (O had we never, never hunted there!),
> Pattern'd by that the poet here describes,
> By nature made for murthers and for rapes.   (4.1.54 58)

Unlike King Lear's mad interrogation of nature and the gods, Titus's stops short of the ultimate question, of what there is in nature that causes these hard hearts.

That Titus looks to Ovid for answers is not surprising, for the scene of the "solemn hunting" centers upon two Ovidean myths, both of which involve the hunt: those of Philomel and Actaeon. The scene begins with yet another classical hunting story, that of Dido and Aeneas, whose hunting is interrupted by a storm that forces them to take shelter in a cave. The source of this allusion is Tamora, who, in her attempt to seduce Aaron, plays "Dido" to his "wand'ring prince" (2.3.22), inciting him to imagine them both "curtain'd with a counsel-keeping cave," "wreathed in the other's arms," and possessed of "a golden slumber,"

> Whiles hounds and horns and sweet melodious birds
> Be unto us as is a nurse's song
> Of lullaby to bring her babe asleep.   (2.3.24–29)

To this Aaron replies that although Venus may "govern" *her* desires, Saturn dominates his (30–31); he proceeds to inform her of his plans for Bassianus's murder and Lavinia's rape. Like a travesty of Aeneas, Aaron abandons love for the higher destiny of war.

Having been deprived of a Virgilian role by Aaron's uncooperativeness, Tamora is immediately assigned an equally grotesque antithesis, that of Diana, goddess of chastity and the hunt. When Bassianus and Lavinia see Tamora alone with Aaron, they suspect romantic intrigue, and Bassianus slyly asks Tamora whether she might be not "Rome's royal Emperess" but Diana herself, "Who hath abandoned her holy groves / To see the general hunting in this forest" (55, 58–59). Stung by this obvious insult, Tamora transforms Bassianus into Actaeon:

> Had I the pow'r that some say Dian had,
> Thy temples should be planted presently
> With horns, as was Actaeon's, and the hounds
> Should drive upon thy new-transformed limbs,
> Unmannerly intruder as thou art!   (61–65)

The spontaneous insult provides a metaphoric structure for the events that ensue. When Lavinia is raped, Bassianus is indeed given the cuckold's horns, and by an action that Tamora encourages. When Bassianus is killed, by Chiron and Demetrius, he falls prey to characters who, if not hounds, are tigers, and is thrown like an animal into a pit. Aaron has earlier implied a likeness between Bassianus's death and that of a hunted animal in his observation to Tamora that her sons will "wash their hands in Bassianus' blood" (2.3.45); here the imagery of human sacrifice merges with the ritual that marks the death of the deer. The grotesque and nightmarish world of the play has more affinity with Ovid than Virgil. Whereas Shakespeare's travesty of Dido and Aeneas undermines the Virgilian possibilities in his story, his use of Ovid, here and throughout, exaggerates the ironic horrors of stories already macabre.[19]

Unlike the stories of Dido and Actaeon, that of Philomel does not center on the hunt; an allusion to hunting within the story, however, might have triggered off the grisly symmetry of Shakespeare's ending. In Ovid, when Philomel goes into hiding after her rape and mutilation, her sister, Procne, searches for her in disguise, wearing over her shoulder the deer-skin of a Bacchante and carrying a lance. Later, when in revenge she seizes Tereus's son, Itys, she does so "like some tigress on the Ganges' banks, dragging an unweaned fawn through the thick forest."[20] The child is then hacked to bits, with some parts boiled and some roasted, and served up to his father. In Shakespeare's version Philomel herself, Lavinia, becomes a doe, and her rape and mutilation recall the death and dismemberment of a deer. The hunt to avenge this deed is led by Titus, who dismembers Chiron and Demetrius and serves them up to Tamora as a "pasty." Shakespeare's substitution of a pasty for the boiled and roasted meat of his source suggests his desire to keep the irony of the hunting theme alive, for, as the *Oxford English Dictionary* makes clear, pasties were often made of venison. The ceremonial nature of this feast would increase the likelihood of such meat, for venison was considered a special delicacy, as is clear from accounts such as William Harrison's.[21]

The assault on Lavinia is motivated primarily by the lust of Chiron and Demetrius. Once they are persuaded by Aaron to join forces, however, the crime becomes not merely personal but political and familial. The hunt becomes an attack upon the Andronici. When Lavinia pleads with Tamora to save her, "for my father's sake," Tamora replies,

> Even for his sake am I pitiless.
> Remember, boys, I pour'd forth tears in vain
> To save your brother from the sacrifice,
> But fierce Andronicus would not relent.   (2.3.158,162–65)

The assault on Lavinia, then, becomes an act of retaliation, a "sacrifice" that atones for the death of Tamora's eldest son. As such, her violation serves as a constant reminder of the original sacrifice. The revenge is not exactly symmetrical: Alarbus is killed, dismembered, and burned; Lavinia is raped and mutilated. In the Roman logic of the play, however, as witnessed by the reactions of both Titus and Lavinia, rape is a fate worse than death. The play's central visual symbol, moreover, is that of Lavinia's maimed body. Before Alarbus is sacrificed, Lucius asks "that we may hew his limbs" (1.1.97); afterwards, he exultantly tells his father that the "limbs are lopp'd" (1.1.143). When Marcus first encounters the maimed Lavinia, he asks "what stern ungentle hands" have "lopp'd and

hew'd" her (2.4.16–17). At the end of the play, upon his capture of
Aaron, Lucius must endure the description of his own sister having been
"wash'd, and cut, and trimm'd" – a "trim sport for them which had the
doing of it" (5.1.95–96).

Lavinia is thus not merely a "doe" but one that belongs to Titus
Andronicus. When Marcus describes how he found the violated Lavinia
"straying in the park, / Seeking to hide herself, as doth the deer / That
hath receiv'd some unrecuring wound," Titus responds, "It was my dear,
and he that wounded her / Hath hurt me more than had he kill'd me
dead" (3.1.88–92). By shifting the locale from forest to park, Shakespeare
accentuates both the sense of ownership and the sense of pathos. The
attack upon Titus's daughter is an attack upon him, her loss of honor a
loss of his own.

In the metaphoric terms of the hunt, Titus has been the victim of
poaching; someone has attacked his "deer." Demetrius himself views the
attack upon Lavinia in precisely this way, when in anticipation of the
chase he reminds Aaron and Chiron of the pleasures of poaching. The
exchange joins images of illicit hunting and illicit sexuality:

> *Dem.* What, hast not thou full often strook a doe,
> And borne her cleanly by the keeper's nose?
> *Aar.* Why then it seems some certain snatch or so
> Would serve your turns.
> *Chi.*   Ay, so the turn were served.
> *Dem.* Aaron, thou hast hit it.
> *Aar.*   Would you had hit it too!
>
> (2.1.93–97)

The viciously jocular puns on "strook," "snatch," and "hit" all serve to
link the joys of sexual violence not merely to the violence of the hunt
but to the special pleasures of poaching.

Aaron, Chiron, and Demetrius can thus be seen as nightmare versions
of Elizabethan poachers. They are swaggerers. They delight in wanton
destruction. They use the hunt to take revenge against an enemy, as an
act of symbolic warfare. They make a trophy of the victim, confronting
the enemy with a reminder of their power over his property. And of
course their action begets a corresponding revenge-action, the killing of
Chiron and Demetrius as animals, to be served up in a pasty.

Tensions within the Elizabethan culture of the hunt, then, underlie
the representation of violence in *Titus Andronicus*. The conflict between
civilization and bestiality enacted and ideally resolved in the ritual dismemberment of the hart is played out with Erasmian effect: the sacrifice

of the hunt reveals the beasts within the hunters. In the case of Titus, Shakespeare focuses on the ironic breaking apart of this ritual tension, with his noble but naive aspirations towards ceremony themselves precipitating the social descent into savagery. The "irreligious piety" of Titus's initial attempt to ritualize savage revenge through the lopping and burning of Tamora's first-born son fuels another revenge of murder, rape, and dismemberment, which fuels yet another revenge of murder, dismemberment, and cannibalistic feasting. The festive yet "solemn" hunting celebrating the marriage of Saturninus and Tamora becomes transformed into the wild and parodic rites of poaching, with humans as both predators and prey. In the play's final abhorrent actions, the hunt theme reaches its logical conclusion: Tamora the tigress eats her sons, and Titus kills his own "dear" Lavinia. In *Praise of Folly*, the hunters become savage beasts. In *Titus Andronicus*, these same beasts end by devouring themselves.

In *Julius Caesar*, Brutus, like Titus, is a ceremonialist. His complicity in the plot against Caesar depends upon his ability to persuade himself that the assassination is not a murder but a solemn sacrifice. A staunch republican, whose ancestors drove Tarquin "from the streets of Rome . . . when he was call'd a king" (2.1.53–54), Brutus justifies the assassination of Caesar as an act of "pity to the general wrong of Rome" (3.1.170). "What villain touch'd his body," he asks, "that did stab / And not for justice?" (4.3.20–21). For Brutus, as for Titus, personal, familial, and civic honor require the imaginative conversion of live human beings into mere ceremonial victims, sacrifices to the common good. In both cases the motives of the sacrificers are tainted, and their action does not redress the "general wrong of Rome" but intensifies it.[22]

   The most powerful statement of Brutus's ceremonialism occurs, ironically, in his dispute with Cassius over the necessity of killing Antony along with Caesar. Cassius rightly perceives Antony as a serious political threat and advocates his murder as the necessary corollary of Caesar's. Brutus counters with a visionary but confused mixture of political strategy and political principle. He turns first to the issue of Antony:

> Our course will seem too bloody, Caius Cassius,
> To cut the head off and then hack the limbs –
> Like wrath in death and envy afterwards;
> For Antony is but a limb of Caesar.   (2.1.162–65)

At this point the question remains a political one, that of the potential impact of the murder of Antony upon the people. Brutus is capable of thinking tactically, and even during the assassination, as we shall see, he reveals a sensitivity to the symbolic nature of political action. Unfortunately, however, his tactical thinking is invariably wrong, and Cassius, confusing moral with political authority, invariably yields to it.

The source of Brutus's political misjudgment, it seems, is his moral sensitivity, which finds expression as this speech continues and he turns to the murder of Caesar himself:

> Let's be sacrificers, but not butchers, Caius.
> We all stand up against the spirit of Caesar,
> And in the spirit of men there is no blood;
> O that we then could come by Caesar's spirit,
> And not dismember Caesar! But, alas,
> Caesar must bleed for it! And, gentle friends,
> Let's kill him boldly, but not wrathfully;
> Let's carve him as a dish fit for the gods,
> Not hew him as a carcass fit for hounds;
> And let our hearts, as subtle masters do,
> Stir up their servants to an act of rage,
> And after seem to chide 'em. (166–77)

Unlike Cassius, Brutus shows genuine moral feeling for the deed he is about to commit, and for this he is celebrated at the end of the play by Antony himself.

Brutus's attempt to define assassination as a moral, even a religious act, however, is intellectually and morally evasive. He first attempts to distinguish sacrificial killing, the death of the spirit, from butchery, the death of the body, but then must admit that the only way to the spirit is through the body: "alas, / Caesar must bleed for it!" Having conceded the necessity of blood, Brutus then focuses on the method of bloodshed, distinguishing between the sacrificial "carving" accorded to a noble dish and the "hewing" accorded to a carcass for hounds.[23] Yet even here he must admit the devious psychology upon which the distinction rests: that one can stir oneself to an act of rage and then pretend to reprove oneself by respectful action – that one can, in short, stir oneself to murderous rage, and then convert the action into one of solemn sacrifice.

The deviousness that underlies this last image – of stirring one's servants to a rage and then pretending to chide them – continues as Brutus returns once more to the political effect of their action:

> This shall make
> Our purpose necessary, and not envious,
> Which so appearing to the common eyes,
> We shall be call'd purgers, not murderers. (177–80)

His final remark is to belittle the political threat represented by Antony:

> And for Mark Antony, think not of him;
> For he can do no more than Caesar's arm
> When Caesar's head is off.   (181–83)

The movement of thought throughout the speech is from amoral political strategy to religious sacrifice and back to amoral political strategy.
Either Brutus is guilty of intellectual and moral confusion or he is pretending to think politically for the sake of Cassius.

The contrast between "carving" and "hewing," and the notion of an
act of killing that requires not only rage but the suppression of rage both
anticipate the imagery of the death and dismemberment of the hart that
will later dominate the scene of the assassination itself. As we have seen
earlier, the dismembering of a stag is a ceremonial and potentially
sacrificial act, an act that in both *A Jewell for Gentrie* and *Love's Labor's Lost*
is described as "carving"; it is also an act of respect or even reverence
for the worth of the dead animal, which dies so that humans may live.
As René Girard observes of Brutus's image, "in the carving metaphor
all aspects of culture seem harmoniously blended, the differential and
the spiritual, the spatial, the ethical, and the aesthetic."[24] Brutus's reductive alternative to this ceremony, the brutal "hewing" of a "carcass fit for
hounds," ironically anticipates Antony's later description of the savage
nature of the assassination itself. Brutus's image of stirring up "servants"
to rage that must be later suppressed recalls the dependency of the hunt
on the ferocity of the hounds, which not only characterizes the process
of the pursuit and the attack but is re-enacted in the ritual of their
reward.

The underlying issue in these allusions to the hunt is the one we have
already observed in Erasmus's *Praise of Folly*: Is the hunt a solemn
sacrifice, or is it a mere act of savage bestiality? And, more precisely, does
the act of hunting itself, with all its ceremony, simply encourage humans
to suppress their humanity, to become no more than beasts themselves?
Brutus's attempt to "carve" rather than "hew" Caesar is an attempt,
through ceremony, to legitimize and sanctify the act of killing. In this,
Brutus is like Burkert's Paleolithic hunters, for whom the shock of the
kill requires a ritual form within which it may be overcome. Both Brutus
and Titus Andronicus are basically good men who recoil from the
bloody acts that "justice" requires of them, and whose recoil is marked
by the desire to transform the bloodshed into a sacrificial rite.

Brutus's image of the assassination as a solemn sacrifice is important not merely because it reflects his inner motivations but because it prepares for the event itself, which is the climactic moment of the play. In this scene Brutus becomes a kind of priest, who attempts to translate his ritualistic conception of the meaning of the plot into stage action. In this, Brutus fails, for, whether we imagine the killing of Caesar to be staged ritualistically or with frenzied brutality, the contrast between Brutus's bloodless aspirations and the bloodiness of the deed cannot help but unnerve an audience. Despite his aspirations to spiritualize the action, the "sacrifice" becomes the very "savage spectacle" (3.1.223) he sought to avoid. The encircling of Caesar by the conspirators; their thrusting forward of petitions, which makes Caesar think of fawning dogs (45–46); the multitude of the wounds; the bathing of the conspirators' hands "up to the elbows" (107) in Caesar's blood – the actions of Brutus's "sacrifice" undermine his ritual purpose.

After the event, when Antony enters and looks down at the corpse of Caesar, he converts the underlying symbolism of the scene into explicit verbal statement:

> Here wast thou bay'd, brave hart,
> Here didst thou fall, and here thy hunters stand,
> Sign'd in thy spoil, and crimson'd in thy lethe.
> O world! thou wast the forest to this hart,
> And this indeed, O world, the heart of thee.
> How like a deer, strooken by many princes,
> Dost thou here lie![25]   (3.1.204–10)

The link between Caesar and a hunted animal, as we have seen, is foreshadowed in North's Plutarch, in which he is described as "hacked and mangeled amonge them, as a wilde beaste taken of hunters." In specifying that the "wilde beaste" is a hart, Antony both ennobles and creates sympathy for the subject, since the hart is the most magnificent and royal of the animals hunted, and not itself a predator. The image may also have sprung to mind because of the common tradition that harts belonging to Caesar had been found alive throughout Europe hundreds of years after his death, with collars around their necks indicating his ownership.[26]

Antony's description of Caesar's death as that of a hart reverses Brutus's earlier attempt to ritualize and thereby sanitize it. In juxtaposing the two men's opposed views of the same event, Shakespeare exploits tensions that underlie the Elizabethan hunt itself. Antony's image of the hunters "signed" and "crimsoned" in the life-blood of the deer, like Brutus's earlier exhortation to the conspirators to "bathe our hands in Caesar's blood / Up to the elbows" (3.1.106–7), derives from the customary action of "blooding" at the end of a hunt. The notion of "blooding" may have indeed inspired the episode, since nothing like it occurs in the source descriptions of Caesar's assassination.[27] Both characters see the conspirators' action as symbolic, but for both the symbolism points in opposite directions. For Brutus, the bloody hands signify "peace, freedom, and liberty" (3.1.110); for Antony, the "purpled hands" that "do reek and smoke" (3.1.158) signify utter bestiality.

In the discourse of the hunt, one might locate this conflict in the opposition between the views of James I and those of Erasmus. For James, daubing his courtiers' faces with the blood of a deer was a ritual sign of their valor, to be worn proudly and displayed until the stain wore off. King James also used the blood of a deer killed in the hunt for curative purposes, as when he "killed a buck in Eltham Park, and bathed his bare feet and legs in the blood, as a cure for the gout."[28] For Erasmus, the bloodshed of the hunt had no ritualistic or curative value but merely incited human bestiality. Brutus's attempt to ritualize the death of Caesar arouses discomfort in Cassius, whose views are more pragmatic than spiritual. When Brutus exhorts the conspirators to "bathe our hands in Caesar's blood," Cassius responds with the curt directive, "stoop, then, and wash" (3.1.111). Bathing suggests ritualistic immersion; washing, ironically, mere cleansing. The public display of bloody hands is for Brutus a ritual demonstration of the conspirators' honor; for Cassius, however, it is mere theater: "How many ages hence / Shall this our lofty scene be acted over" (111–12).

Antony's image of Caesar as a deer struck "by many princes" might also be situated in cultural anxieties surrounding the ritual of the hunt. On the one hand, the word "princes" euphemistically elevates the action of the conspirators, masking Antony's true opinion for the sake of his own safety. The use of the plural form of the word, however, conveys a subtle irony, for the killing of a stag was almost certainly not a group action.[29]

The moral ambiguities that lie within the killing of the hart surface in George Gascoigne's account of the event. In order to illustrate the great danger in killing a hart, Gascoigne recounts the story of the Emperor Basil, who, although heroically victorious in many battles, was slain by a hart as he attacked it. The tragic irony in the Emperor's death – that a great warrior should be slain by a "fearefull beast" forced to defend itself – leads Gascoigne to moralize the event as "a mirrour to al Princes" not to proffer "undeserved injuries" or to "constrayne the simple sakelesse man to stand in his owne defence." Having drawn his moral, however,

Gascoigne realizes to his dismay that, if taken seriously, it would undermine the very idea of hunting. So he is forced to backtrack:

I woulde not have my wordes wrested to this construction, that it were unlawfull to kill a Deare or such beasts of venerie: for so should I both speake agaynst the purpose which I have taken in hande, and agayne I should seeme to argue against Gods ordinances, since it seemeth that suche beastes have bene created to the use of man and for his recreation: but as by all Fables some good moralitie may be gathered, so by all Histories and examples, some good allegorie and comparison may be made.[30]

In chapter 1 we have already observed Gascoigne's complex attitude towards the hunt. In this instance, the death of a hart becomes the source of a moral tension remarkably similar to that evoked by Shakespeare in his treatment of the death of Caesar. Gascoigne's ambivalence is expressed in two contradictory attitudes: either the hart is innocent and the deed reprehensible, or the hart is innocent but a legitimate sacrifice to human need. In Shakespeare's play, Antony takes the former view, Brutus the latter.

As soon as the conspirators leave, Antony bursts through the sentimental image of the stricken deer, an image which insulates the conspirators from the real horror of their action and protects him from their fury. In soliloquy, he vents his passion for revenge: "O pardon me, thou bleeding piece of earth, / That I am meek and gentle with these butchers!" (3.1.254–55). Brutus's hopeful imagery is thus turned against him; his attempt to create a solemn ritual, to be perceived as a sacrificer, not a butcher, has achieved the opposite effect. By the end of Antony's speech, the roles of Brutus and Caesar have been reversed, and Caesar's spirit becomes a hunter, pursuing the conspirators for his revenge:

> And Caesar's spirit, ranging for revenge,
> With Ate by his side come hot from hell,
> Shall in these confines with a monarch's voice
> Cry "Havoc!" and let slip the dogs of war,
> That this foul deed shall smell above the earth
> With carrion men, groaning for burial.   (270–75)

The image is terrifying for a number of reasons, not the least of which is the fact that Antony himself not merely prophesies the dreadful civil war but deliberately incites it. Caesar's "spirit" lives within him, and he urges the hounds to violence.

Antony's ferocious call for vengeance combines the language of hunting and of war, and thus depends upon the long-standing convergence of the two activities in vindications of the hunt as a preparation in the arts of war. The word "range," according to the *Oxford English Dictionary*, is used of both persons and animals, and in the latter case, especially, of "hunting dogs searching for game." The word "confines," an odd choice for a civil war that will later encompass the Mediterranean, suggests the enclosed space of a park. The cry "havoc," primarily a military term, a call for utter destruction of the enemy, takes on overtones of hunting through the association with letting slip "the dogs of war"; Roger B. Manning notes that the term is "occasionally used in Star Chamber complaints to describe poachers who wantonly killed more deer than they could possibly carry away, leaving many carcasses behind to spoil."[31] In *Coriolanus*, Menenius uses the term in the context of the hunt: "Do not cry havoc where you should but hunt / With modest warrant" (3.1.273–74). The notion that Caesar is a "spirit" hunter might link his avenging ghost to the mythological figure of Herne the hunter, whose wildly destructive night-hunts, suggestive of poaching raids, are alluded to in *The Merry Wives of Windsor*. The image of the hunt that underlies this passage is thus not that of the "solemn" or ceremonial hunt, but that of a revenge-hunt, an act of poaching.

The social context invoked by Antony's lines may be illustrated by one of the more dramatic instances of such poaching warfare in the period – an attack in 1572 by the Earl of Leicester upon his enemy, Henry, eleventh Lord Berkeley, that implicated the Queen. While on progress, accompanied by Leicester, Elizabeth arrived at Berkeley Castle. Lord Berkeley, absent at the time, was an avid hunter and kept a herd of red deer in the adjoining park. Leicester and the Queen decided to hunt them. "Such slaughter was made" during their brief stay at the Castle that "27 stagges were slayne in the Toiles in one day, and many others in that and the next stollen and havocked." Furious at this insult, Berkeley destroyed his own park. A few months later, however, he received a "secret freindly advertizement from the Court" relating Elizabeth's warning to him to beware of Leicester's designs. Leicester had "drawn" the Queen to the Castle, according to this report, and, contrary to her desire, "purposely had caused that slaughter of his deere." Leicester, the report said, "might have a further plott against his [Berkeley's] head and that Castle, whereto he had taken noe small liking, and affirmed to have good title thereto . . ."[32]

More was at stake in this affair than appears at first glance. Berkeley's absence was probably a deliberate slight, for Elizabeth's main purpose in the visit was to warn him that the followers of his brother-in-law, the recently executed fourth duke of Norfolk, should end their resistance;

the slaughter of his deer was thus an emblem of royal power. By traveling with Leicester, moreover, Elizabeth was also signaling her support of his side in his dispute with Berkeley over the Lisle inheritance. The attack upon Berkeley's deer was thus part of a long-standing feud between powerful nobles. The attack itself had significant consequences: it "reverberated through the Vale of Berkeley and precipitated a poaching war lasting nearly fifty years between Lord Berkeley's gamekeepers and the adherents of Sir Thomas Throckmorton, Leicester's henchman in Gloucestershire."[33] In Elizabethan England, then, as in the Rome invoked by Mark Antony, the language of civil war and the language of wild hunting converge.[34]

Under Antony's direction the war of revenge that he envisages takes on overtones of a hunt. The scene in which he and Octavius, like deathly accountants, decide who is "prick'd to die" depends so heavily upon repetitions of the word "prick" or "prick'd" (three times in sixteen lines, 4.1.1–16) that it may allude to the special role of "prickers" in the hunt, whose job it was to goad the chosen animals to their death.[35] Later, when Brutus mocks him before Philippi, Antony converts his earlier image of Caesar as a hart stricken by many princes into that of a man bitten to death by sycophantic apes and dogs:

> You show'd your [teeth] like apes, and fawn'd like hounds,
> And bow'd like bondmen, kissing Caesar's feet;
> Whilst damned Casca, like a cur, behind
> Strook Caesar on the neck. O you flatterers! (5.1.41–44)

Both Brutus and Cassius see themselves finally as prey. As he awaits the battle at Philippi, Cassius observes fatalistically that the eagles that have heretofore perched on his foremost banner have flown away and been replaced by "ravens, crows, and kites" looking at them as if they were "sickly prey" (5.1.84, 86). When he later has himself killed by Pindarus, Cassius calls attention to the irony in the weapon used: "Caesar, thou art reveng'd, / Even with the sword that kill'd thee" (5.3.45–46). Brutus too notes the irony of his own suicide: "Caesar, now be still, / I kill'd not thee with half so good a will" (5.5.50–51). Brutus takes his life, moreover, shortly after he likens his end to that of a driven animal:

> Our enemies have beat us to the pit.
> It is more worthy to leap in ourselves
> Than tarry till they push us. (5.5.23–25)

In true Roman fashion, both conspirators take their own lives, having been gradually transformed from hunters of Caesar into Caesar's prey and finally into hunters of themselves. Although rather more decorously tragic than the final actions of Tamora and Titus in *Titus Andronicus*, these deaths too show predators finally preying upon themselves.

In both *Titus Andronicus* and *Julius Caesar*, Shakespeare exploits the conventional image of the hunt as a ritual of death and dismemberment, a means of civilizing bloodshed. In both plays the contrast between a civilized and barbaric Rome is articulated in the equivocal ritualism of the hunt – a ritualism that for Elizabethans was itself a source of ideological conflict. In both plays, Shakespeare explodes the ritual ideal of civilized violence by depicting the inner tensions and hypocrisies that characterize it, even in high-minded ceremonialists like Titus and Brutus. The ceremonial ideal ultimately finds only parodic expression in the wild and anarchic vendettas of poaching. The anti-ceremonial thrust of both plays recalls the satiric perspective of Erasmus, for whom the ritual of the hunt itself accentuates the human tendency towards cruelty and violence, transforming men into beasts.

Shakespeare's plays, unlike Erasmus's satire, are not directed at hunting. They exploit an Erasmian view of the hunt, one might say, to probe the discordances between the ceremonial ideals of a high civilization and the savage realities that underlie them. This tension is a familiar one in Shakespeare, appearing in theatrical moments as diverse as Henry V's soliloquy on ceremony the night before Agincourt (4.1.225–84), Othello's attempt to see Desdemona's murder as a sacrifice (5.2.65), and King Lear's anguished action of ripping off his clothes to find the "poor, bare, fork'd animal" beneath (3.4.107–8). The ritual of the hunt, with its uniquely literal attempt to bring the bestial within the order of civilization, provided Shakespeare with a vivid set of images for a problem he pursued throughout his career: the tragic inability of ceremonial ideals to withstand the violent impulses within human nature.

CHAPTER FOUR

The "manning" of Katherine: falconry in The Taming of the Shrew

Since at least the end of the nineteenth century, when G. B. Shaw lamented that "no man with any decency of feeling" could sit out the play "in the company of a woman" and not be "extremely ashamed of the lord-of-creation moral" of its ending, *The Taming of the Shrew* has been a critical and theatrical problem.[1] How are we to enjoy a play that not only centers upon the brutal farce of "taming" a woman but concludes with the woman's own celebration of the doctrine of the tamer? As the critical and theatrical traditions suggest, the question permits a variety of possible answers. We can consign the play to the shelf, at least theoretically (it continues to be performed and discussed). More realistically, we can take the shame out of the ending by overturning or at least softening its apparent "lord-of-creation moral": we can show Katherine as remaining essentially untamed; or as having achieved the upper hand herself; or, more romantically, as having fulfilled herself through marriage. As Lynda E. Boose has wittily observed, the latter option in particular, which emphasizes affection more than submission, has become the most popular way to "save the play from its own ending."[2]

There are other options. We can keep the play and its ending, according to Robert B. Heilman, if we simply remember that the play is a farce, that farce "anesthetizes" us from thought or emotion, and that the repressive patriarchal doctrine which the play celebrates, like that of the divine right of kings and other bizarre Elizabethan notions, can be easily ignored as archaic and irrelevant. The problem with this view, however, anesthesia aside, is that the play resists either generic or ideological taming. Even Heilman, who begins by reducing the play emphatically to farce, admits later that both Katherine and Petruchio are given "a good deal of intelligence and feeling that they would not have in elementary farce."[3] Peter Saccio, in another discussion of the play as farce, avoids this trap but only by defining the play as a humane or "kindly" farce.[4] Once we begin to move from farce towards romantic comedy, however, the anesthesia of farce begins to evaporate and the problem of taming returns.

The ideological problem of the ending is as vexing as the generic. Here too the critical drift is towards romanticizing the ending. As John C. Bean and others have observed, if read historically the doctrine enunciated in Katherine's final speech is far less repressive than its counterpart in the closely related play, *The Taming of A Shrew*, and can be positioned at the liberal end of the spectrum of Elizabethan views on marriage. Historicizing the speech, in short, can soften the edges of its apparent antifeminism and sanction readings that stress mutuality and affection. Solving the problem of the ending in this way, however, as Bean shrewdly perceives, merely poses a new problem, that of the manner in which the ending is achieved: Katherine's speech is uttered at Petruchio's command and after a long period of brutal and coercive "taming." In her final performance, observes Bean, Katherine "still has some of the vestiges of a trained bear."[5] That she voices a relatively progressive view of marital relations is in this context hardly reassuring.

The more liberal and romantic our reading of the play, it seems, the more difficult becomes its title and the more problematic the main action of the play. How can we reconcile the practice of taming with even the most mildly progressive gestures of the play, as in its tendency to move beyond farce and to liberalize contemporary doctrines of marriage? The problem, moreover, is not merely that of reconciling Shakespeare with contemporary views. Fletcher's sequel to the play, *The Woman's Prize or the Tamer Tamed*, which features the taming of Petruchio by his second wife and concludes with a homily on mutuality in marriage, shows that *The Taming of the Shrew* was at the very least controversial and capable of evoking protest among Elizabethan and Jacobean audiences. In addition, there is the problem of reconciling the *Shrew* with the rest of Shakespeare; although his other plays often reflect patriarchal attitudes towards women and marriage, none does so with such apparently zestful brutality as this one.

The difficulty posed by the play may help explain why, although it is often acknowledged, the metaphor of taming in the title is rarely considered at any length. Instead of basing their interpretations of Petruchio's courtship of Katherine on the taming of falcons, the metaphor that Petruchio himself uses, critics tend to prefer other, more benign metaphors. For Joel Fineman, Petruchio follows the logic of homeopathic medicine, by which he holds "his own lunatic self up as mirror of Kate's unnatural nature."[6] For Peter Saccio Petruchio is a teacher of games; he "teaches" Katherine "to play."[7] The metaphor of game is important for many critics, including Marianne Novy, who in adopting it acknowledges the irony that "the leader of the game" is always Petruchio.[8]

Each of these metaphors, it is fair to say, has some warrant in the text, and each evokes certain real qualities in the relationship between the two characters. The tendency in using them, however, as Novy observes in the case of "game," is to soften and romanticize the process, to imply a mutuality that only begins to appear, if at all, at the very end of the play. To respond adequately to this play, we must come to terms with its central metaphor, articulated both by Shakespeare and by Petruchio, that of taming falcons. The metaphor appears not only in the title of the play but in Petruchio's crucial soliloquy in act 4 scene 1, in which he rationalizes his approach to courtship by means of a detailed and technical description of the process of taming a falcon. If we understand the full implications of the metaphor, and of the social context it evokes, we might discover, by a circuitous route, a way of "saving the play from its own ending" without either evading or romanticizing its main action, that of "taming" a woman.

As a play about taming, and especially taming in the context of hunting, the *Shrew* is implicitly about "man's" dominion over nature. The right to tame animals, like the right to hunt them, derives from God's exhortation in Genesis to "subdue" the earth and to "rule over the fish of the sea and over the foule of the heaven, and over everie beast that moveth upon the earth."[9] As Gervase Markham rather smugly notes, in defending the legitimacy of recreational hunting, "a man so good and vertuous as the true *Husband man* is, should not be deprived any comfort, or felicity, which the earth, or the creatures of the earth can affoord unto him, being indeed the right Lord and Master (next under God) of them both . . ." The very notion of taming, in this context, implies the rightful domination of man over nature in a double sense: the tamed animal, the dog or falcon, becomes man's weapon against the wild prey. In an age like our own, in which hunting is dominated by technology, it is difficult to appreciate the extent to which Elizabethan hunting emphasized the discipline and control of animals. So accustomed is Markham to the use of dogs in the chase, in fact, that he defines hunting itself simply as "a curious search or conquest of one Beast over an other."[10] The training of a beast to subordinate its own instincts to man's will is a triumph of human ingenuity. "Suche and so great is the singular skill of man," says George Turbervile of the successful training of a falcon, "when by arte he is resolved, to alter the prescribed order of nature, which by industrie and payne we see is brought to passe and effect."[11]

Throughout the *Taming of the Shrew*, Petruchio is shown in constant relation with animals and servants. He dominates them both with farcical brutality, and with boisterous and good natured tyranny. In his first appearance in the play, he wrings Grumio's ears after a heated exchange over the meaning of his equivocal order to "knock me here soundly" (1.2.8). He appears at his wedding on a horse both ill-caparisoned and wracked with disease: "possess'd with the glanders and like to mose in the chine, troubled with the lampass, infected with the fashions, full of windgalls, sped with spavins, ray'd with the yellows," and more (3.2.50–53). On the journey to his home, he beats Grumio because the horse stumbles in the mire. Once arrived, he rages at his servants for their lack of attendance, strikes both the servant who attempts to take off his boots and the servant who brings water to him, throws over the table of food, and beats all the other servants in sight.

Some of these violent antics can be explained as ploys to "educate" Katherine into an awareness of his power, which extends over all the people, property, and animals he controls:

> I will be master of what is mine own.
> She is my goods, my chattels, she is my house,
> My household stuff, my field, my barn,
> My horse, my ox, my ass, my any thing . . .   (3.2.229–32).

Petruchio's impetuous rages and outrageous posturing cannot be explained away, however, as mere "educational" theater. The opening knock-about with Grumio has no other witnesses and creates a "personality" that informs the more overtly theatrical gestures that follow. Petruchio's braggadocio may be calculated in part, and may partly disguise an inner humanity, but it expresses nonetheless his own powerful sense of self: "Have I not in my time heard lions roar?" (1.2.200). He sets out to master Katherine not only for the money but for the challenge; the wooing has about it the stereotypically masculine love of the dare and the competitiveness that accompanies it. For Petruchio, marriage is a sporting event. His energy, his noise, his self-assertiveness, his violent physicality, his swaggering relish of the life of a soldier amidst the "Loud 'larums, neighing steeds, and trumpets' clang" (1.2.206) – all bespeak his affinity with the aggressively masculine culture of the hunt.

Petruchio is not nearly as rough physically on Katherine as he is on his servants and animals. He never hits her. As Anne Barton observes, moreover, if we compare him to the usual husband in shrew-taming stories, who is prone to bind, beat, or bleed his wife, or wrap her in the salted skin of a dead horse, he seems "almost a model of intelligence and humanity."[12] This is so, ironically, not because Petruchio is a model husband but because he is a model tamer of hawks. His guide to courtship is not a book of sonnets or a handbook on marriage but a book of falconry: he adapts the methods of taming and training a hawk to the task of domesticating Katherine. Since we will be dealing closely with the language of falconry in the play, I shall quote the entire speech in which he declares this intention and italicize the technical terms:

> Thus have I politicly begun my reign,
> And 'tis my hope to end successfully.
> My *falcon* now is sharp and passing empty,
> And till she *stoop*, she must not be *full-gorg'd*,
> For then she never looks upon her *lure*.
> Another way I have to *man* my *haggard*,
> To make her come, and know her keeper's call,
> That is, to *watch* her, as we *watch* these *kites*
> That *bate* and beat and will not be obedient.
> She eat no meat to-day, nor none shall eat;
> Last night she slept not, nor to-night she shall not;
> As with the meat, some undeserved fault
> I'll find about the making of the bed,
> And here I'll fling the pillow, there the bolster,
> This way the coverlet, another way the sheets.
> Ay, and amid this hurly I intend
> That all is done in reverend care of her,
> And in conclusion, she shall watch all night,
> And if she chance to nod I'll rail and brawl,
> And with the clamor keep her still awake.
> This is a way to kill a wife with kindness,
> And thus I'll curb her mad and headstrong humor.
> He that knows better how to tame a shrew,
> Now let him speak; 'tis charity to shew.   (4.1.188–211)

As this speech demonstrates, Petruchio has mastered the jargon of falconry; he uses easily and naturally terms like "stoop," "lure," "man," "watch," and "bate." He knows that the tamer must keep the hawk hungry and sleepless, and that the tamer's ultimate goal is a bird that returns obediently to the call. More strikingly, he has mastered the paradoxical psychology coupling cruelty and kindness that underlies the process: "amid this hurly I intend / That all is done in reverend care of her." He perceives, moreover, that the goal of taming is power: "Thus have I politicly begun my reign." He is a benignly Machiavellian falconer, a sporting parody of Richard III, determined "to kill a wife with kindness." The phrase captures perfectly the paradoxical nature of the falconer's art.

Shakespeare's use of the language of falconry to characterize Petruchio's "taming" of Katherine must have had considerable impact upon contemporary audiences. When John Fletcher came to write his sequel to *The Taming of the Shrew*, entitled *The Woman's Prize or The Tamer Tamed* (1611), he acknowledged Shakespeare's metaphor by having his own "shrew," Maria, subvert it to her own purposes:

> Hang these tame hearted Eyasses, that no sooner
> See the Lure out, and heare their husbands halla,
> But cry like Kites upon 'em: The free Haggard
> (Which is that woman, that has wing, and knowes it,
> Spirit, and plume) will make an hundred checks,
> To shew her freedome, saile in ev'ry ayre,
> And look out ev'ry pleasure; not regarding
> Lure, nor Quarry, till her pitch command
> What she desires, making her foundred keeper
> Be glad to fling out traines, and golden ones,
> To take her down again.[13]

In contrasting herself to a tamed hawk, Maria sees herself as a "free Haggard" that flies at will and is drawn back to her tamer only with the lure of "golden" rewards. Having alluded to his Shakespearean original in this passage, Fletcher drops the metaphor of falconry and develops his lovers' conflict in the more conventional imagery of siege warfare. In Shakespeare's play, Katherine is tamed like a falcon; in Fletcher's, Maria wins a war.

The paradoxical effect of falcon-taming is foreshadowed in Petruchio's witty pun on the word "stoop" (191). In its technical sense the word conveys the astonishing speed and power of the falcon itself, referring to the "swift swoop or thunderbolt descent of the falcon on the quarry from above."[14] In its common meaning, in contrast, it refers to a lowering of the self, as in a gesture of submission. The "stooping" of the falcon thus expresses simultaneously its own and its master's power: the falcon fulfills its instinctual will, one might say, by lowering itself. Such a gesture of victorious submission occurs at the very end of the play when

Katherine, having outdone the other wives, offers to stoop and place her hand below Petruchio's foot. "'Tis my hope to end successfully," Petruchio tells us in his soliloquy, "And till she stoop, she must not be full-gorg'd." In such a context, the comic convention of the feast that ends the play takes on new meaning. Katherine feasts after she has "stooped" to defeat the other wives and "stooped" to honor her husband.

For Petruchio, Katherine is a "haggard . . . falcon" (4.1.193,190). The name "falcon," although used variously in the manuals, refers most commonly to "the female of all long-winged hawks."[15] Katherine is thus placed among the noblest of hunting birds, those that tower above their prey, not those that pursue it from the side or below. As a "haggard," she is a mature bird captured in the wild, not an "eyas," a bird stolen from the nest before it has learned to hunt. The haggard is often considered superior to the eyas because of its wild and hardy nature. Symon Latham, for example, ranks the haggard falcon above all other birds of prey.[16] As Edmund Bert observes, however, because the haggard has "lived long at liberty, having many things at her command, . . . she is therefore the harder to be brought to subjection and obedience."[17] As a haggard falcon, Katherine is a challenge worthy of her powerful lord.

As the numerous books on the subject make clear, taming a haggard falcon is an excruciatingly difficult art. The goal is "subjection and obedience," as Edmund Bert puts it, the complete subordination of the will of the bird to that of its master. The difficulty lies not only in securing obedience but in securing it in such a way that the bird is not destroyed as a hunter in the process. Taming requires that the bird suppress some of its most basic instincts, such as the fear of man, while at the same time fulfilling others, such as the will to hunt, only at the direction of the master. At its best, the sport aspires towards a union of two wills, animal and human, each devoted to the same exhilarating and instinctive end, the pursuit of prey. Any such union must be one-sided, however, for ultimate power resides with the falconer alone. In the language of the sport the falconer does not merely "train" his bird but "makes" it; the process of taming results in a new identity, a new creation. Edmund Bert exemplifies the pride of such a maker: "I have made so many and so extraordinary good Hawkes, as they could not be bettered both for flying and good conditions."[18]

Taming a falcon is necessarily a variable and fluid process, but it can be divided roughly into three general stages: the "manning," the training to the lure, and, climactically, the test of unrestricted flight.

Petruchio's "taming" of Katherine follows a similar pattern. The bulk of the "courtship" – including the first meeting, the wedding debacle, and the stay at Petruchio's – consists of "manning," the most difficult, intense, and time consuming part of the job. The trip home, including the meeting on the road with old Vincentio, might be considered Katherine's training to the lure. The final banquet, in which Katherine demonstrates her new status as an obedient wife, is the test of unrestricted flight towards which the entire exercise drives. Viewing Petruchio's "courtship" of Katherine from the perspective of falcon-taming illuminates the inner logic of his sometimes bizarre and puzzling behavior.

According to Frederick II of Hohenstaufen, taming a falcon "consists chiefly in persuading her to live quietly among men."[19] The first stage of the process, that of "manning," is devoted to making the hawk "acquainted" with the tamer. To achieve this end, the hawk, temporarily blinded by hooding or "seeling" the eyes, is placed on the wrist of the falconer, fed very sparingly, and kept awake for about three nights. The hawk's natural tendency is to escape, to "bate," but each time it tries it is returned firmly but affectionately to the wrist. Markham summarizes the process in a way that suggests the subtlety of its psychology:

All Hawkes generally are manned after one manner, that is to say, by watching and keeping them from sleep, by a continuall carrying of them upon your fist, and by a most familiar broaking and playing with them, with the wing of a dead Fowle or such like, and by often gazing and looking of them in the face with a loving and gentle countenance, and so making them acquainted with the man.[20]

As Markham's description suggests, the process drives the opposing forces of discipline and affection to paradoxical extremes. On the one hand, the bird is subjected to cruel deprivations, such as lack of food and what T. H. White calls the "secret cruelty" of sleeplessness.[21] On the other hand, it is treated with ostentatious care and affection. The final result is exhaustion and absolute submission.

Petruchio's treatment of Katherine, which throughout the play combines outrageous cruelty with ostentatious expressions of affection, killing her with kindness, imitates the method of the falconer. In their first meeting he trades insult for insult but refrains from violence even when she strikes him. Throughout their exchange, moreover, he keeps up a barrage of affectionate praise, celebrating the virtues he hopes to create as if her very "shrewishness" embodied them. He simply refuses to be put off:

Kath. I chafe you if I tarry. Let me go.
Pet. No, not a whit, I find you passing gentle:
 'Twas told me you were rough and coy and sullen,
And now I find report a very liar;
For thou art pleasant, gamesome, passing courteous,
But slow in speech, yet sweet as spring-time flowers.   (2.1.241–46)

At the wedding ceremony he adopts a similar technique. As he seizes Katherine to take her home with him, refusing her the ceremony of the wedding feast, he declares in one breath that she is "my horse, my ox, my ass, my any thing," and in the next that he will chivalrously protect her against the "thieves" who beset them: "Fear not, sweet wench, they shall not touch thee, Kate! / I'll buckler thee against a million" (3.2.232, 238–39). He is both brute and chivalric hero.

At Petruchio's country house Katherine experiences complete bewilderment. Sleeplessness, lack of food, and lectures on continency take their toll. "She, poor soul," says the sympathetic Curtius, "Knows not which way to stand, to look, to speak, / And sits as one new risen from a dream" (4.1.184–86). Her greatest shock, however, comes from what we might call the falconer's paradox:

But I, who never knew how to entreat,
Nor never needed that I should entreat,
Am starv'd for meat, giddy from lack of sleep,
With oaths kept waking, and with brawling fed;
And that which spites me more than all these wants,
He does it under name of perfect love;
As who should say, if I should sleep or eat,
 'Twere deadly sickness, or else present death.   (4.3.7–14)

Petruchio intends that "all is done in reverend care of her"; Katherine is here utterly mystified because his brutal actions carry the "name of perfect love." The falconer, says Edmund Bert, must show the falcon he dominates both "diligent care" and "loving respect."[22]

Perhaps the most striking sign of this paradoxical combination of cruelty and kindness is Petruchio's use of Katherine's name to assert both the imperiousness of his will and his affection. Katherine's very first words to him consist of a vain attempt to assert her identity by denying that her name is Kate: "They do call me Katherine that do talk of me" (2.1.184). Throughout the play she never calls herself anything but "Katherine." With only a few insignificant exceptions, moreover, she is "Katherine" or the equivalent "Katherina" to everyone else in the play. Petruchio uses "Katherine," however, only three times: once with ironic intent, in their first meeting (2.1.267), and twice in the final scene of the play, when he commands her to step on her cap (5.2.121) and lecture the wives on obedience (5.2.130). The formality of the latter instances suggest that he is engaged in a subtle form of bribery, a sign of a lingering doubt about the strength of Katherine's conversion. For the remainder of the play – at least sixty times, by my count – Petruchio re-creates Katherine's identity by imposing upon her his own version of her name, a version that in its intimacy puts him immediately in the position of a husband and master.

The most forceful attack on her sense of identity occurs in their first meeting, the point at which the tamer's power must be asserted unequivocally. In overwhelming her with the name "Kate" – he uses the name eleven times in five lines – Petruchio probably takes his cue from Baptista, who has referred to her by the intimate family name a moment before.[23] He therefore usurps the patriarchal role. As Katherine's taming proceeds and she becomes increasingly pliant, Petruchio's tone becomes increasingly affectionate, the name "Kate" becoming less wittily insulting and more endearing. It remains to the end, however, Petruchio's chosen name, not Katherine's, symbolizing not only his affection but his power even in the famous "kiss me, Kate" which marks both their public embrace and their final union at the end of the play (5.1.143; 5.2.180). The falconer thus not only "makes" his falcon but names it, as Adam "gave names unto all cattel, and to the foule of the heaven, and to everie beast of the field."[24] The continuing power of Petruchio's naming can be felt, ironically, in the language of most critics of the play, who follow Petruchio's choice, not Katherine's.

As the many allusions to affection between hawk and tamer in the manuals of falconry suggest, the process of taming is erotically charged, making the metaphor peculiarly apt for Petruchio's "courtship" of Katherine. The most highly prized hawks were female, and, although women of the gentry and above often hunted with hawks, the trainers and authors of manuals seem to have been invariably male. Whenever a hawk is mentioned in the manuals, it is almost always a "she," the falconer invariably a "he." The result is a persistent rhetoric of sexual attraction and domination throughout the entire process, the first and most difficult stage of which even goes by the provocative name of "manning." As George Turbervile puts it, a falcon is "made and manned" by a trainer who should take such "syngular delyght" in his bird that "hee may seeme to bee in love."[25] Edmund Bert advises the falconer to make the hawk "much in love with thy sweet and milde using her."[26]

The complex combination of cruel discipline, courtesy, and eroticism required in the taming of a falcon gives to Shakespeare's metaphor of taming far greater subtlety than one often finds in the critical and stage traditions. Neither the handbooks on falconry nor the play itself represents a view of the tamer like that imagined by G. B. Shaw, who sees Petruchio as a "coarse, thick-skinned money hunter, who sets to work to tame his wife exactly as brutal people tame animals or children – that is, by breaking their spirit by domineering cruelty." Nor does the metaphor of taming sanction the long-standing stage custom which provides Petruchio with a whip.[27] The whole point of taming a falcon is not to break its spirit but to attract, focus, and control its wild energy.

Once the falconer has induced submission to his own will, the hawk is gradually exposed to human society and to the normal disruptions of social experience which it must learn to tolerate if it is to be taken into the fields and among people. "Manning" thus involves not only the submission of the hawk to "man" but its submission to one man above all others, its refusal to be distracted from this peculiar allegiance by any external temptations. The customary practice of hooding the eyes lessens the danger of distraction by sight, but since the bird must eventually use its eyes to hunt, it must learn to look without distraction. The bird must be exposed to the world yet remain fixated upon the will of its master. T. H. White's goshawk was much upset by the cars, cyclists, and crowds it encountered on its first outing.[28]

The importance of training a falcon to live at the same time in the world and apart from it, to tolerate society but to act only upon the will of the master, helps to explain a peculiarity in Petruchio's "courtship" of Katherine: his repeated manipulation of tests that pit her loyalties to family and society against her devotion to him. Each of these tests requires that she accept his will, no matter how absurd or arbitrary, and defy the conventions and conventional ties that threaten to distract her. Among her own family, she must forgo a proper wedding ceremony, enduring a misattired bridegroom, a travesty of a church service, and the culminating insult of Petruchio's refusal to attend the feast. At Petruchio's country house she must endure humiliation before the servants and the haberdasher, whose attempts to provide her with respectable clothing are foiled by her husband. Even at the very end of the play, when Petruchio has won his will, he demands, and receives, a kiss in the streets. These tests are too obviously social to be explained simply as arbitrary manifestations of Petruchio's authority. As Camille Wells Slights observes, however, critics contradict each other in explaining their rationale, with some holding that Petruchio is trying "to rescue Kate from a repressive society" and others that he is trying "to teach her by negative example how insupportable such antisocial eccentricity is."[29] If viewed from the perspective of falconry, Petruchio's social tests have a single unifying purpose: to assert the absolute power of the master, whose will must become the unchallenged source of all authority, and to assert that power even in the face of the most compelling demands from the world at large.

Once the falcon is "manned," it is gradually trained to hunt and to return to the call of the falconer. To ensure that the hawk does not escape, the falconer attaches a fine cord, or "creance," to the bird before encouraging it to fly to a lure. If the hawk returns when called, it is rewarded with meat. With success, the falconer gradually increases the length of the cord, providing greater and greater distances for flight and return. Petruchio follows a similar method. When he is convinced that Katherine is "manned," he agrees to take her to visit her family, thus exposing her to the world outside. On the road, he tests her obedience by commenting on the brightness of the shining moon. When she objects, insisting that "it is the sun that shines so bright," he starts to turn around; she reverses herself immediately, however, affirming that the sun is not the sun when he says it is not and, slyly, that "the moon changes even as your mind." Her reversal convinces both Petruchio and Hortensio that she has been successfully "manned." "Petruchio," gasps Hortensio, "go thy ways, the field is won" (4.5.5–23).

The proof of Petruchio's victory lies in the mutual sport that both he and Katherine take in confusing old Vincentio, who enters at that moment. By now Katherine needs no orders to follow Petruchio's will. When he addresses Vincentio as if he were a "gentlewoman," she treats him as such without a pause to gather her wits, even embellishing her performance for their mutual delight; when required to reverse Vincentio's gender, she responds with equally instinctual ease. She has taken the lure, in the form of an innocent and disinterested stranger, and has demonstrated not only obedience but the spirited love of the sport that shows she is ready for public competition.[30]

In many readings and productions, the play takes a decidedly romantic turn at this moment. Because Katherine plays her new role before Vincentio with such obvious delight and theatrical exuberance, one cannot help but feel the joy and exhilaration of the sport. From the vantage point of falconry, however, such loving and responsive behavior is the mark of successful taming. A well trained hawk, says Symon

Latham, one that should be rewarded and treated with special kindness, is one that is "familiar," "lovingly reclaimed," gives "care to you, and to your voice," comes quickly when called, and when she comes seems "eager and hot to cease [seize] upon that which you shall throw or give unto her, and be familiar with your selfe, without starting or staring about her, or otherwise to be coie or waiward"; when she does the falconer's will, moreover, she looks up for the fist "and willingly and redily" jumps onto it.[31] The bond between falconer and successfully trained falcon thus blurs the boundaries between free will and subjection, pleasure and obedience; the bird's apparent delight in service creates the illusion of complete independence. The bond not only unites falcon and falconer against the prey which is the object of their pursuit but against any competitor who might seek to better them at their own game.

In Elizabethan and Jacobean England falconry was a competitive sport. The mere possession of such exotic and valuable properties as hawks fueled competitive energies, with owners and their falconers vying over methods of training and care and the quality and abilities of their favorite birds. Shakespeare evokes this general atmosphere in the very opening of the play, when the lord and the huntsman debate the various abilities of their hounds. But falconry was also competitive in a much more direct and obvious sense. Matches were held, wagers laid, and great sums won or lost, as moralists often lamented. A telling theatrical example of this custom is provided in Thomas Heywood's *A Woman Killed with Kindness* (1603). In the opening scene of the play, which depicts the wedding feast of Anne and John Frankford, Sir Charles Mountford proposes a hawking match the next day at Chevy Chase with the bride's brother, Sir Francis Acton; the wager is set at a hundred pounds, with an additional hundred on the dogs. The match takes place and, after a heated, complex, and technical dispute over whose hawk and dogs are victorious, a fight ensues, in which Sir Charles kills two of Sir Francis's men. In this case a friendly hawking match ends in murder. A desire to mitigate the anti-social tendencies in such competitions, one suspects, must have been in part responsible for the fanfare which accompanied Robert Dover's celebration of the Cotswold Games in 1636. The book of poems published in honor of these games, which includes figures such as Drayton, Jonson, and Heywood, portrays them as the heroic reincarnation of the ancient Olympics. In the Cotswold Games, both coursing and hawking were formal competitive events, with prizes awarded to the winners.[32]

The wager that takes place at the end of *The Taming of the Shrew* is thus the logical culmination of the process of taming. The banquet at Baptista's house evokes the sporting atmosphere of the hunt. Hortensio and his Widow begin the festive competition by taunting Petruchio with insinuations about Katherine's shrewishness. When Katherine takes offense, the conflict becomes a metaphoric hunt, with Petruchio and Hortensio imitating the orders that a huntsman gives to his dog in the chase: "To her, Kate," "To her, widow!" (5.2.33–34).[33] "A hundred marks," says Petruchio, "my Kate does put her down" (5.2.35). When Bianca is in turn attacked, she shifts the metaphor to birding and leads the women from the room: "Am I your bird? I mean to shift my bush, / and then pursue me as you draw your bow" (5.2.46–47). Once introduced, the metaphor of the hunt expands to encompass not only the immediate conflict but virtually the entire action of the play:

> *Pet.*   Here, Signior Tranio,
> This bird you aim'd at, though you hit her not;
> Therefore a health to all that shot and miss'd.
> *Tra.* O, sir, Lucentio slipp'd me like his greyhound,
> Which runs himself, and catches for his master.
> *Pet.* A good swift simile, but something currish.
> *Tra.* 'Tis well, sir, that you hunted for yourself;
> 'Tis thought your deer does hold you at a bay.
> *Bap.* O, O, Petruchio, Tranio hits you now.
> *Luc.* I thank thee for that gird, good Tranio.
> *Hor.* Confess, confess, hath he not hit you here?
> *Pet.* 'A has a little gall'd me, I confess;
> And as the jest did glance away from me,
> 'Tis ten to one it maim'd you [two] outright.   (5.2.49–62)

Fowling, coursing, stag-hunting – the language of the hunt, used throughout to characterize the taming of Katherine, at this point expands to encompass the play's entire treatment of courtship.

The play thus ends as it begins, by invoking the atmosphere of the hunt.[34] Petruchio, finding himself at this point hunted and at bay, decides to gamble upon his wife's obedience. The challenge is whether the wives will return upon the call of their husbands, a test of obedience that mimics precisely the test required of a hawk trained to the lure. The wager, moreover, links Katherine's "taming" explicitly to that of hawks. "Twenty crowns!" exclaims Petruchio in response to Lucentio's offer, "I'll venture so much of my hawk or hound, / But twenty times so much upon my wife" (5.2.71–73). He accepts an offer of a hundred crowns, and wins. Katherine, it seems, has been "manned" and "made."

Viewing the main action of the play as an instance of falcon-taming thus seems to lead to a reductive conclusion. Petruchio is more than falconer, we might want to object, Katherine more than falcon, and the play more than farce. The metaphor of taming is capable of a more romantic interpretation, indeed, and one is provided by Margaret Loftus Ranald. Ranald's interpretation provides a useful test for my own reading not only because it represents a rigorous and sustained attempt to situate the play within the context of falconry but because it develops from the metaphor romantic implications. Through the metaphor of falconry, Ranald argues, the play subverts the "antifeminist genre" of "the wifebeating farce," reinterpreting "that traditionally male-oriented view of marriage which requires the molding of a wife, by force if necessary, into total submission to her husband." The play celebrates instead the "success of the relationship of equality between the sexes personified by Kate and Petruchio."[35]

Ranald's argument, like my own, depends to a great extent upon the most striking feature of the process of taming a hawk, its goal of "mutual respect between bird and keeper."[36] She develops at length, and with considerable sensitivity, the parallelism between the two activities, that of taming a hawk and courting Katherine. In Katherine's final speech, she argues, Shakespeare conveys "the ideal matrimonial situation. Both keeper and falcon, husband and wife, have their own areas of superiority, but when both work together at a given hunting task they are incomparable."[37] Although she does not exploit it, Ranald's argument carries a nicely ironic paradox: that Shakespeare humanizes marriage by treating the relationship between husband and wife as that between falconer and falcon. The play achieves a liberal view of marriage, in short, because the taming of falcons was so humane.

It may be true, regrettably, that the treatment of hawks was more humane than the treatment of wives in Elizabethan England; Shakespeare implies, certainly, that the hunting lord's treatment of his hounds is at least as humane as his treatment of Christopher Sly. To use words such as "mutual agreement," "mutuality," or "equality" to characterize the relationship between tamed hawk and lord, however, is to lose sight of the actual nature of the relationship. To tame a hawk is to achieve mastery over it, to secure its obedience. The process requires affection, as we have seen, and it ends, if successful, with mutual respect and mutual exhilaration in the hunt. But affection, respect, and exhilaration of this sort have nothing to do with equality. The bird has simply learned to fulfill its instinctual desires by expressing them upon the command and under the control of its master. It hunts, but not of its own will. The art of training a falcon, George Turbervile reminds us, testifies to "the singular skill of man."[38] Ranald's "positive evaluation of falconry as a model for marriage," as Frances E. Dolan observes, "downplays the significant disparities between the two parties," ignoring the fact that the bond between bird and man is "hardly between equals."[39]

The difficulty of reconciling the metaphor of falconry with a liberal reading of the play is illustrated by Brian Morris's attempt to develop the familiar motif of Petruchio as Katherine's teacher. Morris's admirably wide-ranging introduction to the Arden edition includes separate sections on Petruchio's role as falconer and as educator. In the former, he notes how the last two acts of the play "focus intensively on the single action of manning a wild hawk, translating it relentlessly into human terms"; in the latter, he discusses Petruchio as an innovator in "educational methodology." To see Petruchio as a teacher, Morris must argue that education is always paradoxical, designed on the one hand "to liberate" individuals and on the other to reduce them "to social conformity." "To some extent," he observes, education is "always a taming procedure, at odds with the very human desire for liberty." In *The Taming of the Shrew*, he concludes, the "tension between these contrary impulses" is "uncomfortably evident." Although the admission of discomfort acknowledges the ultimate irreconcilability of teaching and taming, it does not keep Morris from romanticizing the final union of pupil and teacher. When Katherine kisses Petruchio in the streets at the end of act 5 scene 1, according to Morris, her words demonstrate "a mutuality, a gentle and loving concern for union which shows that the teaching is over, the pupil has graduated, and all that is left is love."[40] How the discomfort vanishes is never explained.

The entire thrust of the metaphor of falconry in *The Taming of the Shrew*, as we have seen, is to identify Petruchio as tamer and Katherine as hawk. To treat taming as education is to blur the boundaries between activities that are fundamentally at odds. As the manuals of falconry make clear, hawks are not tamed by free choice. They are "killed with kindness." Hence the language applied to the successfully tamed hawk is that of creation. One "makes" a hawk. Katherine herself is similarly "made." She is "manned," exposed to the lure, and, finally, tested in competition. For her owner, she becomes not only a creature of delight, capable of imagining and fulfilling his desires without even the necessity of command, but, like other hunting animals, an instrument of playful aggression. She can beat the competition.

As critics such as John C. Bean have shown, the notion of "mutuality" in marriage can be found in the more enlightened Elizabethan treatments of marriage.[41] The liberalizing of doctrines of marriage that occurred in the Elizabethan and Jacobean periods, however, depended essentially upon Christian theology. Underlying the Puritan emphasis upon marriage as a kind of friendship, for example, was the notion that husbands and wives, although not physically, intellectually, or socially equal, were equal in the eyes of God, equally capable of salvation.[42] Such a view of marriage does not necessarily challenge the patriarchal social order, especially because of the biblical injunctions that sustain it, but it does not accommodate metaphors of taming animals. As Keith Thomas has amply demonstrated, fundamental to all thinking about animals in the period was acceptance of the Christian notion that only human beings have immortal souls.[43] In such a context, to compare a wife to a tamed hawk is not to liberalize marriage. The humanizing of marriage, then, depends upon a theology that divorces humans from animals; the metaphor of falconry identifies humans with animals, or, more precisely, wives with falcons.

If focusing on the reductive implications of the metaphor of taming seems too cynical, we might consider the play's satiric depiction of other marital and familial relationships. Baptista seems a kind man and caring father, but his views of marriage are in essence simply economic. He is embarrassingly eager to foist Katherine upon Petruchio, so much so that he is willing to take an unusual business risk: "Faith gentlemen, now I play a merchant's part, / And venture madly on a desperate mart" (2.1.326–27). As for Bianca, he assures Tranio and Gremio that "deeds must win the prize," but for him the word "deeds" means contracts, not worthy actions: "he of both / That can assure my daughter greatest dower / Shall have my Bianca's love" (2.1.342–44). In contrast to Baptista, Lucentio is delightfully romantic, but his romanticism is as automatic and conventional as Baptista's mercantilism; the two incongruous discourses – of mercantile and romantic love – are played off against each other for broadly comic effect. If the relationship between Katherine and Petruchio looks good at the end of the play, it is not because it embodies a Shakespearean ideal of marriage but because the alternatives are so absurd.

The name for the kind of comedy that treats humans as animals is farce, a label that seems both inadequate and inescapable in response to this play. The label is ultimately inadequate, it seems to me, not so much because it obscures the play's richness of characterization or romantic tone but because it ignores its metadramatic nature. If we are given something close to farce in the courtship of Petruchio and Katherine, it is farce made self-conscious. The relationship is framed by our awareness that we are watching a play-within-a play, an entertainment for Christopher Sly. In this sense the play might be called, paradoxically, a self-reflexive farce, one in which farce recoils upon itself and in the process becomes intellectually provocative. True farce is notoriously anti-intellectual, of course, the kind of comedy that depends upon slapstick, horseplay, caricatures, broad verbal humor, and ludicrous situations – all of which appear in the play. Farce is also notoriously reductive, implying a "debased" view of life, in which instinct is all, and in which success, if it comes, depends upon cunning, physical strength, and an obsessive and child-like egotism. *The Taming of the Shrew* is reductive in much the same way, it seems to me, but self-consciously so. In this sense the farce of taming Katherine might be considered an experiment or hypothesis in human relations, requiring us to confront, in comic terms, the full implications of a traditional metaphor. What does it mean to "tame" a wife? Or, as Petruchio himself demands of the audience, "He that knows better how to tame a shrew, / Now let him speak; 'tis charity to shew" (4.1.210–11). The self-conscious farce of taming the shrew works like a peculiarly mad version of scientific reductionism: it pares life down to its most basic drives, de-humanizing individual relationships in order to reveal their essential natures.

This concentration on essentials, which underlies the entire representation of falconry in the relationship between Katherine and Petruchio, climaxes in Katherine's final speech (5.2.136–79). The bulk of this speech is in this respect of little consequence, although it has attracted most of the commentary. Katherine spends most of her time wittily and theatrically developing the conventional images and arguments in favor of benign patriarchal marriage: a woman's beauty is marred by frowns; the husband is lord, life, and keeper; the wife owes the duty of obedience to her husband; her place is in the home, under his protection and authority; and so forth. In this part of the speech one recognizes the theatrical delight in her new role displayed earlier in her address to old Vincentio.

More revealing, and more essentially true to the dynamics of Katherine's taming, is her conclusion, which centers upon the brute fact of weakness:

My mind hath been as big as one of yours,
My heart as great, my reason haply more,
To bandy word for word and frown for frown;
But now I see our lances are but straws,
Our strength as weak, our weakness past compare,
That seeming to be most which we indeed least are.   (5.2.170–75)

Everything that Katherine says about wifely duties and obligations derives from this recognition and acceptance of Petruchio's greater strength. The formal rhetoric of benign patriarchal marriage which she elaborates with such gusto is here revealed as an ideological result of female weakness. This admission is the one part of her speech that grows directly out of the play's experience. Petruchio has simply overwhelmed Katherine, and the pleasure she takes in her new role is coupled with the rueful acceptance of defeat. The play ends, in short, with the metaphor of taming carried unflinchingly to its logical conclusion.

The most insidious implications of this metaphor lie not in its mere elevation of male power but in the very "humanity" with which such power is invested. As Petruchio and the manuals of falconry develop it, the metaphor actually enables us to imagine the very Katherine who appears in productions and critical essays of the romantic kind. She is not brutalized in body or cowed in spirit. She is vibrant, alert, so ready for competition that she performs far beyond the expectations of her master or the demands of the occasion. She carries with her a sense of play, as if in following orders she herself is achieving the fulfillment of her own desires, as if her very freedom were to be found in obedience itself. The very "romantic" spirit which Katherine demonstrates at the end of the play, in short, if read in the context of the metaphor of taming, is not a mark of true independence and mutuality but of successful taming. Katherine seems a more vibrant and fulfilled human being from this perspective because she behaves like an ideal hawk. Since man was "appointed by God to have dominion over the beasts," observes C. S. Lewis, "the tame animal is . . . in the deepest sense the only 'natural' animal – the only one we see occupying the place it was meant to occupy."[44] The metaphor of falconry is insidious precisely because the relationship between tamer and bird is so intensely and lovingly "human."

If we accept such a reading of the play, one that takes the metaphor of taming to its reductive extreme, do any consolations remain? Is there any way, to adopt Shaw's Victorian phrasing, for a "man" with "decency of feeling" to attend this play, with or without the company of a woman?

Not if we look for serious "mutuality" in marriage, it seems to me, or even for the anesthesia of pure farce. Consolation is to be found, if at all, only in more desperate measures. If we value the resistance of wives to patriarchal coercion, for example, we might take some solace in the behavior of Bianca and the widow, neither of whom respond on call to the commands of their husbands. Bianca's behavior is itself characterized in the language of hawking. At the beginning of the play, both Gremio and Tranio protest at Bianca's being "mew'd" up, caged like a falcon, because of Baptista's desire to marry Katherine first (1.1.87, 183). When Hortensio discovers her affection for the disguised Lucentio, he likens her to a hawk that is distracted by every decoy, that casts its "wand'ring eyes on every stale" (3.1.90), and later he renounces his love for this "proud disdainful haggard" (4.2.39). He leaves Bianca in the futile hope of finding a more docile and obedient bird in the widow. The irony of the play's ending depends upon a sharp contrast between the birds that merely seem tame and the one who is. If one prefers wild to "manned" hawks, then there is perhaps some consolation to be found in the continuing wildness of the widow and Bianca.

A more likely source of consolation is to be found in Katherine herself. In many productions of the play, actresses playing Katherine have undermined her apparent subjection by signaling, usually through a wink to the audience, her secret resistance to the role that she accepts for the moment. Such a gesture is sanctioned by the motif of "seeming" which runs throughout this metadramatic play. The motif cuts two ways: if Bianca "seems" a docile wife at first, Katherine may "seem" so at the end. Petruchio's decision to use the name "Katherine" twice in calling her to him at this point, as we have seen earlier, suggests a certain anxiety about her obedience. The play's final line, moreover, is Lucentio's "'Tis a wonder, by your leave, she will be tam'd so" (5.2.189).

This male anxiety about the possibility of relapse is one that audiences familiar with falconry would take for granted. From the vantage point of falconry, the issue is not so much whether Katherine has been truly tamed – her speech gives no reason to believe otherwise – but how long she will remain so. In this context, Petruchio's nervousness and Lucentio's wonder are predictable responses to the situation. As all of the manuals make clear, tamed hawks require vigilant care. The more valuable they are as hawks, moreover, the more likely they are to seek their freedom. The falconer therefore always flirts with disaster, encouraging in his hawk the most highly spirited and soaring flight, making himself vulnerable to the possibility that wildness will reassert itself and the hawk be lost forever. Symon Latham, for example, warns his readers about the special need to remain watchful over haggards:

Now must it needes bee that these kindes of *Hawkes* have, and evermore will have some wildnesse in them, which disposition, although I have formerly shewd you how to alter and change, and to keepe them loving and familiar with you: yet that being wrought and effected by art you must beware that nature do not get the upper hand, or beare the greatest swaie, for if it doe, then your skill failes you, and your art deserves no commendation.[45]

In the language of the play, as we have seen, Katherine is a "haggard"; any falconer would know that such hawks "evermore will have some wildnesse in them." The metaphor of taming a haggard thus carries with it a continuing potential for escape, a continuing male anxiety. We too may wonder, with Lucentio, that Katherine "will be tam'd so."

But perhaps there is a more radical way to save the play from its own ending – by probing more fully than is customary the implications of its beginning. The play opens with an Induction, which features a hunting lord's practical joke at the expense of the tinker and beggar, Christopher Sly. The motif of taming is introduced upon the first appearance of this lord, for he enters "*from hunting, with his* Train," and to the sound of horns(Ind.i.16.s.d.). He has just returned from hunting deer with his hounds, and for the next fifteen lines he gives directions to his huntsman for their care. The dialogue between lord and huntsman establishes at the outset of the play the atmosphere of the hunt, and their concern for their dogs later modulates into the "taming" of Christopher Sly which, for the brief period of a joke, transforms his identity. The scene as a whole, as has often been observed, mirrors the major action of the play, with the lord transforming Sly from a "monstrous beast" (Ind.i.34) to a nobleman and Petruchio transforming Katherine from a shrew to an obedient wife.

In the brief exchange between the lord and his huntsman (Ind.i.30), Shakespeare evokes the ethos of the hunt that underlies the role of Petruchio throughout the play.[46] Like Petruchio, the lord is a forceful man: he "charges" his young huntsman to care for the hounds and calls him, with affectionate brusqueness, a "fool" for preferring the wrong dog. Like Petruchio, too, he has a playful wit, for it is he who instigates the jest against Sly and directs the various performances. As striking as his mastery over his world, however, is his care for those dependent upon his power. He takes pains to protect Sly against the "over-merry spleen" of his servants, "which otherwise would grow into extremes" (Ind.i.137–38), and his care for his dogs accords with the best models of the manuals of the hunt. The pack as a whole, he tells his huntsman, is to be "tendered" well; poor Merriman, "embossed" (foaming at the mouth) from an exhausting chase, is to be given special attention, as is Clowder, who is to be coupled with "the deep-mouth'd brach," perhaps because he is a young hound and requires the stability of a mature bitch, or perhaps because the music of their voices is harmonious.

Training even a domesticated animal for the hunt requires affection, discipline, and reinforcement. The hunting lord's hounds, for example, would have been taught first to respond to the "hallow" of both voice and horn and then gradually introduced to the hunt itself by the method preferred by their trainer. In *The Noble Arte of Venerie*, George Gascoigne recommends "entering" the hound first to the hare, since it is easily weaned from such hunting to that of the stag; he admits, however, that they can be also "entered" to fat or wounded stags, for they are easily pursued. In their first attempts the young dogs benefit from the guidance of mature dogs in the pack. Their desire to hunt is reinforced by immediate reward at the end of the hunt, the neck of the hart being flayed for that purpose.[47] As we have seen in chapter 3, the hunting instincts even of mature hounds must be reinforced with every kill, the rewarding consisting of an abbreviated mimicry of the hunt itself, with each dog being allotted its rightful share in the carcass. Successfully trained hunting dogs achieve a difficult balance between obedience to man and instinctual wildness; they pursue and kill, but only on command.

Moralistic objections to the hunt often focused on the lavish indulgence of hounds, which were usually treated better by aristocrats than the common people themselves. Keith Thomas quotes an early Stuart commentator who complains that when masters returned from the hunt they would often show "more care for their dogs than of their servants and make them lie down by them, and often the servant is beaten for the dog; you may see in some men's houses fair and fat dogs to run up and down and men pale and wan to walk feebly."[48] The care recommended in Gascoigne's *Noble Arte of Venerie* is typical. The kennels are to be spacious, well aired, clean, heated by a fireplace, provided with running water, lightened by whited walls and windows, and each dog is to be assigned a "little bedstead" on rollers, so that when it returns from the chase it can be rolled "as neare the fire as you wil." After a chase in inclement weather, the hounds are to receive special care: their coats are to be warmed, brushed and cleaned and, if necessary, their feet are to be washed with a mixture of water, salt, egg yolks, vinegar and herbs. Although the *Noble Arte of Venerie* defines a "good keeper of hounds" as

"gratious, curteous, and gentle, loving his dogs of a naturall disposition,"[49] the care of the animals was not disinterested, for they were
essential instruments in the hunt. "Sup them well, and look unto them
all," says Shakespeare's lord of his hounds, "To-morrow I intend to hunt
again" (Ind.i.28–29).

Intertwined with the lord's directions to his huntsman about the care
of his hounds is a jocular debate about the abilities of the various dogs.
The lord praises Silver for picking up a cold scent at the hedge-corner,
but the huntsman counters with the example of Belman, who "twice to-
day picked out the dullest scent" and is the "better dog" (Ind.i.24–25).
The lord in turn objects, praising Echo, despite his slowness, as "worth
a dozen such" (Ind.i.27). Such bantering is as characteristic of the
culture of the hunt as the lord's care of his hounds. Were the hunter and
his huntsman social equals and the dogs from different packs, bets might
be placed. The careful appraisal of the virtues of the hounds, the competitive ranking of one against the other – these activities are as much a
part of the sport as the chase itself. This competitive male spirit, as we
have seen, is one of the driving forces of the taming plot, especially of
the wager that brings it to a close.

The world that Shakespeare evokes at the opening of the play, then,
is the bantering, playfully aggressive and stereotypically masculine world
of the hunt. Its presiding spirit is a lord, who dominates both the social
and natural orders as master of his hounds, his servants, and drunken
tinkers. He rules with rough care, affection, and wit. The "dream" that
he creates in jest for Christopher Sly is not an arbitrary fantasy but one
that projects the distinctive ethos of his own world. In his offers to Sly he
lists the usual accoutrements of a nobleman – servants, music, a soft and
lustful bed – but his vision of a lord's life climaxes with the prospect of
riding, hawking, and hunting:

> Or wilt thou ride? Thy horses shall be trapp'd,
> Their harness studded all with gold and pearl.
> Dost thou love hawking? Thou hast hawks will soar
> Above the morning lark. Or wilt thou hunt?
> Thy hounds shall make the welkin answer them
> And fetch shrill echoes from the hollow earth. (Ind.ii.41–46)

Even the titillating pictures offered by the lord and his servants feature
eroticized versions of the hunt, with Venus in pursuit of Adonis, and
Apollo chasing Daphne. Sly is presented with a vision of life as lived and
imagined not by any lord but by a hunting lord.

To have this life, even in the brief unreality of a dream, Sly must do two things. He must repudiate his former identity: "Upon my life, I am a lord indeed, / And not a tinker, nor Christopher Sly" (Ind. ii. 72–73). He must also repress his sexual desire for his "wife," the indulgence of which would jeopardize his cure: "But I would be loath to fall into my dreams again. I will therefore tarry in despite of the flesh and the blood" (Ind.ii.126–28). The bargain he makes, trading the drunken life of a tinker for the dream life of a lord, makes him analogous to a hound or bird of prey: he is "tamed." For the price of a few instincts and a name, he receives the treatment of a lord, which is guaranteed for as long as he continues to provide amusement. His first reward is the performance of a play. Why does he see a play that involves the taming of a shrew?

Throughout his career Shakespeare invariably connects his plays-within-plays to the character of the rulers or nobles who request them. The practice surely imitates normal custom, for one would expect the person who pays the players to choose the nature of the entertainment. In *A Midsummer Night's Dream*, Theseus is given his choice of entertainments, such as it is, and selects "Pyramus and Thisbe," having rejected others as too familiar or as "not sorting with a nuptial ceremony" (5.1.55); in its tragical-comical rendition of the violence of love, the playlet sorts rather more well with the nuptial ceremony than its audience imagines. In *Love's Labor's Lost*, Holofernes, having been ordered by Navarre to entertain the Princess, chooses the pageant of the Nine Worthies as most "fit" for the audience and the occasion (5.1.123); both the theme and the performance of the entertainment mock the aspirations of the young male aristocrats who have commissioned it. In *Hamlet*, the visiting actors receive instructions from the prince for a play that is designed to "catch the conscience of the King" (2.2.605). In *The Tempest*, finally, Prospero designs and choreographs his own entertainment; the masque that he presents before Ferdinand and Miranda not only blesses the betrothed couple but embodies his idealized celebration of chaste love.

With these analogues in mind, it is not difficult to see the play performed at the request of the hunting lord in *The Taming of the Shrew* as a projection of his own values. The performance focuses on Christopher Sly, of course, as the guest of honor. The lord prepares the actors for his eccentric habits and warns them that he has never seen a play. When the play is announced, the messenger tells Sly that a comedy has been selected upon the recommendation of the doctor, as an antidote to his melancholy. Implicit in these preparations is the notion that the performance will speak both to the hunting lord who has called for it and to the lord who is his guest; the hunting lord's life has become Sly's fantasy.

It should come as no surprise, then, that the play which ensues depicts the successful courtship of another hunting lord, one who tames a wife by using the methods of a falconer and who triumphs over wooers whose methods are contemptibly sentimental or mercenary or both. The fantasy projected before Christopher Sly is not his own fantasy but that of the hunting lord himself. The play he witnesses shows the triumph of the culture of the hunt over the mercantile and romantic culture embodied in the courtships of Bianca and the widow, and over a woman who needs to be tamed. It is a play that catches the conscience of a hunting lord.

The device of the Induction, then, allows us to experience *The Taming of the Shrew* as an image not of *the* world but of *a* world – a world characterized by a distinctive social atmosphere and inhabited by distinctive social types with their own ways of thinking and behaving in society. This is not our world, we may say, but it is also no more than a self-consciously farcical and satirical slice of Shakespeare's. The ironic framework established by the Induction lends support to Coppélia Kahn's unconventional and brilliantly provocative argument that the play is a satire and its target "the male urge to control woman." From Kahn's perspective, Petruchio's outrageous exaggerations of the typical attributes of male supremacy – his oaths, his brutality, his arbitrariness and irrationality, his reduction of Katherine to the status of an animal – are a source of satiric laughter.[50] The dominant motifs of hunting and taming throughout the play locate this male braggadocio in the culture of the hunt.

The metadramatic potential of the Induction has only recently begun to be realized on stage. From 1754 to 1844 Garrick's *Catherine and Petruchio* was the sole version performed, and it eliminated both the Induction and the subplot. Even after 1844, when Shakespeare's text became the basis for performances, the Induction was omitted more often than not until the 1950s, when a series of productions stressed its potential to distance the audience from the farcical action of the taming and to highlight theatrically the notions of role-playing and illusion. Emphasis on the Induction, of course, can provide very different theatrical meanings. Graham Holderness, for example, contrasts the effects achieved in John Barton's Royal Shakespeare Company production of 1960 with those achieved in Di Trevis's Royal Shakespeare Company touring production in 1985. The former, he shows, used the Induction to emphasize harmony and reconciliation at the end of the play, whereas the latter created a Brechtian effect, distancing audiences from the drama they had just seen. In Barton's version, the prominence of the Induction and Christopher Sly highlighted a cheerful romanticism in the main plot; in Di Trevis's, it highlighted the link between Sly and Katherine, who appeared alone on stage at the end as victims of their capricious lords.[51] It is not difficult to imagine a production that could present the play-within-the-play as a version of life seen through the eyes of a hunting lord.

As Leah Marcus has shown, most of the recent productions of the play that have exploited the Induction have merged the text of *The Shrew* with that of *A Shrew*, in which the Sly framework is much more systematically deployed. In *A Shrew*, Sly not only interrupts the proceedings on several occasions, the lord at his side, but is returned to the streets at the end. The play closes with his awakening from a "dream" and determining to put his new knowledge to use by taming his wife. Productions that frame the taming plot with the misadventures of Sly, Marcus observes, deflect its "reality" by making shrew-taming "the compensatory fantasy of a socially underprivileged male." According to Marcus, this reading of the play, which depends upon a text that most editors dismiss as a "bad" quarto, represents the recovery of an interpretative possibility foreclosed by editors who have traditionally preferred their texts authoritative and their women obedient. Modern texts of the play, edited so as to exclude consideration of *A Shrew*, enforce patriarchy by representing Katherine's taming as "real"; theatrical productions, adapting the framework of *A Shrew*, cast the whole patriarchal system constructed by the taming plot into "doubt and unreality."[52]

Although Marcus's appeal to re-open consideration of the text of *A Shrew* is convincing, her argument depends upon two questionable assumptions: that any metadramatic irony is evoked from the play only by the full Sly framework, and that the irony is necessarily focused on Sly alone. Even the text of *The Shrew*, it seems to me, implies sustained irony in the use of the framework. Although Sly interrupts the proceedings only once, the Induction as a whole is rich enough to carry its ironies throughout, especially since, as we have observed, the final scene of the play restates its dominant motifs of hunting, taming, and joking. The absence of stage directions, moreover, makes it possible either to keep both Sly and the lord on stage throughout the play or to double the parts of the lord and Petruchio; either choice would keep alive the ironies of the Induction. To say that *The Shrew* represents a "real" taming because the play does not close upon Christopher Sly thus overstates the case considerably. The difference between the two texts is one of degree, not kind.

The emphasis upon Sly's "fantasy" created both by Marcus and the productions she cites, moreover, fails to address the role of his host, the hunting lord. In either version of the text, the fantasy is Sly's only because the lord directs the actors to present a play. In *A Shrew*, moreover, the role of the lord is even more emphatic than in *The Shrew*. In the former version he explicitly selects the play, greeting the player's proposal with, "the taming of a shrew, that's excellent sure" (1.65); he converses with Sly during each interruption; and he orders Sly returned to the street at the end. Sly may interpret the play as a "compensatory fantasy," but it is a fantasy selected by the hunting lord and developed by players devoted to his entertainment.

To see the taming of Katherine as the wish-fulfillment fantasy of a hunting lord, of course, does not necessarily resolve the problem of the ending. One can imagine a production of the play, indeed – one at court, perhaps – that would give full weight to the Induction and highlight the motifs of taming and hunting throughout, not to satirize the swaggering masculinity of the world of the hunt but to celebrate it with playful mockery. In such a case, male members of an audience sharp enough to perceive the mockery could indulge simultaneously in a wish-fulfillment fantasy of taming and a rueful acknowledgment of their own braggadocio. At the very least, however, acknowledgment of the ironic treatment of the culture of the hunt throughout the play makes it impossible to take the taming of Katherine straight. It complicates our perspective on the taming, forcing us to see its most insidious implications as emblems not of reality itself but of the social world of the hunt. By disallowing the reductive extremes of stark antifeminism or evasive romanticism, it brings the play within the more familiar patriarchal boundaries of Shakespearean comedy.

To appreciate the distinctive social world evoked by Shakespeare's Induction, and by the "play" that ensues, it might be useful to consider the life of a true Elizabethan hunting lord, one for whom Petruchio's taming of Katherine would have provided a welcome "compensatory fantasy." In the early seventeenth century, John Smyth of Nibley, having served for many years as steward of the manors of the great Berkeley estate, wrote a history of the family from 1066 to 1628.[53] Smyth's own employer was Henry Lord Berkeley (1534–1613). If we attend closely to

Smyth's family history of Lord Henry, his wife, and one of their falcons, we can uncover a remarkably immediate social context, and perhaps even a new "source" for the atmosphere of the hunting world that so deeply permeates Shakespeare's play.

In the long section devoted to the life of his employer, Smyth at one point recalls his lord's fondness for falconry, and his own delight, as a young, new employee, in watching Lord Henry's famous pair of haggard falcons soar out of sight. The falcons "lasted twelve or more years," notes Smyth, and were

famous with all great faulconers in many counties, and prized at excessive rates, esteemed for high and round flying, free stooping, and all other good conditions, inferior to none in Christendome; whom my self in my younger years waiting upon his son Thomas, then not twelve years old, at Binly Brooke, have in the height of their pitch, lost the sight of, in a cleer evening . . . (363)

Since Lord Henry's son Thomas turned twelve in 1587, and since the falcons lasted "twelve or more years," these magnificent and superbly trained birds were almost certainly famous throughout the territories favored by Lord Henry – Gloucestershire, Warwickshire, and London among them – during the years in which Shakespeare must have composed *The Taming of the Shrew*.[54]

Lord Henry's falcons are of particular interest because they had evocative names. One, which we shall ignore, was called Stella, perhaps after the heroine of Sidney's *Astrophil and Stella*.[55] The other was named Kate, probably after its mistress, Lady Berkeley, whose name was Katharine. As we have seen, this name resounds in various forms throughout Shakespeare's play – 8 times as Katherina, 19 times as Katherine, and 71 times as Kate. The name does not occur in any of the works usually proposed as sources for the play. Around 1590, then, we have the coincidence of three Kates: one is a falcon, one owns a falcon, and one is tamed as a falcon in a comedy.

I begin with Smyth's image of a soaring haggard falcon because, as we have seen, *The Taming of the Shrew* develops the idea of taming primarily through metaphors from falconry. In the case of Lady Katharine, the association between wife and falcon was more than metaphoric. Lady Katharine was an avid falconer herself. Although Smyth says nothing about her relationship to the falcon named Kate, a comment he makes about her general treatment of hunting birds suggests that it may well have been close: she "kept commonly a cast or two of merlins, which sometimes she mewed in her own chamber; which falconry cost her husband each yeare one or two gownes and kirtles spoiled by their mutings" (285). Since Lady Katharine went so far as to keep molting falcons in her chamber, she might even have played an active role in their taming; if so, she would have been unusual indeed, for, although hunting with falcons was common among aristocratic women in the period, contemporary handbooks on falconry never refer to women as trainers. In any event, Smyth's anecdote implies an exceptional intimacy, perhaps an implicit kind of identification, between Lady Katharine and her birds of prey.

Like many other female aristocrats, Lady Katharine hunted not only with falcons but with dogs. She was known, indeed, as an extraordinary huntress. She was a strong woman, "somewhat tall," according to Smyth, and "of pace the most stately and upright all times of her age that ever I beheld" (382). In hunting she used both a cross bow and a long bow, and in her younger days was "amongst her servants soe good an Archer at butts, as her side by her was not the weaker" (285). Smyth expresses wonder at her physical courage, as when she refused to "take notice of the paine" while watching a surgeon cut off her finger (385).

Lady Katharine was exceptional in other respects as well. As a Howard, she was a member of one of the most prominent, cultivated, and troubled families in the kingdom. She had remarkable intellectual interests and abilities and had received an extraordinary education. Smyth describes her as

of speech passing Eloquent and ready; whom in many years I could never observe to misplace or seem to recall one mistaken, misplaced or mispronounced word or sillable; And as ready and significant under her pen; forty of whose letters at least at severall times I have received; her invention as quick as her first thoughts, And her words as ready as her invention; Skillfull in the french, but perfect in the Italian tongue, wherein shee most desired her daughters to bee instructed; At the lute shee played admirably, and in her private chamber would often singe thereto, to the ravishment of the hearers . . . (382–83)

Like Shakespeare's heroine, Lady Katharine is eloquent, outspoken, and quick-witted; she is also a master at the very instrument that Katherine breaks across Hortensio's head (2.1.142.s.d.). In "her elder years," observes Smyth, Lady Katharine studied natural philosophy and astronomy, and she often discussed the rules of Latin grammar with him to "continue her knowledge in the latin tongue."

Although he admired Lady Katharine for her intelligence, learning, and spirit, Smyth clearly found her difficult. To illustrate her character, he quotes a letter she wrote to him in May 1595, which conveys an impression of strong, manipulative control of both Lord Henry and the household (383–84). After reading Lady Katharine's letter, it comes as no surprise that she and her husband had a rather stormy marriage. Smyth calls attention to her proud bearing. She was "of stomacke great and haughty, no way diminishing the greatnes of her birth and marriage by omission of any ceremony, at diet or publike prayers; whose book I have usually observed presented to her with the lowest courtesies that might bee, and on the knees of her gentlewoman . . . " (382). She seems to have been more intelligent than her husband and was certainly more highly educated. Smyth notes that Lord Henry reproached himself for his own lack of education and, when appointed Justice of the Peace for Gloucester, he "brought his servant Thomas Duport into equall authority with him, whereby his own unaptnes was less perceived, and the buisines of the Country not worse discharged" (287).

For Smyth, the conventions of the patriarchy counted for more than mere ability, and he minces no words about Lady Katharine's domineering tendencies as a wife. Despite occasional expressions of wonder at Lady Katharine's abilities and power in the household, Smyth's overall judgment of her is strongly patriarchal and censorious. He speaks the dominant language of the day. Lady Katharine's spending far exceeded her income, an offense that must have rankled with the man who was largely responsible for keeping the finances of the household in order. More offensive than her spending habits, however, which were shared by her husband, was her desire to "rule her husbands affaires." Smyth's judgment of this aspiration is worth quoting at length:

It cannot bee said That any apparant vice was in this lady, But it may bee said of a wife as of money, they are as they are used, helpers or hurters; money is a good servant but a bad master: And sure it is that shee much coveted to rule her husbands affaires at home and abroad, And to bee informed of the particular passages of each of them, which somtimes brought forth harshnes at home, and turning off of such servants as shee observed refractory to her intentions therein.

Not only did she use the servants as spies, but she took regularly without her husband's knowledge a percentage of the fines levied upon his tenants, a practice that Smyth notes was "by us all disliked, but by none of us to bee helped" (386–87).

Smyth concludes his account of his mistress by drawing a conventional moral from her behavior, one that Petruchio himself seems to live by:

Most just it is that all Toll should come into the right Tolldish: For the most part it falleth out That where wives will rule all they marre all, words I lately heard from wise lords in the Starchamber in the cases of the lady Lake, the Countesse of Suffolke, and some others: These verses are ancient;

> Concerning wives, take this an certaine rule
> That if at first, you let them have the rule
> Your self with them at last shall bear no rule
> Except you let them evermore to rule.   (387)

Highly educated, eloquent, quick-witted, unconventional in behavior, Lady Katharine "awed" the household, ruled over her husband, and manipulated his financial affairs. She was the kind of woman who could prompt even a steward to quote poetry.

As one would expect from his "ancient" verses, Smyth assigns the blame for this inversion of the patriarchal order to Lord Henry, who abrogated his responsibilities as a husband. In a section entitled "The Application and use of his life," in which he draws from Lord Henry's life morals that might be useful for his heirs, Smyth singles out his inability to control his wife as one of his major faults. From Lord Henry's treatment of Lady Katharine, Smyth observes, the family "may learne That nothing is more necessary in the person of a master of a family, according as his estate and greatnes shall bee, then Majesty," and he urges "every master" to "remember Esops fable of the frogs, how contemptibly they esteemed their heavy and blockish king" (411). Smyth sees this marital misrule, moreover, as of more than local significance. Noting Lord Henry's "sufferings and losses by [too] indulgently following the wills and Counsells" of both his mother and Lady Katharine, Smyth reminds the family

That when Eve went about to expound the text shee mistooke the text and hurt her husband: And that English wives challenge more liberty and enclyne to more soveraignty then those of other nations: That female counsells are to bee suspected, as proceeding from an unproper sphear . . . And that prodegy of witt whose excellencies have conquered both example and imitation [*marginal note: Sir Walter Raleigh*], hath told his son that wives were ordained to continue the generation of men; To obey, not to rule their affairs: that they are like marchants in a common wealth, the greatest good or the worst of evills that can happen to a man; And to ballence them and their Counsells thereafter. (413–14)

For Smyth, Lady Katharine represented not only an imperious mistress, one who domineered over her husband and manipulated his servants, but a threat to the patriarchy itself. The stridency and repetitiousness of his attacks suggest the degree of anxiety that such a figure could arouse

in the period. Smyth's response to marital relations within the household
may explain why the epithet he chooses for Lord Henry is "Henry the
harmlesse" (265).

Lord Henry, who clearly failed in his role of wife-tamer, seems to have
had three dominant passions in his life: lawsuits, gambling, and hunting.
The lawsuits, although they take up much of Smyth's narrative, shed no
light on his resemblance to Petruchio, except perhaps that they illustrate
a disputatious nature and a tendency towards impetuous anger, which
was easily dissolved "when the cause [was] removed" (413). The love of
gambling is more suggestive, since Petruchio shows himself willing to
take risks in his courtship of Katherine and, more importantly, since, in
the final scene of the play, Petruchio proposes a wager to test the wives'
obedience. Smyth notes admiringly that Lord Henry's "longe and
slender lady-like-hand knew a dye as well and how to handle it as any of
his ranke and time" (363).

Lord Henry's "chief delights," however, and those which link him
most directly to both the hunting lord and Petruchio in *The Taming of the
Shrew*, are in hunting and hawking:

But his cheife delights wherein hee spent near three parts of the yeare, were, to
his great charges, in hunting the hare fox and deere, red and fallow, not wanting
choice of as good hunting horses as yearly hee could buy at faires in the North;
And in hawking both at river and at land: And as his hounds were held inferior
to no mans, (through the great choice of whelps which with much care hee
yearly bred of his choicest braches, and his continuall huntings,) soe were his
hawks of severall sorts; which if hee sent not a man to fetch from beyond seas,
as three or fower times I remember hee did, yet had hee the choice as soone as
they were brought over into England, keeping a man lodging in London, in
some years a month or more, to bee sure of his choice at their first landing. (363)

It is easy to recognize in this description the hunting lord of *The Taming
of the Shrew*, who enters the play "*from hunting*," instructs his huntsman to
"tender well" all his hounds, gives precise directions for the care of
"Brach Merriman" and "Clowder," and admires Silver so much that he
"would not lose the dog for twenty pound" (Ind.1.16–21). Shakespeare's
emphasis upon the lord's care of his dogs captures a familiar attribute of
the type, but it is worth noting that Smyth mentions Lord Henry's pride
in his dogs several times (282, 285). Petruchio, whose taming of
Katherine parallels the hunting lord's joke upon Christopher Sly, continues the play's hunting motif with his swaggering, his taming methods
drawn from falconry, and his numerous hunting jests in the final scene
(5.2.49–62). The ethos that characterizes the hunting lord of the

Induction, Petruchio, and Lord Henry is that of the Elizabethan culture of the hunt.

It would be difficult to imagine a better example of an Elizabethan hunting lord than Lord Henry, whose "chief delight" lay in the sport. In his early years he hawked en route to his various properties, leading his 150 servants in livery between "Yate, Mangottesfeild, London, Callowdon, and other places" (284). In July 1558 he initiated a pattern of hunting that was to last throughout most of his life. When he arrived at Callowdon, near Coventry,

> the first worke done was the sending for his buckhounds to Yate in Gloucestershire: His hounds being come Away goes hee and his wife a progres of buck hunting to the parks of Barkewell, Groby, Bradgate, Leicester forrest, Toley, and others on that side his house: And after a small repose, Then to the parks of Kenilworth, Ashby, Wedgenocke, and others, on the other side his house: And this was the course of this lord (more or lesse) for the thirty next somers at least: not omitting his own at Callowdon and in the county of Gloucester. (285)

Lord Henry hunted not only often but with abandon. In about 1560 he "extreamly heated himself by chasing on foot a tame Deere in Yate Parke," an escapade that caused an immoderate nose-bleed which he tried to stop by thrusting "his whole face into a bason of cold water"; the action caused in turn a "flush and fulnes of his nose . . . [which] could never bee remedied" (287). In his "middle age," he indulged in nostalgia for such episodes, and would "often comfortably remember" his near escapes from death, two of which involved falling from horses while galloping at full speed in pursuit of his hounds and deer (380). Even Lord Henry's political and legal affairs were intertwined with hunting, as when, in an episode recounted in chapter 3 (92–93), Queen Elizabeth joined the Earl of Leicester in a riotous slaughter of his deer in Worthy Park.

A case can be made, then, for Lord Henry, Lady Katharine, and their falcon as raw material from which Shakespeare fashioned his central characters. Lady Katharine was an independent, intelligent, and powerful woman, a huntress and falconer, a dominant force in household affairs, and a perceived threat not only to marital tranquillity but to the entire structure of patriarchal values. Lord Henry, or "Henry the harmless," was not only the husband of a difficult wife named Katharine and the owner of a "famous" falcon named Kate but the epitome of an Elizabethan hunting lord – a falconer and stag-hunter, a man who lavished care on his dogs, who hawked while traveling, who roamed the hills of Warwickshire every summer for thirty years chasing deer, who, if Smyth is to be believed, spent "three parts of the year" hunting (363). The relationship between Lord Henry and Lady Katharine, moreover, seems complicated in much the same way as that between Petruchio and Katherine. Despite the evidence of conflict provided by Smyth, the couple lived, traveled, and hunted together from their marriage in 1554 until Lady Katharine's death in 1596, when her husband gave her an impressive funeral at Coventry. She bore Lord Henry six children, only three of whom survived into adulthood. The relationship is thus compatible with the mixture of conflict and affection that Shakespeare depicts in Petruchio and Katherine, and in his hunting couple, Theseus and Hippolyta, in *A Midsummer Night's Dream*. Smyth's description of Lord Henry's inability to control his wife, and the ironic title of "Henry the harmless" that highlights it, suggest that this hunting lord might have found in Petruchio's successful taming of his wife a delightful wish-fulfillment fantasy.

If one finds the parallels between the Berkeley family and *The Taming of the Shrew* suggestive, a question still remains: Is there evidence that Shakespeare would have known, or known of this couple and their "famous" falcons? The likelihood that Shakespeare knew of the falcons, of course, increases with the likelihood that he knew of their owners.

Lord Henry was often in London. In the mid-1550s he and Lady Katharine lived with his mother in the city, and he achieved a kind of notoriety through his hunting, gambling, lawsuits, extravagance, and 150 liveried servants. Under Elizabeth the couple continued to spend wildly beyond their means, the victims, according to Smyth, of captains, scholars, poets, and cast-off courtiers. Even as late as 1595, when Lord Henry was negotiating over the marriage of his son, Thomas, Lady Katharine attempted to keep her husband out of London, fearing his susceptibility to the influence of "younge crafty Courtiers" (384). Lady Katharine's controversial family and Lord Henry's lawsuits would have kept them both in the public eye throughout their lives, and Lord Henry spent much time pursuing his legal affairs in London. A single feud with Sir Thomas Throckmorton, for example, led Lord Henry to file numerous complaints in the Court of Star Chamber between 1576 and 1596, charging Throckmorton and "eighty-eight of his kinsmen, gamekeepers, servants, tenants, and allies" with unlawful hunting.[56] Throughout his life, then, Lord Henry's presence as a hunting lord would have been manifest in London: he hunted there himself, imported his falcons there, and, as Justice Shallow threatens to do to Falstaff in *Merry Wives*, he brought his enemies to the Star Chamber on charges of poaching. His only "notorious vice," Smyth notes ironically, was that "hee was too great a lover of law, knowing it noe better" (409). It is difficult to imagine Shakespeare or his audiences unaware of or uninterested in the activities of the Berkeleys.

Although many opportunities existed for close observation of the couple in London, Shakespeare would almost certainly have encountered them as a boy in Stratford and remained aware of their activities through his close relationship with the region throughout his life. When he died, Lord Henry had holdings in the counties of Gloucester, Somerset, Warwick, Leicester, and Sussex. Throughout his life he traveled regularly with his family from one estate to another. Smyth's account suggests that one of his favorite residences, and certainly one in which he spent a great deal of time, was Callowdon, an estate in the liberties of Coventry, about twenty-five miles from Stratford. Binly Brook, where Smyth watched the falcon Kate soar out of sight, ran through the estate. Every summer from 1558 until at least 1588, according to Smyth, Lord Henry hunted in the parks surrounding this estate – "Barkewell, Groby, Bradgate, Leicester forrest, Toley, and others" towards the north, and "Kenilworth, Ashby, Wedgenocke, and others" towards the south (285). Kenilworth was about fifteen miles from Stratford, Wedgenocke Park less than ten. Shakespeare could not easily have been unaware of these activities, especially given the highly public nature of Elizabethan hunting and the size of the Berkeleys' retinue.

As far as the falcon named Kate is concerned, Smyth observes that both she and Stella were "famous with all great faulconers in many counties." He recalls seeing the birds in 1586 or 1587 at Binly Brook, near Callowdon. Since Lord Henry hawked nearly all the time and everywhere – in London, on his many estates, en route from one place to another – Shakespeare would have had many opportunities to learn of the feats of these birds. Since they lived for at least twelve years, as we have seen, the falcons were almost certainly famous at the time that he composed *The Taming of the Shrew*.

Shakespeare's interest in the Berkeley family would have been accentuated by Lord Henry's association with the world of the theater. He himself had a troupe of actors, Lord Berkeley's Men, for which we have records from 1581 to 1610. The troupe seems to have performed mainly in the country, since only one record, an account of a brawl with Inns of Court men in 1581, links them to London. But Shakespeare is likely to have been aware of at least two of their performances, since they took place at Stratford-upon-Avon in 1580–81 and 1582–83, when he was between the ages of sixteen and twenty.[57]

An even closer connection between Lord Henry and Shakespeare seems likely through the Russell family of Strensham, a village in Worcestershire not far from Stratford. Sir Thomas Russell was a Protestant member of Parliament and an adviser to Bishop Sandys. During 1569 and 1570, according to Smyth, Lord Henry and his wife and family "sojourned" for an extensive period with Sir Thomas (376). At this time Shakespeare would have been five or six years old and living in Stratford, less than thirty miles away. Sir Thomas's second son, born in 1570, was also named Thomas, and he eventually became one of the overseers of Shakespeare's will. When Thomas was four, his father died, and his mother married soon after a cousin of Lord Henry – another Henry, Sir Henry Berkeley of Bruton, Somerset. Thomas grew up in their household with his stepbrothers and later went to Queen's College, Oxford. Although we do not know when he first met Shakespeare, Thomas had property in Alderminster, Worcestershire, only four miles south of Stratford, and by 1597 / 8 he was identified as residing in that place.[58]

Although highly speculative, there is also a possible connection between Lord Henry and Lady Katharine Berkeley and the first performance of *A Midsummer Night's Dream*. When in her letter to John Smyth in 1595 Lady Katharine expressed her anxieties over her husband's going to London to negotiate their son's marriage, the son in question was Thomas Berkeley, and the potential bride, Elizabeth Carey, daughter of Sir George Carey, and the granddaughter of Henry, Lord Hunsdon, the Queen's Lord Chamberlain. Shakespeare's company at this time was the Lord Chamberlain's Men. The marriage took place on 19 February 1596. Many scholars have suggested that *A Midsummer Night's Dream* was composed for this wedding and first performed at the event.[59] If so, and there is admittedly no evidence that the play was performed for any special occasion, the hunting of Theseus and Hippolyta might have taken on a special meaning. Their paradoxical love, combining affection and aggression, is embodied in the voices of their hounds, which astonish Hippolyta with "so musical a discord, such sweet thunder" (4.1.118).

Speculations aside, there seems to be sufficient evidence in the foregoing account of the activities and relationships of the Berkeleys in London and the nearby counties to establish the probability of

Shakespeare's interest in and perhaps even intimate knowledge of the family. The Berkeleys were much in the public eye, were famous for their prowess in hunting and hawking, resided often in the environs of Stratford and London, and were connected – through their acting company, their misadventures with scholars, poets and cast-off courtiers, and the Russell family – with individuals to whom Shakespeare would have had ready access.

If Lord Henry and Lady Katharine are somehow the "originals" of Petruchio and Katherine in *The Taming of the Shrew*, their shadowy presence in the play is unlikely to be explained by a sustained allegorical intent on the part of Shakespeare. It is far more likely that stories of Lord Henry, Lady Katharine, and their falcons were simply engrained in Shakespeare's imagination – some deriving from his boyhood in Stratford, some from his own travels in the region as an adult, and some from his experiences in London. From such a perspective, one can imagine Shakespeare shaping his plot and characters independently of these "sources" but aware of their potential recognition, on occasion, by knowing members of an audience; one can imagine as well individual performances exploiting this allusive potential in many different ways, both satiric and celebratory. If such is the case, the lives of the Berkeleys simply become another source for Shakespeare's drama, a living source, filtered through his imagination along with the literary documents which we more customarily privilege with the title. This "source" takes on added interest when one considers that, in none of the most commonly proposed sources or analogues of *The Taming of the Shrew* – whether in folklore, oral tradition, or literary document – do hunting and falconry figure as a significant motif.[60]

Critics agree that one of the most striking features of *The Taming of the Shrew* is its evocation of the Warwickshire countryside. Ann Thompson notes that "the whole atmosphere of rural Warwickshire with its hunting lords, drunken tinkers and fat alewives is clearly drawn (perhaps somewhat rosily) from [Shakespeare's] own youthful experience." She observes as well that, "despite the Paduan setting, Petruchio and Katherine's marriage seems to take place in a world of country courtship practices and sports (hunting, falconry) readily comprehensible to a Warwickshire tinker."[61] When we consider the importance of this Warwickshire atmosphere, and its absence from any other known sources, the activities of the Berkeleys become as suggestive a backdrop for the play as Gascoigne's *Supposes* or folktales of tricking artisans or

taming shrews. Even if the argument for the Berkeleys as a "source" fails
to convince, the social atmosphere that their lives so vividly evoke tells
us much about the imaginative world of Shakespeare's play.

If we attend to the culture of the hunt, as represented both within and
outside *The Taming of the Shrew*, it might be possible to acknowledge the
insidiously oppressive nature of Katherine's taming and at the same
time "save the play from its own ending." Even from the limited perspective of the hunting lord, the taming of Katherine has ironic potential,
for any falconer knows that the most highly trained hawk might suddenly
revert to wild behavior. From the wider perspective of the audience, the
entire play-within-the-play might become ironical, the taming of
Katherine a wish-fulfillment fantasy of a hunting lord, a man whose
imagination is infected with the values of his "sport." The lives of the
Berkeleys and their falcon named Kate help us to reconstruct a part of
that world with great particularity. Seen as a response to its distinctive
ethos, the play might become more familiarly Shakespearean, in its sly
social criticism, its metadramatic energy, and in its satiric framing of the
more blatant and unreflective symptoms of the male dominance of the
time. Perhaps a modern setting of the play with the culture of the hunt
in mind could offer us a new and unsentimental way of appreciating its
rich comic texture.

CHAPTER FIVE

The "rascal" Falstaff in Windsor

In act 5 scene 4 of *1 Henry IV* Prince Hal kills Hotspur in single combat on the field at Shrewsbury. While doing what he calls "fair rites of tenderness" (98) to honor Hotspur's corpse, Hal spies Falstaff on the ground, dead. He responds with a speech filled with wordplay. He calls Falstaff an "old" acquaintance. He muses on the incongruity of Falstaff's bulk: "Could not all this flesh / Keep in a little life?" He salutes Falstaff as "poor Jack," the name both a familiar and affectionate substitute for "John" and a synonym for "knave." He weighs his loss both morally and emotionally: "I could have better spar'd a better man" (102–4). The wit of the lines brings together affection and moral judgment, playfulness and regret, crystallizing Hal's complex relationship to his companion throughout the play.

As his speech draws to a close, Hal introduces a novel metaphor for Falstaff, transforming him from a man into a deer:

> Death hath not strook so fat a deer to-day,
> Though many dearer, in this bloody fray.
> Embowell'd will I see thee by and by,
> Till then in blood by noble Percy lie.   (5.4.107–10)

For a brief moment, the bodies on the field at Shrewsbury become a quarry of deer and Falstaff the fattest among them. The metaphor triggers off yet another pun – "though many dearer" – and sustains its force in the word "embowell'd" and the phrase "in blood." Emboweling in preparation for salting or cooking was the inevitable fate of a dead deer, especially a fat one in the prime of life, one "in blood."[1] To compare Falstaff to a deer "in blood" is to subject him to a triple thrust of wit. As a man, Falstaff is ignoble, and therefore not "in blood." The chief mark of his ignobility at this moment, moreover, which Hal himself does not perceive, is his retention of his blood: he does not lie in blood but is "in," or full of, blood. As a deer, finally, Falstaff is hardly "in blood"; although old and fat, he is by no means in his prime, and Hal's irony acknowledges that fact.

The appropriate metaphor for Falstaff is not that of a deer "in blood" but a "rascal." Although the term is often used in the period in a general sense, to mean a "rogue" or "knave," it also carried a technical meaning, as "the young, lean, or inferior deer of a herd, distinguished from the full-grown antlered bucks or stags" (*OED*). Shakespeare plays on both meanings of the term earlier in the play when Hal calls Falstaff a "fat-kidney'd rascal" (2.2.5–6), an "oily rascal" who is "known as well as Paul's" (2.4.526), and an "impudent, emboss'd rascal" (3.3.157). The latter phrase, "emboss'd rascal," captures both Falstaff's swollen girth and breathlessness, for the word "embossed" refers not only to something molded or carved in relief but to a hunted animal, in this case a "rascal," foaming at the mouth from exhaustion.[2] As a deer, then, Falstaff is as paradoxical as he is as a man. He is a rascal, an inferior specimen, but neither young nor lean; he is an old fat rascal. He himself notes the incongruity of the metaphor in *2 Henry IV* when Doll Tearsheet calls him a "muddy rascal." He replies, "You make fat rascals, Mistress Doll" (2.4.39–41).

Because they are inferior specimens, rascals are less likely to be killed than deer "in blood." Hotspur dies at the end of *1 Henry IV*, but Falstaff, the rascal, feigns death, wounds Hotspur, and gains honor. Arising from the ground after Hal's exit, he gasps in outrage at the implications of Hal's metaphor: "Embowell'd! if thou embowel me to-day, I'll give you leave to powder me and eat me too tomorrow" (5.4.111–13). Hal's fat rascal comes back to life, desperate to prevent the emboweling and salting that would lead to his being eaten. The dead Percy becomes food "for worms" (87), but the live Falstaff refuses to become venison. As has often been observed, the "resurrection" of Falstaff is reminiscent of the ritualistic English folk drama, in which a challenger is first killed by the hero and then resurrected by a doctor. The metamorphosis of Falstaff into a deer at this point accentuates the ritualistic quality of the moment, for the participants in such folk-plays often wear or carry parts of animals, such as skins or tails. In the horn dance of Abbots Bromley, indeed, the dancers carry the horns of reindeer.[3]

Although Falstaff is called a "rascal" several times in the play, the metaphor is hardly significant enough to warrant its centrality in the "death" of Falstaff at Shrewsbury. As John Dover Wilson has shown, Falstaff is characterized throughout *1 Henry IV* primarily through the language of the taverns, and particularly that of feasting on meat.[4] Falstaff is Sir Loin-of-Beef. "Call in ribs, call in tallow" (2.4.111), says Hal of the man he later calls "my sweet beef" (3.3.177). He is also "that roasted manningtree ox with the pudding in his belly" (2.4.452–53). As befits the lord of the Boar's Head Tavern, moreover, he is the boar himself: "guts" (2.4.452), "chops" (1.2.136), "brawn" (2.4.110). In *2 Henry IV* Hal asks, "doth the old boar feed in the old frank?" (2.2.146–47), and Doll calls him her "whoreson little tidy bartholomew boar-pig" (2.4.231). All of these metaphors associate Falstaff with domesticated meat, not venison. Elizabethan social custom, indeed, makes venison a somewhat unlikely choice for Falstaff. Although the numerous complaints about the marketing of poached deer make clear that venison would have been available at least occasionally in the tavern world of London, it could not easily be made into a symbol of that world or of the traditional holidays that the play exploits. Venison connoted a higher social world than the one we customarily associate with Falstaff; the meat was normally reserved for gifts among the gentry and for formal occasions such as the Lord Mayor's feast.[5] Given these associations, it is not surprising that Hal's reference to Falstaff as a deer at the end of *1 Henry IV* is the only significant instance of its kind in either the *Henry IV* plays or in *Henry V*.

Why, then, should the metaphor of Falstaff as deer engage Shakespeare's imagination at this climactic moment in *1 Henry IV*? One answer, I suspect, lies in a poem that could well be a submerged source for the play, the ballad "The Hunting of the Cheviot," more commonly known as "Chevy Chase." The ballad was of ancient origin and was well known throughout the Elizabethan period. Sidney, for example, praises it in the *Defence of Poetry* as an example of the power of primitive lyric poetry: "Certainly, I must confess my own barbarousness, I never heard the old song of Percy and Douglas that I found not my heart moved more than with a trumpet; and yet is it sung but by some blind crowder, with no rougher voice than rude style . . ."[6] Although the evidence is only circumstantial, both the overall plot of the ballad and certain details suggest that it might have been in Shakespeare's mind when conceiving the battle of Shrewsbury.

"Chevy Chase" recounts in fictitious form the battle of Otterburn. The ballad account is historically anomalous in a manner suggestive for the *Henry IV* plays, for it sets the battle not in the reign of Richard II where it belongs but in that of Henry IV. The plot of the ballad has little relationship to Shakespeare's play, but mysterious echoes of names and events make it seem a fantasy on the themes of the Henriad. The protagonists of "Chevy Chase" are Percy and Douglas. The battle is initiated when Percy crosses the Scottish border to hunt deer, hoping to encounter his enemy Douglas on the other side. Percy and his men hunt all morning, and by noon a hundred fat harts have been killed. When Percy goes to see the breaking of the deer, Douglas appears and challenges him. Percy answers his challenge with defiance, and Douglas replies in turn with an offer of single combat. When one of Percy's men refuses to sit by and watch, a general battle breaks forth, and Douglas is killed by an arrow as he fights with Percy. Percy honors him in death and is then killed himself. The ballad ends with both armies virtually destroyed and with Henry IV vowing to avenge Percy's death at Holmedon. In this brief and ancient ballad, then, we find a kaleidoscope of elements that appear in *1 Henry IV*: a border raid, a challenge of single combat between two heroic protagonists, a refusal of one soldier to allow single combat to proceed, opposition between characters called Percy and Douglas, and a victor honoring his dead opponent. The ballad ends, moreover, with Henry IV looking forward to avenging his dead hero at the battle of Holmedon, the very battle with which Shakespeare's play begins.

Even more curious are certain verbal echoes that link ballad to play. Three times in the ballad the fatness of the harts is emphasized. They are the "fattiste hartes in all Cheviat" (st. 2).[7] By noontime "a hondrith fat hartës ded ther lay" (st. 7). Percy taunts Douglas by saying, "The fattiste hartës in all Chyviat / we have kyld, and cast to carry them away" (st. 17). The imagery of fat harts dead on the field is oddly close to Hal's "Death hath not strook so fat a deer to-day" (5.4.107). In honoring Douglas in death, moreover, Percy uses words that recall Hal's of Falstaff. Holding the dead man's hand, Percy comments, "For a better man, of hart nare of hande, / was nat in all the north contrë" (st. 39); Hal's words are "I could have better spar'd a better man" (5.4.104). In the ballad, finally, when Henry IV vows to avenge Percy's death, his use of the word "brook" links his speech to Hotspur's own dying words in Shakespeare's play. Henry IV says, "But Persë, and I brook my lyffe, / thy deth well quyte shall be" (st. 62). Hotspur, also thinking of whether his death has been well recompensed, says, "I better brook the loss of brittle life / Than those proud titles thou has won of me" (5.4.78–79).[8]

Although probably inadequate to establish "Chevy Chase" as a definite source for *1 Henry IV*, the many resemblances between the two works seem more than coincidental. The sheer arbitrariness and obliquity of the echoes, however, if that is what they are, forestall any attempt to explain them as conscious allusions. If the ballad was in Shakespeare's mind as he composed his play, it was likely to have been present at a barely conscious level, with fragments of the narrative, setting, and language reassembling themselves by a process of association. If such a scenario seems plausible, we may ask why these memories should have been triggered off by Falstaff's mock-death at the battle of Shrewsbury.

Part of the answer, of course, is provided by the detailed resemblances we have already examined: the names of the characters, the battlefield setting, the situation of two great heroes fighting in single combat. At a deeper and perhaps less conscious level, however, the two episodes are linked in a way that will eventually lead to the Falstaff of *The Merry Wives of Windsor*. The link is that between hunting and war, and, more precisely, between poaching and social rebellion.

In the ballad of "Chevy Chase," Percy's hunting raid has as its object not merely the killing of deer but the humiliation of Douglas, the chief ranger of the parks and chases of Scotland, under whose protection the deer exist. "Who gave youe leave to hunte in this Chyviat chays," asks Douglas when he accosts Percy, "in the spyt of myn and of me" (st. 15). The poem as a whole, moreover, treats the hunting raid and the battle as symbolic equivalents. The battle itself is introduced as a continuation of the hunt (st. 24), and is identified with the hunt in the final stanza:

> Ihesue Crist our balys [torments] bete [assuage],
>   and to the blys us brynge!
> Thus was the hountynge of the Chivyat:
>   God send us alle good endyng!   (st. 68)

The ballad, in short, depends upon the same symbolism that underlies Elizabethan poaching. In slaughtering his deer, Percy is destroying Douglas's honor, thereby symbolically slaughtering both him and his army. As Roger B. Manning's account of the ballad makes clear, the action is both a literal instigator of war and its symbolic equivalent.[9]

Shakespeare's imagination works in a similar manner. In an Elizabethan context, the field of battle, unlike the world of the taverns, does not evoke images of boar or beef; it evokes images of the hunt. The field of a hunt, like the field of a battle, was often filled with corpses, and with the victors surveying the nobility of those that had been killed. The hunt was not merely associated with war but was even conducted as a kind of war itself.[10] For Hal, the battlefield at Shrewsbury, littered with corpses, becomes a quarry of deer and the "dead" Falstaff the fattest of the lot.

Although both Hal and Hotspur aspire to elevate the battle of Shrewsbury into chivalric warfare, the conflict actually pits rebels against a rebel-king who peoples the field with counterfeits wearing his own armor. The men killed at Shrewsbury, like the deer killed at Chevy Chase, are not ceremoniously hunted but poached. Rebellion is to chivalric warfare what poaching is to the ceremonial hunt. In this sense, Falstaff may be considered a poacher, since he steals from Hal the honor of killing Hotspur. From this perspective, Hal's fat rascal avenges himself upon the "hunt" of war by stabbing the noblest hunter in the thigh and carrying him home as a trophy. Falstaff will not be eaten. The hunted becomes the hunter, and sheer animal vitality triumphs. The fat rascal survives and prospers.

Although the man Falstaff gets his comeuppance at the end of *2 Henry IV*, when the newly crowned Henry V rejects and banishes him, the fate of the fat rascal Falstaff, the dear deer of Shrewsbury, is suspended until he meets the wives of Windsor. In *The Merry Wives*, the metaphor that surfaces momentarily upon Falstaff's "death" at Shrewsbury appears throughout the play. In Windsor, the rascal Falstaff plays the roles of a literal poacher of deer, a metaphoric poacher of wives, Herne the Hunter, and a Windsor stag. To appreciate the significance of these roles, it is necessary to consider not merely the figure of Falstaff but his place within the play as a whole.

The Merry Wives poses special problems for critics. The date of composition, the occasion for which the play might have been written, the relationship between the Quarto and Folio texts are all uncertain and the subject of continuing controversy.[11] The anomalous position of the play among Shakespeare's comedies, moreover, has encouraged a kind of disparagement by exclusion: *The Merry Wives*, it seems, offers neither the delights of the romantic comedies, with their exotic locales, their vibrant heroines, or their marvelous plots, nor the wit, energy, and gritty realism of the Falstaffian history plays. A recent interest in local history and local readings of plays, however, has begun to provide a context within which to appreciate the play's most distinctive qualities, the most important of which is its depiction of Elizabethan town life. The Windsor of the play, as R. S. White observes, is "solidly rooted in its specified town planning, its diurnal activities, its local customs."[12] In a lively and insightful essay, "Falstaff and the Comic Community," Anne Barton stresses the dramatic significance of that distinctive world, observing that "Windsor itself, as a corporate entity, is the true protagonist of the comedy, not Falstaff, the shadowy lovers, or even the merry wives themselves, who uphold its values so well."[13]

Although I shall later want to qualify Barton's characterization of the wives as mere upholders of Windsor's values, I believe she captures the single quality that makes this play most distinctive and is most important to its critical appreciation: *The Merry Wives* is the one Shakespearean comedy that represents the social dynamics of Elizabethan town life. In placing a generalized "Windsor" at the center of the play, moreover, Shakespeare not only achieves a high degree of comic realism but subjects the very social practices he imitates to comic scrutiny. In this way the play provides not only a representative image of an Elizabethan community, "Windsor," but a comic meditation on some of the forces that drive Elizabethan communal life, forces for which poaching becomes a central metaphor. In so doing, the play also turns our gaze upon its own form – upon the capacity of comedy to resolve social tensions of the kind it imitates. The play thus reflects the customs of Elizabethan town life, reflects upon them, and probes their adaptability to traditional comic form.

The most important fact about Windsor is conflict. The opening words of the play, Shallow's "I will make a Star chamber matter of it" (1.1.1–2), are only the first of many demands for retribution – so many that, as Linda Anderson observes, the play seems "not merely concerned with revenge" but "obsessed with it."[14] Each plot of the play develops a different kind of social conflict and a different mode of attempted resolution. Shallow wants to bring Falstaff to the Star Chamber for poaching his deer, although he still hankers after the sword-fights of his youth. Slender accuses Falstaff's men of stealing his purse. Evans and Caius attempt to fight a duel over Anne Page, but are thwarted by the jocular peacemaking of the Host, who becomes in turn the victim of their revenge, the "theft" of his horses. Mistress Page and her husband compete against each other as matchmakers for Anne, both attempting to arrange a secret marriage, a legal but strongly anti-social bit of trickery. Falstaff arouses the wrath of Pistol and Bardolph by dismissing them, the wrath of Mistress Ford and Mistress Page by insulting them, and the wrath of Master Ford by threatening to cuckold him – all actions that precipitate counter-plots of revenge. Pistol and Bardolph become informers against Falstaff, while Master Ford attempts to entrap him, using his own wife as bait and, according to Mistress Quickly, beating her "black and blue" (4.5.112) when his efforts fail. The merry wives, finally, devise a series of informal punishments which climax in Falstaff's humiliation before the entire community. In the range and variety of conflicts and attempted resolutions, the play provides a casebook of conflict in an Elizabethan town. Local and national law, the private code of the duel, trickery, neighborly intervention, and public humiliation are all part of the social repertory of the citizens of Windsor.

From a modern perspective, what is most striking about the various attempts to resolve conflict is their dependence upon informal and communal methods of "justice." Although Shallow and Slender threaten the use of the national and local legal system, they are thwarted in their designs, and social peace is essentially left in the hands of the community itself. To resolve disputes, the citizens of Windsor take the "law" into their own collective hands. Since the play opens with Shallow's ineffectual attempt to bring Falstaff before the Star Chamber and ends with Falstaff punished by the community, we might say that the plot itself replaces legalistic with informal and communal methods of achieving peace.

Keeping order in Windsor is both a local and a highly collaborative activity. Evans attempts to settle Slender's complaint against Falstaff's men with a panel of "three umpires" – Page, the host of the Garter, and himself (1.1.137). Page holds a dinner of venison pasty in hopes that Shallow, Slender, Falstaff, and his men will "drink down all unkindness" (1.1.196–97). Mistress Page and Mistress Ford band together in their punishments of Falstaff. Page, Shallow, and Slender join the Host in preventing the duel between Caius and Evans. In her indiscriminate good will as a match-maker, Mistress Quickly scrambles to keep everyone happy, parodying the role of peacemaker. In his efforts to catch Falstaff in the act of courting his wife, Ford brings Page, Caius, and Evans as witnesses, hoping to transform the shame of cuckoldry into communal applause: "to these violent proceedings all my neighbors shall cry aim" (3.2.43–44). The erstwhile opponents, Caius and Evans, join forces to revenge themselves against the Host. And the play climaxes in a scene that shows almost the entire community united against Falstaff. In a society that seems as obsessively driven by the bourgeois motive of economic gain as that of revenge, it is worth observing that the resolution of conflict involves the whole community in ways that largely transcend differences in wealth and social status.

When placed against the backdrop of what we know about Elizabethan town life in the late sixteenth and early seventeenth centuries, the play's preoccupation with conflict, and with informal, communal modes of conflict resolution, sharpens in focus. In the 1590s most Elizabethan towns experienced serious social and economic disorder, brought on by a wide variety of causes, among them harvest failure, plague, and overseas war. In the early seventeenth century demographic change, enclosure, and an increase in class divisions accentuated by Puritanism continued this destabilizing trend. Partly in response to these social tensions, the civic authorities and moralists of the period seem almost obsessed with fears of civil disorder.[15]

In a way that is difficult for moderns to appreciate, this anxiety about civic order was expressed within a social system that had few legal and institutional resources. The national system of law enforcement and local administration, for example, depended upon "the diligence and co-operation of essentially amateur, unpaid local officers,"[16] such as Justice Shallow. For this and other reasons – including the desire for independence and local control – informal, local mediation of disputes was usually preferred to legal means: "Local gentlemen, clergymen and prominent neighbors were commonly involved in mediation of this kind and local officers could also take a hand."[17] At the level of the town and village, according to Keith Wrightson, "'order' meant little more than conformity to a fairly malleable local custom which was considerably more flexible than statute law."[18] In cases not amenable to informal mediation, the community had available numerous traditional sanctions, ranging from the relatively benign method of gossip to more violent methods, such as the charivari.

In order to be effective, these communal methods of conflict resolution depended upon the small size of the towns, which fostered among individuals, for better and worse, close involvement in each other's affairs. Informal peacemaking also required a reasonable consensus about the nature of social relations in the community. Central to this consensus, according to Mildred Campbell, was an ideal of "good neighborhood": "Neighborliness stands perhaps first in the criteria by which the social and ethical standing of an individual in a country community was measured."[19] Keith Wrightson offers a definition of this social ideal, which he sees as complementary with two other social norms, paternalism and deference. Neighborliness, he observes, "involved a mutual recognition of reciprocal obligations of a practical kind and a degree of normative consensus as to the nature of proper behaviour between neighbors . . . it was essentially a horizontal relationship, one which implied a degree of equality and mutuality between partners to the relationship, irrespective of distinctions of wealth or social standing."[20] In general, neighborliness was manifested in a willingness, among other things, to lend implements or money (without interest), to share in parish administration, to help at shearing or harvest time, to assist the needy, to engage in genial social relations, to mediate disputes, and to promote harmonious social relations.[21]

Such a social ideal, of course, was commonly much diluted when put into practice, and the informal power and responsibility it conferred on individuals and groups could have negative and sometimes dangerous implications. A good example of the equivocal nature of "good neighborhood," as we shall see in some detail later, is the charivari, an informal method of social punishment that could be coercive not only to offenders but to those in the community who might have prevented the offense. In some charivaris, for example, a neighbor served as a surrogate victim, as if the neighborhood itself were somehow implicated in the offense.[22] Neighborliness was thus not a matter of choice but an obligation, involving, in some cases, both the offender and the peacemaker in a network of socially coercive behavior. In cases of extreme conflict, "good neighborhood" might be difficult to distinguish from social violence.

A comic representation of the way in which "good neighborhood" might have worked in Elizabethan towns is provided in the opening scene of *The Merry Wives*, which serves as an overture to the play as a whole. The scene begins with Justice Shallow's threat to make a Star Chamber matter out of Falstaff's poaching of his deer. Sir Hugh Evans, as a good neighbor and cleric, attempts to mediate – "I am of the church, and will be glad to do my benevolence to make atonements and compremises between you" (1.1.32–34) – but Shallow insists that "the Council shall hear it, it is a riot" (35), and then sputters that if he were only young again, "the sword should end it" (40–41). Evans's reply to this threat gives us, in a thick Welsh accent, the cryptic insight of the fool, an insight, as we shall see, that the remainder of the play explores: "It is petter that friends is the sword, and end it" (42–43). The opening moments of the play thus outline three potential modes of conflict resolution: the socially (and personally) anachronistic method of the duel, the law, and the informal mediation of neighbors.

Shallow is too old for sword-fights and, initially, too stubborn for informal mediation. He is Justice of the Peace and Coram, and *Custa-lorum*, too, and he wants the law. His opening confrontation with Falstaff, however, demonstrates the limitations of this approach. Falstaff knows the law and how to evade it. This becomes most obviously clear in Slender's accusations against Bardolph, Nym and Pistol for stealing his purse. Because he was too drunk at the time to make a positive identification, Slender's charge cannot hold up, and Falstaff can conclude, triumphantly, "You hear all these matters denied, gentlemen; you hear it" (186–87). Slender's only recourse at this point is to restrict himself henceforth to getting drunk in "honest, civil, godly company" (182). The law will do him no good.

Shallow's charge of poaching involves subtler matters of law and a subtler evasiveness. Since the nature of Falstaff's triumph in this matter tends to escape critical notice, it is worth special attention. The chief theatrical question raised by the episode is why, after so insistent a demand for a trial in the Star Chamber, Shallow (or Shakespeare) lets the matter drop. Although the issue is not resolved in this scene, it is never referred to again. The image of Falstaff as a poacher is obviously important, however, for it reappears in his disguise as Herne the hunter at the end of the play.

To understand the significance of the episode, one must consider the legal treatment of poaching in the period. In its most destructive and dangerous form, the offense had nothing to do with the occasional desire of a commoner for meat; it constituted instead both a symbolic and real assault by one member of the gentry against another and often involved serious injury, destruction of property, and loss of honor, or what Evans calls "disparagements" (31). For such offenses, usually treated as a form of riot in the courts, recourse to the Court of Star Chamber was fairly common and appropriate.[23] In the case of Falstaff, the motive for the poaching is unclear. Both the theatrical and social contexts imply that drunken sport was the most likely motive, with perhaps the addition of a riotous challenge to Shallow and the social order in general. Since Falstaff needs money, however, the motive might also have been economic. Commercial poaching became a major problem at the turn of the century, and inns and alehouses were well-known distribution points in the illicit trade; speaking in Star Chamber in 1616, James I complained "of Ale-houses, for receipt of Stealers of my Deer."[24] Much of the venison sold illegally in London, moreover, came from the grounds of Windsor Castle.[25] Whatever Falstaff's motives, it is clear that Falstaff has not only "beaten" Shallow's men, "kill'd" his deer, and "broke open" his lodge (111–12), but assaulted his dignity: "If he were twenty Sir John Falstaffs, he shall not abuse Robert Shallow, esquire" (2–4). The raid, in short, constitutes a symbolic assault.[26]

Why, then, does Shallow let the matter drop? Because Falstaff outmaneuvers him procedurally by admitting his crime outright. When Shallow demands "this shall be answer'd," Falstaff's replies give him little choice but to allow Page's efforts at informal mediation:

Fal. I will answer it straight: I have done all this. That is now answered.
Shal. The Council shall know this.
Fal. 'Twere better for you if it were known in counsel. You'll be laugh'd at.

(114–19)

Implicit in this exchange is not only the recognition of both men that Falstaff might have influence at court but that Shallow would disgrace himself by invoking the Star Chamber for a relatively minor offense. Crucial to the legal process in cases of poaching was a distinction between those who admitted the crime and those who did not. Admission downgraded the offense from a felony, at least technically punishable by death, to a misdemeanor, an offense with less severe consequences.[27] By admitting the offense, Falstaff has reduced its severity significantly. Since the Court of the Star Chamber was seriously overburdened with litigation during this period, and since Justices of the Peace like Shallow were under the Court's authority and had numerous formal and informal means to settle such disputes, the likelihood of the Court looking sympathetically upon such a case would have been very small indeed.[28] In such circumstances, Shallow would be well advised to follow Falstaff's advice and keep his own counsel. In his quest for justice, Shallow is thus driven back upon his own and the community's resources.

The scene concludes, therefore, not with a summons to the Star Chamber but with an invitation to a dinner of venison pasty. "Come," says Page, having taken over the peacemaker's role from Evans, "we have a hot venison pasty to dinner. Come, gentlemen, I hope we shall drink down all unkindness" (195–97). Shakespeare does not stage this dinner, but it seems a very curious affair. Conventionally in Shakespearean comedy, as in Elizabethan society, feasting marks the resolution of conflict and binds society together in a rite of incorporation; in this case, however, the feast seems at best premature, for Falstaff's conflict with Shallow and Slender has not been resolved. This feast, one might say, includes hostility within the festive form itself, as if eating together might bring the kind of peace that a feast would ordinarily celebrate.

Even more curious is the meal itself, which consists of venison. Where did it come from? Literally, the deer is a gift from Shallow to Page, presumably a neighborly gesture intended to foster their proposed family alliance; metaphorically, however, it might be called an inadvertent gift from Falstaff, for, as Shallow's apology to Page makes clear, the deer is one that Falstaff poached: "I wish'd your venison better, it was ill kill'd" (82–83). Shallow's statement probably applies in two senses: the deer was killed illegally and, as a consequence, not properly drained of blood. So the very food itself symbolizes the conflict it is meant to resolve. In a precisely literal way, conflict feeds the community, suggesting that Falstaff's relationship with the community is less parasitic than symbiotic. Instead of marking the end of conflict, the festive form "contains" it, in both senses of the word: conflict is both included and kept in check by the feast. That conflict is not ended by such events becomes clear later, when Ford cites his wife's behavior at the dinner to bolster his suspicions against Falstaff (2.1.234–36).

Perhaps the best gloss on this paradoxical interdependency between peace and conflict, order and disorder is Evans's cryptic response to Shallow's threat of the sword, alluded to earlier: "it is petter that friends is the sword, and end it." The statement captures the essence of "good neighborhood" as depicted in the play. It suggests, on the one hand, that the best way to resolve conflict of this kind is not through the sword, or even the Star Chamber, as Shallow proposes, but through members of the community, through friends. Evans's peculiar turn of phrase, however, suggests a deeper meaning, establishing an identity between "friends" and "the sword," as if in taking the place of a duel, the friends themselves were engaged in a surrogate act of violence: "the friends *is* the sword." As we have seen, this paradoxical identification of peace and violence occurs implicitly at Page's dinner of venison pasty; it recurs throughout the play, moreover, in ways that challenge conventional distinctions between order and disorder, harmony and conflict. Evans himself, ironically, the cleric and man of peace who offers to "make atonements and compremises" (1.1.33–34) between Shallow and Falstaff, will later enact the paradox when he prepares to meet Caius in a duel. In its linkage of friendship and force, and more broadly, festivity and violence, the play mirrors in comic form the dynamics of conflict in Elizabethan towns. As Keith Wrightson observes, "such equilibrium as local society possessed was the product of a constant dynamism in its social relations and the impetus of this dynamic came, as often as not, from conflict."[29]

Falstaff poses a special threat to Windsor society because he is an alien, displaced both geographically and socially. A fallen knight, a former frequenter of the world of the court, he resides temporarily in the Garter Inn, the name of which, like the allusion to the Garter ceremonies at the end of the play, casts an ironic shadow on his present condition. His counterpart as an alien threat to the social order of Windsor is Fenton, who also represents the foreign values of the court. Although the comparison may seem strange at first, the two interlopers are curiously alike. Both do not belong in Windsor. Both have squandered their money and, as Page says of Fenton, have "kept company with the wild Prince and Poins" (3.2.72–73). Both are attracted to the women of Windsor for economic reasons. Both become "lovers," and, as such, become involved in intrigues to fulfill their desires. Once they take on the role of lover, moreover, their initial economic motivation becomes complicated by sexual and romantic inclinations: disguised as Herne the Hunter, Falstaff revels at the prospect of bedding both of the merry wives, while Fenton eventually persuades Anne that his love is genuinely disinterested and that he would wed her without dowry, which he does. The Host's appreciation of Fenton – "he speaks holiday, he smells April and May" (3.2.68–69) – suggests that the young wooer represents a benign reincarnation of the old Falstaff, just as Anne represents a more admirable and radical independence even than that manifested by her mother, who is said by Mistress Quickly to have the freedom of her house (2.2.116–20). Falstaff's comment on the couple's successful elopement at the end of the play makes Fenton himself a poacher: "When night-dogs run, all sorts of deer are chas'd" (5.5.238). While Falstaff gets fairy pinches for his poaching, Fenton gets Anne, the blessing of her parents, and the money his elopement had put at risk.

Antagonism between the aristocratic world of the court and the bourgeois world of Windsor runs throughout the play; given the proximity of the castle to the town, the tension probably had a basis in social fact. The local patriotism of Windsorites might have been accentuated at the turn of the century, moreover, because of their concerted but unsuccessful effort to persuade the Queen to renew their charter.[30] As disruptive agents from the court, both Falstaff and Fenton might be said to turn the bourgeois world of Windsor upside down. "He is of too high a region," says Page of Fenton, "he knows too much" (3.2.73–74). It is important to recognize, however, that the society of Windsor actually needs the two wily intruders, in much the same way that the little circle of feasters at Page's house needs Falstaff's poaching. Without Fenton, after all, Anne Page would be doomed to marry Evans or Caius, either prospect a fate worse than being "set quick i'th'earth, / And bowl'd to death with turnips!" (3.4.86–87). Without Falstaff, Ford's obsessive jealousy, for which he is already famous, would doubtless seek out other victims, to the misery of his long-suffering wife. The courtly interlopers do not so much turn the world of Windsor upside down as release disorders already simmering within it; they are catalysts for existing social and personal tensions.

As "foreigners," both Fenton and Falstaff have something in common with two other characters – Evans, the Welsh preacher, and Caius, the French physician. Although to some degree accepted by Windsor society, they remain outsiders, to be treated as comic butts partly for their bizarre behavior, but more consistently for their linguistic deficiencies. Joan Rees's observation about Evans might serve for both characters: "[he] is absorbed into his small town community, certainly, but without honour, dignity or even language, save for a ridiculous version of the tongue of his masters."[31] Although both characters are relatively simple as comic types, they occupy complex social positions. Vocationally they are important to the community: Evans is a "curer of souls," as Shallow observes, Caius a "curer of bodies" (2.3.39). As would have been true in the world outside the play, however, their social status is ambiguous. They are on good terms with the village notables, for example, and Caius has connections at court, but at the same time Shallow, Page, and the Host feel free to make fools of them. The aborted duel provides yet another example of the linkage between festivity and social coercion in the play, for it combines well-meaning merriment, aggression, and public humiliation. Even the Host's act of "good neighborhood" in ordering the combatants disarmed contains an image of violence: "Disarm them, and let them question. Let them keep their limbs whole and hack our English" (3.1.76–78). Like Falstaff's deer, the English language becomes a sacrificial victim, to be hacked and hewn in the interest of social peace. As in Page's dinner of venison pasty, there is no thought here of ending conflict, merely of diverting it into less destructive social forms. As hackers of English, moreover, the two men serve as perpetual outlets for the festive aggression of the community as a whole. They too are "contained" by the community.

The play's most striking instance of trickery as an informal means of social control is provided by the titular heroines of the play, the merry wives. In basing the Falstaff plot upon their witty stratagems, Shakespeare adapts to comic purposes, and subjects to implicit comic scrutiny, a popular form of social control that goes by many names – "rough music," riding, skimmington, and charivari being the most common.[32] Although the charivari took extremely varied forms throughout Europe and England, its essential feature was the public humiliation, by means of raucous noise and symbolic action, of individuals considered guilty of violating social norms. A charivari licensed both festive and derisive laughter, and often included such ritualistic features as processions of armed men, the wearing or display of animals' horns or heads, and mock proclamations, songs, and other kinds of verbal horseplay. The victim or a surrogate was often paraded through the streets on a horse or a wooden pole called a "stang," and subjected to verbal and physical abuse. The social offenses punished in this manner were almost invariably domestic, and in sixteenth-century England the majority occurred because a wife had physically assaulted or dominated her husband, a situation that almost invariably implied cuckoldry. In such cases the victim might vary: sometimes it was the wife, sometimes the husband, sometimes a surrogate, such as, in one instance, "'the next nearest neighbour to the church'"[33] – the latter choice implying, as we have already observed, the coercive nature of the notion of good neighborliness that underlies the entire custom.

Although the forms of charivari are too varied to allow a single instance to stand as a typical example, one cited by Martin Ingram captures some of the essential features. The event took place on 27 May, 1618, in the small market town of Calne, Wiltshire. Thomas Mills, a cutler, and his wife Agnes, the object of the attack, deposed that, after an earlier and smaller group of men and boys was turned away,

about noon came again from Calne to Quemerford another drummer named William Wiatt, and with him three or four hundred men, some like soldiers armed with pieces and other weapons, and a man riding upon a horse, having a white night cap upon his head, two shoeing horns hanging by his ears, a counterfeit beard upon his chin made of a deer's tail, a smock upon the top of his garments, and he rode upon a red horse with a pair of pots under him, and in them some quantity of brewing grains, which he used to cast upon the press of people, rushing over thick upon him in the way as he passed; and he and all his company made a stand when they came just against this examinate's house, and then the gunners shot off their pieces, pipes and horns were sounded, together with lowbells and other smaller bells which the company had amongst them, and rams' horns and bucks' horns, carried upon forks, were then and there lifted up and shown . . .

"Stones were thrown at the windows," continues Ingram, "an entry forced, and Agnes Mills was dragged out of the house, thrown into a wet hole, trampled, beaten, and covered with mud and filth. Her tormentors, however, failed in their final object of riding her behind the horseman to Calne to 'wash her in the cucking stool.'"[34] Agnes's crime, it seems, was having beaten her husband, a crime common enough for Ingram to observe that "the great majority" of such events "in early modern England took place because a wife had physically assaulted her husband or otherwise dominated him."[35]

From this description it is possible to imagine something of the social and psychological impulses behind this potentially dangerous form of social control. Raucous, festive, derisive – the event combines festivity and punishment, creating group solidarity through the expression of righteous aggression. Ingram notes that the custom could range from mild satire to vicious assault, with the individuals sometimes reintegrated into the society and sometimes forced to leave. The basic method, a public humiliation symbolically appropriate to the offense involved, was by no means restricted to popular forms of "justice" but was a popular expression of a pattern already employed in the official punishments of church and state, as in the carting of criminals, the shaming of penitents, and the staging of public executions. As E. P. Thompson observes, "until the early nineteenth century, publicity was of the essence of punishment."[36]

The social significance of any given charivari would depend upon the specific nature of the occasion and its participants. During the sixteenth century the civic authorities seem to have encouraged and sometimes participated in such events, presumably because they were under local control and seen to complement the work of the legal and church hierarchies. By their very nature, however, charivaris were dangerously unstable and could lead to flagrant abuse, not only by causing serious harm to the victim, but, through riotous behavior and the destruction of property, by inciting further social conflict. Individuals, moreover, could subvert such events to their own purposes, using them to settle old scores either against the victim or other neighbors, or merely to vent lawless and destructive energies. It is even possible that such events were inadvertently subversive of their own apparent ends, by creating among women, the usual victims, oppositional attitudes towards patriarchal authority.[37] In the seventeenth century moralistic opposition to charivaris increased, and by 1700 they were declared illegal, although they persisted until the twentieth century.

The equivocal status of such events, which were part festivity and part violent assault, is suggested by the fact that participants commonly referred to them as "sports."[38] Shakespeare's Windsor resonates with a similar use of the term, which is used repeatedly to characterize acts of festive social control that involve public humiliation. Shallow tempts Page to join in the mockery of Evans and Caius with "we have sport in hand" (2.1.197). When Ford invites Page home with him, in hopes of entrapping his unfaithful wife, he promises "you shall have sport" (3.2.80–81); later he assures his witnesses that they may "make sport" at him if his suspicions are wrong (3.3.150), a promise he reiterates during the second search: "If I find not what I seek . . . let me be forever your table-sport" (4.2.161–62). The most evocative use of the term occurs in relation to the charivari against Falstaff: Page calls the event a "public sport" (4.4.13), and asks later that "Heaven prosper our sport!" (5.2.12); Mistress Page, perhaps usurping the role of peacemaker played by her husband in the opening scene, brings the charivari and play to an end by inviting all the participants to "laugh this sport o'er by a country fire" (5.5.242).

Although many details of the charivari are absent from Shakespeare's play, the essence of the form has been preserved in the structure of Falstaff's experience. Falstaff offends against the domestic and social order by attempting to seduce Mistress Page and Mistress Ford, thereby cuckolding their husbands, and in return the society as a whole subjects him to public and symbolically appropriate humiliation. It is important to note, however, as will become clear later, that Falstaff's charivari proceeds in two stages. In the first stage, he is subjected to two symbolic punishments of a relatively private sort, under the exclusive control of the wives: he is first hidden in a buck basket and dumped into the Thames, and then disguised as the old woman of Brainford and beaten. Taken by themselves, these episodes hardly require consideration of the charivari, for such revenge-tricks appear in many plays. In the second stage, however, which takes place under Herne's oak at midnight, Falstaff is subjected to symbolic punishment and public humiliation at the hands of the entire community, children included. This climactic episode, with its mixture of festive and derisive laughter, its use of disguise (including the wearing of the antlers of a stag), its mocking songs and wordplay, its physical abuse, and its raucous noise, adapts the social custom of the charivari to comic theater.

By invoking the charivari, Shakespeare not only brings into the drama the social resonances of a customary popular form; he subjects the form itself to the critique of comedy. For a contemporary Elizabethan audience, Shakespeare's most dramatic departure from social convention would have been the reversal of gender roles in the relationship between punisher and punished. Although the vast majority of charivaris were directed at aggressive and sexually threatening women, the victim in this play is a man. The agents of social justice that undo him, moreover, are strong, aggressive, and sexually secure women. In adapting the charivari, then, Shakespeare has taken a ritual form that threatened women with patriarchal punishment and inverted it, making it a means whereby women achieve their comic revenge. In this sense, the play confers upon married women some of the license of the unmarried and disguised heroines of the romantic comedies. In the *Merry Wives*, the women are subject to the patriarchy, as wives, yet they find in what Mistress Page calls the "sport" (5.5.242) of the charivari a form that enables them to assert a temporary power and freedom. The clash between comic and social form, between matriarchal license and patriarchal restraint, invites among audiences critical reflections upon popular forms of social justice.

The comic revenge inflicted upon Falstaff by the wives is developed in such a way as to accentuate its anti-patriarchal implications. The motives for the revenge, for one thing, are distinctly personal, an expression of the individuality and friendship of the two women; neither woman responds to Falstaff's overtures as an assault upon the good name of her husband, or upon the domestic order. Their outrage springs from his assault upon themselves. Their revenge, moreover, cuts a wide swath. In the first instance, it is directed against Falstaff alone. Falstaff, however, is also a surrogate for Ford; he is not only a potential cuckold-maker but a salaried representative of the potential cuckold himself. In serving the will of a man named Ford, Falstaff is dumped in a "ford" – "I have my belly full of ford" (3.5.36–37), he laments – beaten as someone from "Brainford," and forced to wear the horns that Ford sees upon his own head.[39] He is also hidden in a "buck" basket, which Ford punningly identifies with his own cuckolding: "Buck! I would I could wash myself of the buck! Buck, buck, buck!" (3.3.157–58). The wives make clear, in addition, that behind the individual targets of both the seducer and the jealous husband lies the patriarchy. "Heaven forgive me!" shouts Mistress Page as she reads Falstaff's letter of seduction, "Why, I'll exhibit a bill in the parliament for the putting down of men" (2.1.28–30). This modulation from the particular threat to the general is itself characteristic of the charivari, which can attack either the offender or a surrogate, and which in practice treats the offender as a representative of womankind.

Falstaff's misadventures at the hands of the women, therefore, are appropriately gendered. His first punishment is to be taken out of Ford's house in a buck basket and dumped into a muddy ditch. In 1618, we recall, Agnes Mills was "thrown into a wet hole, trampled, beaten, and covered with mud and filth." In Agnes's case the symbolic intent, it seems, was to cover her with filth that represented her crime, filth being closely allied to sexual misbehavior, and then to cleanse her symbolically "in the cucking stool." Something of the same motif seems embedded in Falstaff's punishment, for although Mistress Ford directs that he be dumped into "the muddy ditch close by the Thames side" (3.3.15–16), the punishment is also linked to the bleaching of sheets, and the victim actually ends up in the Thames itself, as he reports later, drenched and with a bellyfull of water.

The episode is comical for many reasons, not the least of which is its feminist attack on domesticity. Cleanliness is next to godliness, and Falstaff's soul needs whitening as much as Mistress Ford's dirty linen. The comedy is heightened by Falstaff's unaccustomed prissiness as a wooer. In his overtures to Mistress Ford he assumes the role of an effete courtier, and his Sidneyan posturing – "'Have I caught thee, my heavenly jewel?'" (3.3.43) – bespeaks a fastidiousness that will be severely tested by a buck basket of foul linen. The messy business of dealing with soiled linen is women's work, of course, as Mistress Ford reminds her husband in the midst of his questioning about the destination of the buck basket: "Why, what have you to do whither they bear it? You were best meddle with buck-washing" (3.3.154–56). Falstaff is forced to meddle with buck-washing, and one result, as he tells Ford, is an assault upon his olfactory senses – "the rankest compound of villainous smell that ever offended nostril" (3.5.92–93).

Falstaff's second punishment is just as clearly conceived as a woman's revenge. This time he is disguised, says Mistress Ford, as "my maid's aunt, the fat woman of Brainford" (4.2.75–76). This woman is not merely fat, having a gown large enough to fit Falstaff, but she is old and detested by Master Ford, who believes she is a witch: "He cannot abide the old woman of Brainford. He swears she's a witch, forbade her my house, and hath threat'ned to beat her" (4.2.85–87). And Ford is as good as his word. He beats the disguised Falstaff out the door while hurling insults: "you witch, you rag, you baggage, you poulcat, you runnion! out, out! I'll conjure you, I'll fortune-tell you!" (4.2.184–86). In this instance, Falstaff is not merely dirtied by contact with woman's work; he is beaten by taking on the role of a woman who is in some ways a female counterpart. She is old; she is fat; she is unmarried; she is not of the town of Windsor. Whereas Falstaff can overcome these limitations, after a fashion, the woman of Brainford is victimized by them, as Falstaff discovers feelingly. Simple, whose name suggests his capacity as a speaker of unconscious truth, calls the woman "the wise woman of Brainford" (4.5.26–27), and Slender enters the inn later to seek out her advice. Falstaff admits to the Host that there was a wise woman with him, and "one that hath taught me more wit than ever I learn'd before in my life" (4.5.59–61).

Falstaff's words are belied by the rapidity with which he accepts another assignation, and his failure to learn justifies the escalation of private trick into the public ritual with which the play concludes. The modulation between specifically female and more generally communal sanctions occurs when the wives, having satisfied their desire for private revenge, decide to inform their husbands of their actions and to defer to them for any further vengeance. "If they can find in their hearts the poor unvirtuous fat knight shall be any further afflicted," says Mistress Page, "we two will still be the ministers" (4.2.216–19). Mistress Ford anticipates the likely response of their husbands, and accepts its merit: "I'll warrant they'll have him publicly sham'd, and methinks there would be no period to the jest, should he not be publicly shamed" (4.2.220–22). What Master Page later calls a "public sport" (4.4.13) no longer expresses the individuality of the wives but the outrage of the husbands and the community as a whole. As in the romantic comedies, the female protagonists of this play willingly relinquish the power of their own festive liberty in the interest of traditional community values. It is important to recognize, however, that in doing so they take on the untraditional role of "ministers" of the charivari, and that the charivari itself remains untraditional in being directed against a male. While one cannot call this theatrical gesture revolutionary, it suggests the possibility of progressive social change within the patriarchy, as it both absorbs and is modified by potentially rebellious female energies. As elsewhere in the play's vision of social harmony, the final situation of the wives implies an unstable equilibrium, a continuing social tension that has both destructive and creative potential.

The "public sport" directed against Falstaff at the end of the play is designed to chasten rebellious energies at their most dangerously antisocial. The sport combines the two forms of symbolic assault embodied in the charivari and poaching. As a man, in disguise as Herne the Hunter, Falstaff is subjected to the raucous humiliation of the charivari. As a deer, he is poached. If he is a "Windsor stag" (5.5.12–13), as he says he is, and if, as has been argued, the scene is set in the Little Park of Windsor Castle, then the townsfolk are "poaching" the Queen's deer.[40] When the townsfolk conduct their hunt, they resemble a band of poachers: they assemble at night, they wear disguise, they blow hunting horns, they chase their chosen victim, and they encircle him in preparation for the "kill." Their motive, as in poaching, is not venison but punishment and humiliation. As he kneels in abject terror, Falstaff embodies in a single image the fate of the butchered deer and the dishonored landowner in a poaching raid. The play begins with Falstaff poaching Shallow's deer and ends with the townsfolk poaching the rascal Falstaff.

Shakespeare's merger of the charivari with poaching is not surprising. As forms of extra-legal social control, they both have much in common. They bring together bands of people acting in festive and punitive consort; they feature raucous behavior and noise; they attack their victims often through surrogates – deer, neighbors, or spouses. Some instances of poaching were themselves designed as charivari, as when the inhabitants of seven villages in Nottinghamshire, including a bailiff, parson, and schoolmaster, joined in a raucous and festive massacre of George Wastnes's deer, in retaliation for his allowing deer to damage tenants' crops and the manorial woods.[41] The form of charivari that has most in common with Falstaff's punishment, indeed, enacts symbolically a hunt. In the Devon stag-hunt, a surrogate figure disguised as a deer is chased through the streets and symbolically but realistically "killed" on the victim's doorstep.[42]

Falstaff's disguise, however, makes of him a complex and equivocal symbol.[43] On the one hand, he is associated with the destructive energies of nature. He wears the costume of Herne the hunter, an image that links him not only to his own activities as a poacher of deer and women but to the folklore of Windsor, which tells of a hunter who hanged himself on Windsor oak and haunts the place, and to the legendary figure of Herne, the savage Celtic god who leads wild hunts at night. The antlers he wears also link him to Actaeon, who, as John M. Steadman has shown, had become a conventional emblem of lust.[44] Falstaff himself glories in the role of the stag, whose sexual prowess he emulates: "For me, I am here a Windsor stag, and the fattest, I think, i' th' forest. Send me a cool rut-time, Jove, or who can blame me to piss my tallow?" (5.5.12–15).

Although the symbolism of Falstaff's disguise centers upon destructive sexuality, the horns he wears are deeply equivocal, for they represent not only sexual potency but, in relation to the cuckold, emasculation. The horns are thus paradoxically a symbol of sexual power and weakness, just as Falstaff is both a potential cuckold-maker and a surrogate for the potential cuckold, Ford. In one disguise, then, Falstaff plays the role of both male victimizer and male victim. By making Falstaff so obviously a surrogate for Ford, Shakespeare calls attention to the ways in which the victims of the charivari, even if guilty of breaching social norms themselves, may well be scapegoats for social tensions that lie outside their control.

When measured against reports of charivaris, the treatment of

Falstaff is relatively benign. Nonetheless, he is burnt with tapers, pinched by "fairies," made the butt of derisive laughter, and exposed as a fool before the entire community. It is difficult to imagine a stage representation of the event that would not create sympathy for Falstaff, especially since the action mimics the form of the hunt, with horns sounding off-stage, the antlered Falstaff hurling himself face-down on the ground, and the "fairies" encircling, pinching, and burning him with tapers. In that sense the central image of the punishment is the ritual killing of the hart or stag, an image that Shakespeare always treats with pathos, most notably in the death of Caesar in *Julius Caesar*. Having begun the play as an "ill-killer" of deer, Falstaff ends it as a deer himself, the poacher brought down by another extra-legal "sport." The pathos is tinged with irony, however. Falstaff's mock-death parodies that of the heroic Talbot in *1 Henry VI*, who rallies his encircled troops to act like "English deer . . . in blood, / Not rascal-like, to fall down with a pinch" (4.2.48–49). Although he sees himself as a Windsor stag in blood, Falstaff falls down even before he is pinched.

Of the two possible ways to end this charivari against Falstaff – expulsion from the community or reintegration – Shakespeare chose the latter. In keeping with the realistic tone of the play, however, and the nature of his comic victim, Shakespeare provides no gestures towards conversion on Falstaff's part and no feast as a ritual of social communion, merely a "posset" by a "country fire" (5.5.171, 242). Although nonplussed by his experience, which includes a barrage of taunts from the wives, husbands, and Evans, Falstaff remains resilient, able to vent his frustration by assaults upon the Welsh preacher, whose linguistic infelicities make him a safe and enduring object of attack: "Have I lived to stand at the taunt of one that makes fritters of English? This is enough to be the decay of lust and late-walking through the realm" (5.5.142–45). Falstaff draws strength not only from the thrusts of his wit but from the image of virility that his escapade has somewhat unexpectedly thrust upon him. The discovery of the marriage of Anne and Fenton, moreover, affords him a final laugh at his tormentors. His quip at their expense precipitates not only Mistress Page's neighborly invitation to "laugh this sport o'er by a country fire" (5.5.242) but the comical swaggering of Master Ford, whose final taunt ends the play: "Sir John, / To Master [Brook] you yet shall hold your word, / For he to-night shall lie with Mistress Ford" (5.5.244–45). The allusion to honor, and the sardonic use of the title, "Sir John," highlight the degree to which Falstaff continues to threaten both Ford's sexual and social status.

Charivaris, the civic authorities feared, could have unforeseen consequences. In the midst of the well-designed plot against Falstaff, Anne
Page and Fenton elope, to the dismay not only of Slender and Caius,
both of whom discover that they have married boys, but of Mistress Ford
and her husband, whose separate and competing plots have been foiled.
In this victory of Anne and Fenton over the older generation,
Shakespeare further complicates the motif of the charivari with the conventions of comedy. As we have seen, Fenton and Falstaff are in a curious
way mirror images. At the end of the play, however, their fates diverge
sharply. While the town joins together to punish the threat of rampant
sexuality ironically represented by the aging Falstaff, another illicit
suitor, who "capers," "dances," and "has eyes of youth" (3.2.67), is
secretly marrying Anne Page. At the end of the play both Falstaff and
Fenton stand before the community as social rebels, but Falstaff stands
alone and humiliated, while Fenton stands with Anne, his equal in rebellion, and triumphant. By admitting his poaching at the very beginning
of the play, Falstaff evades punishment; by admitting his marriage at the
end, Fenton gets a reward. Whereas Falstaff's degraded version of court
life threatens the community of Windsor, Fenton's, equally and more
permanently rebellious, renews it. Although Anne's rebellion against the
marriage market goes no farther than a husband of her choice, this in
itself is a significant social gesture, and one that goes beyond the more
domesticated rebelliousness of Mistress Ford and Mistress Page.

To pursue this vein, however, and to draw political, social, or economic conclusions from the ending of *The Merry Wives*, is to enforce a
closure that the play itself resists. Critics who take such a tack generally
see the play as socially conservative, and its conclusion as a celebration
of Windsor's ability to resolve conflict without significant social
change.[45] One could mount a progressive, if not radical, challenge to
this apparent consensus by accentuating the recognitions of the protagonists, the residual power of the wives, and the infusion of new values
into the community by the elopement of Anne and Fenton. Either view,
however, risks oversimplifying the complexity of the social vision that
makes the play most distinctive. Although it is the protagonist of the play,
the community of Windsor is finally neither celebrated nor attacked,
merely embodied with comic realism – a realism that cuts to the paradoxical quick of town life in a way that is difficult to generalize in political terms. If the play tests the popular custom of the charivari against
the festive expectations of comic form, it also tests the capacity of
comedy to resolve the social tensions that give rise to such customs.

The comic irresolution of the play's final scene is appropriately embodied in the figure of Mistress Quickly, whose actions throughout the play travesty the notion of "good neighborhood."[46] She is the go-between, the peace-maker, whose indiscriminate good will serves Caius, Shallow, Fenton, and Falstaff. Her motives are obscure, especially to herself. Busybody, trickster, bawd, prude, she is as happy fostering illicit marriages as she is furthering the punishment of Falstaff for lechery. Although her achievements are uncertain at best – Fenton and Anne prosper through their own device, and Falstaff is foiled through the devices of Mistress Page and Mistress Ford – her energy and resiliency make her irrepressible. As the Fairy Queen, she achieves a comic apotheosis, ensuring through her fairy power the virtue of Windsor Castle and the Order of the Garter and bringing Falstaff to "trial-fire" (5.5.84) for his lechery. She and her fairies disappear, ironically, before the outcome of her own plots to marry Caius, Shallow, and Fenton is known. Any social order that depends upon such a presiding spirit is unlikely to be stable.

The play ends more or less as it began, with a "posset" and "a country fire" taking the place of a dinner of "venison pasty" as the backdrop for attempted social reconciliation. One thing has changed, permanently: Anne Page and Fenton are married. The charivari against Falstaff, moreover, and the revelations of the young lovers have provoked a social catharsis, leaving the citizens, for the moment, at least, emotionally purged and enlightened. Essentially, however, the town remains as it was. Whether outsiders like Falstaff and Fenton will eventually be assimilated, or even uneasily "contained," as are Caius and Evans, is left uncertain; perhaps they will both return to a more courtly environment. Whether Ford's obsession has been broken is also unclear, especially in view of his final taunt against Falstaff. Shallow's complaints against Falstaff are unresolved, as are the Host's against Caius and Evans, whose revenge has left him without his horses. The future roles of the wives, too, are left somewhat in doubt: Ford's concluding taunt not only mocks Falstaff but asserts his sexual mastery over his wife, and even Page invites Falstaff to "laugh at my wife" (5.5.172) in anticipation of his success in the wedding plot. The play's vision of social life, while comic, is distinctly unsentimental, suggesting the resiliency of the community and its capacity to absorb conflict, but suggesting as well that conflict is only absorbed, never resolved, and that social tensions are paradoxically both creative and destructive of social order. The town of Windsor will survive, but any peace it achieves will be restless and unstable, for "good neighborhood"

●

carries the motto that "friends is the sword" and is nourished by "ill-killed" deer, whether poached from Shallow or pinched by fairies in Windsor Forest.

The Merry Wives is not a play about hunting. But the town of Windsor, as befits a royal seat located near both the Little and Great Parks of Windsor Castle and the immense tract of Windsor Forest, is touched at many levels by the culture of the hunt. Its gentry give venison to cement relationships, threaten poachers with the Star Chamber, go birding, imagine themselves with buck's antlers when anxious about cuckoldry, and devise charivari that make full use of the ritual of the hunt. When confronted with an alien poacher, the citizens unite, transforming the hunter into the hunted. And the mark of their unity, ironically, the charivari, is itself poaching in another guise – a kind of rough justice, a symbolic assault by means of which the offender is harassed and humiliated for social deviance. In its representation of Falstaff as the "stag" of Windsor Forest, the comedy of *The Merry Wives* captures something of the rough humor of poaching, in which society both destroys and renews itself in the "killing" of rascals.

CHAPTER SIX

Pastoral hunting in As You Like It

If, as Paul Alpers suggests, the central and defining fiction of pastoral is the representation of "herdsmen and their lives," then it is not surprising that hunting appears infrequently in the genre.[1] The life of the shepherd, as conceived by pastoral poets, centers upon the tending of flocks, and both the activities and values associated with that life contrast sharply with those associated with the life of a hunter. The hunter spends time in vigorous action, the shepherd in patient watching, whiling away the hours in contemplation, discussion, and song. The hunter lives to kill animals; the shepherd, although required to slaughter lambs on occasion, lives to nurture and protect them. The hunter enters wild nature and assaults it; the shepherd lives within domesticated nature, intertwining his own life with that of the animals he tends.

Despite these sharp contrasts in the two modes of life, Virgil allows at least a little space for hunting in his *Eclogues*. In the Second Eclogue, for example, the shepherd Corydon sings of his frustrated love for the absent Alexis. In his song he yearningly envisions the simple but joyful life they could lead together: "If only you could bring yourself to live with me under some humble roof in the homely countryside, to shoot the stag, and drive a herd of goats with a green marshmallow switch!" The implied equivalency between shooting the stag and driving a herd of goats suggests that for Virgil, as for Corydon, the two activities coexist as part of the natural rhythm of a shepherd's life, a rhythm that includes both the nurturing and killing of animals. In Eclogue I, Tityrus speaks of taking "new-weaned lambs" to the marketplace; in Eclogue II, as we have seen, Corydon imagines killing stags for food. In Eclogue I, Tityrus promises to "stain" an altar with "the blood of a young lamb" to honor the man who has made his leisure possible; in Eclogue VII, Corydon promises a boar's head and stag's antlers to the goddess Diana.[2] Although the bloodshed of both hunting and shepherding is kept discreetly in the background, both activities are treated as part of the natural routine of a shepherd's life. For Virgil, the life of a shepherd includes occasional hunting.

In Spenser's *Shepheardes Calender*, in contrast, hunting is scarcely mentioned. The sole reference to an actual hunt occurs in the December Eclogue, when Colin briefly recalls chasing "the trembling Pricket" and hunting "the hartlesse hare" as a youth (27–28), an image that recalls the conventional association between hunting, especially poaching, with adolescence. With this single exception, Spenser's shepherds live without hunting. The rural landscape, although filled with flowers, brambles, hills, dales, grazing lambs, greenwood, and even an occasional wolf or fox, provides no sustenance from deer or hare. Even the goddess Cynthia, invoked in the April Eclogue to celebrate Queen Elizabeth, does not appear as a huntress. Aside from Colin's momentary nostalgia for his youthful escapades, the only image of the hunt that appears in the work captures not the normal rhythms of the shepherd's life in nature but the searing and destructive heat of July. In this astrological image, the sun of the July Eclogue "hunts" the "rampant Lyon" with "Dogge of noysome breath, / Whose balefull barking bringes in hast / pyne, plagues, and dreery death" (21–24).[3] In Virgilian pastoral, hunting is a minor but unexceptional part of the shepherd's life; in Spenserian pastoral, hunting is virtually irrelevant, appearing only as a fleeting memory or as an astrological sign.

The reason for this difference probably lies in the social and legal position of hunting in the two cultures. Virgil could assume that a shepherd might hunt deer or boar, but Spenser certainly could not. For the Romans, both the forests and the wild beasts were *res nullius* (belonging to no one); even wild animals that inhabited private land were not legally the property of the owner.[4] For Elizabethans, shepherds could not hunt, at least legally, for hunting was restricted by the Game Laws to those of wealth and social standing. Hence any allusion in pastoral to hunting hare or deer might imply that characters intended to represent natural innocence were actually poachers. To associate hunting with shepherds as Virgil does, moreover, would be to characterize it as a necessity rather than a sport. If they hunt at all, shepherds hunt for sustenance. The dominant Elizabethan and Jacobean attitudes towards the hunt, however, express contempt for what Elyot calls hunting "for the pot."[5] Hunting is admirable not because it sustains human life but because it provides a "manly" recreation suitable for future warriors.

The social tensions that divide hunting from the pastoral in the Elizabethan period are evident in Sidney's treatment of hunting in the

Arcadia. In the *Old Arcadia*, hunting does not appear in the narrative at all, and appears in the eclogues only twice, both times in relation to Philisides, who is not a shepherd, but an exile, and, in addition, Sidney's own persona. The first allusion to hunting is insignificant: the old shepherd, Geron, advises Philisides to "hunt fearefull beastes" as a means of overcoming love-melancholy. The second is both significant and strongly negative: Philisides himself sings a beast fable, "On Ister Bank," that depicts hunting as the final stage in the development of man's tyranny over the beasts. The climactic moment of that process occurs when man turns from killing for food to killing for sport: "At length for glutton taste he did them kill: / At last for sport their sillie lives did spill."[6]

When Sidney revised the *Old Arcadia*, transforming it from pastoral romance into a kind of epic, he brought hunting within the narrative as an aristocratic sport. In a brief episode, Kalander, as a noble host, takes Pyrocles and Musidorus stag-hunting. Kalander recalls his youthful joys as a hunter, and Sidney describes the chase from beginning to end. Although Sidney treats the death of the stag in a way that hints at his own critical attitude towards the hunt – the "poor beast" weeps to show "the unkindness he took of man's cruelty" – he also praises Kalander for his compassion in despatching the deer quickly.[7] Nothing in the episode as a whole indicates that the hunt is unworthy of Kalander's hospitality or the participation of his young guests. For Sidney, then, attitudes towards the hunt are generically marked. In the pastoral *Arcadia*, hunting is either ignored or condemned outright as a mark of tyranny; in the heroic revisions, hunting is accepted as a lively, if slightly disturbing, aristocratic entertainment.

If treated as an aristocratic sport, the hunt itself may evoke traditional pastoral attitudes. In Drayton's *The Muses Elizium*, for example, Silvius, the forester, celebrates the life of the hunter for its reveling in the beauties of nature:

> I am the Prince of sports, the Forrest is my Fee,
> He's not upon the Earth for pleasure lives like me;
> The Morne no sooner puts her Rosye Mantle on,
> But from my quyet Lodge I instantly am gone,
> When the melodious Birds from every Bush and Bryer
> Of the wilde spacious Wasts, make a continuall quire . . .

The list of joys continues with flowered meadows, soft breezes, dryads, fairies, bubbling brooks, groves, and more.[8]

Even the hunting manuals occasionally strike the same note. In *The Master of Game*, Edward Duke of York asserts that "hunters live in this world more joyfully than any other men." When the hunter "riseth in the morning," he "sees a sweet and fair morn and clear weather and bright, and he heareth the song of the small birds, the which sing so sweetly with great melody and full of love." With the rising of the sun, "he shall see fresh dew upon the small twigs and grasses."[9] Such celebrations of nature are not restricted to the rising of the hunters; they appear as well in descriptions of the assembly, in which the hunters enjoy a woodland feast and review the plans for the pursuit. In the *Noble Arte of Venerie*, George Gascoigne even provides a poetic description of the assembly, which centers upon a contrast between its natural pleasures and the unhealthy artifice of the court. The setting is a "pleasant gladsome greene" with a stream nearby. The colors of the ground provide a tapestry, the aromas of the flowers, perfume. It is a place "where pleasure dwels at large, / Which Princes seeke in Pallaces, with payne and costly charge."[10]

The difficulty with this aristocratic "pastoralizing" of the hunt is that the joys of nature are incidental to the main business of the day, the pursuit and killing of deer. This fact produces some ironic incongruities. Immediately after describing the hunter's joy in the beauties of nature, for example, Edward Duke of York turns to joys of a rather less pastoral kind: "And when the hart be overcome and shall be at bay he [the hunter] shall have pleasure. And after, when the hart is spayed and dead, he undoeth him and maketh his curée and enquireth or rewardeth his hounds, and so he shall have great pleasure . . ."[11] Even in Gascoigne's poetic description of the assembly, the description of the beauties of the place yields to a fanciful battle for supremacy between the cooks and butlers, as if peace and harmony were inappropriate to the festive setting. The only hunting manual in the period that gestures toward the traditional pastoral experience is Gascoigne's French source, *La Venerie de Jaques Du Fouilloux*. Du Fouilloux includes a long poem, "L'Adolescence de Jacques du Fouilloux," in which the hero, an adolescent hunter and a persona for the author himself, encounters while hunting a group of shepherdesses tending their flocks. He falls in love with one of them, courts her, and wins her, and the two experience the joys of love in an idyllic pastoral setting. In *La Venerie*, then, the hunt provides a setting for a pastoral experience, but the two modes of activity remain completely separate. For Gascoigne, the inclusion of an amorous pastoral episode merely degrades the hunt. He refuses to translate "L'Adolescence de Jaques du Fouilloux" because these "unsemely verses . . . are more apt for lascivious mindes, than to be enterlaced amongst the noble termes of

Venerie."[12] The insistence upon the nobility of the terms of venery suggests that Gascoigne feared not merely the moral taint of lascivious love but the social taint of mixing shepherd lasses with aristocratic hunters.

The closest one comes in Elizabethan England to a pastoral version of the hunt is in the ballads, folk-customs, and plays associated with Robin Hood. The celebration of the greenwood that characterizes these materials evokes the joys of a simple, spartan life in the forest, a life made festive by an abundance of venison and communal merry-making. The ballad "A Gest of Robyn Hoode," for example, evokes the surge of relief that Robin feels after returning to Sherwood Forest after a stay in the court:

> Whan he came to grenë wode,
>   In a mery mornynge,
> There he herde the notës small
>   Of byrdës small
> Of byrdës mery syngynge.
>
> 'It is ferre gone,' sayd Robyn,
>   'That I was last here;
> Me lyste a lytell for to shote
>   At the donnë dere.'
>
> Robyn slewe a full grete harte;
>   His horne than gan he blow,
> That all the outlawes of that forest
>   That horne coud they knowe,
>
> And gadred them togyder,
>   In a lytell throwe.[13]

In this version of the greenwood, the pleasures of the merry morning and the small birds singing harmonize with the pleasure of shooting a deer, and the deer itself will provide the communal meal bringing Robin together once more with his merry band.

As versions of pastoral hunting, however, the Robin Hood stories were deeply implicated in social conflict. In his traditional form, Robin is a commoner and an outlaw, carrying out from his sanctuary in the forest attacks upon the rich, the church, and the civil authorities. Hunting in this context is poaching; in the ballad just quoted, Robin actually serves the King one of his own deer. Hence the Robin Hood stories may celebrate life in the greenwood and the delights of pursuing the stag, but they do so in a way that subverts the aristocratic culture of the hunt. Some of the popularity of the Robin Hood stories, one suspects, derives not merely from his protests against social injustice but from his direct assault on the King's control of the forests and the deer. It is therefore not surprising that in the Elizabethan and Jacobean periods bands of poachers, including both gentry and commoners, sometimes linked themselves to Robin Hood and his merry men.[14]

The gentrification of the Robin Hood materials that took place during the sixteenth century drained away their subversive potential. In Munday's play, *The Downfall of Robert Hood, Earle of Huntingdon*, for example, Robin is a nobleman (Robert, Earl of Huntingdon), forced into the forest by injustice; he takes the name of Robin Hood upon becoming an outlaw. His love, Matilda, becomes Maid Marian, and lives with him in the forest, scrupulously retaining her virginity until he is able to make her his lawful wife. The pleasures of the forest life are many. In one scene Robin sleeps on a green bank while Marian strews him with flowers. In another, Robin evokes a pastoral contrast between the greenwood and the court: "*Marian,* thou seest though courtly pleasures want, / Yet country sport, in Sherewodde is not scant." Instead of instrumental music, they have the songs of "winged quiristers." Instead of rich tapestries, they have "natures best imbrothery." Instead of mirrors, they have the "Christall brooke." "What in wealth we want," Robin concludes, "we have in flowers, / And what wee loose in halles, we finde in bowers."[15] The play as a whole concludes with Robin welcoming the King himself to his bower. Munday's elevation of Robin not only sentimentalizes the treatment of nature and love but transforms the social context of the hunt. No longer does it represent a commoner's assault against social privilege. The Earl has hunted deer before, presumably, and will do so again when returned to his rightful position; his pursuit of deer as an outlaw in Sherwood Forest merely converts an aristocratic sport into a temporary means of survival. His hunting thus represents only a superficial threat to aristocratic and royal privilege.

The relationship between hunting and the pastoral in the Elizabethan and Jacobean periods is thus fraught with literary and social tension. To treat the hunt within the traditional pastoral context is to threaten the traditional values that the shepherd's life represents, which center upon the nurturing, not the destruction of animals, and to threaten an aggressive radicalizing of the form by making law-abiding shepherds into poachers; as politically oriented studies of the pastoral tend to show, the form itself seems to have displaced or contained serious political and social subversion rather than provided a forum for it.[16] To step outside the pastoral, and to "pastoralize" the hunt itself is to introduce still other problems, among them the inevitable prominence of the kill and the subversive implications of the greenwood motif, as celebrated in the stories of Robin Hood. It is within this complicated literary and social context, it seems to me, that we can best understand the treatment of the hunt in *As You Like It*.

The genteel and "masculine" status of hunting is reflected in the play by a delicate separation between the worlds of hunters and shepherds and an implied hierarchy which advantages the former. Duke Senior and his men survive by hunting deer, and their activities and imaginations center on the forest itself. Duke Senior's first words concern the hunt, and Jaques first makes his presence felt in Amiens' description of him weeping over a wounded deer. The Duke and his men are dining in the forest when Orlando, who will later become one of the Duke's foresters, accosts them in search of food. Towards the end of the play, the Duke's men mark a successful hunt with festive song and merriment. The shepherds in the play, in contrast, whether "real" like Corin or "artificial" like Silvius and Phebe, exist in what Rosalind calls "the skirts of the forest" (3.2.336), an image that subtly feminizes the pastoral landscape. Rosalind and Celia buy a shepherd's cottage from Corin's landlord, and, with the exception of their meetings with Orlando, both the women and Touchstone spend their time among shepherds. Until the end of the play, the two social realms are kept separate for the most part, with only occasional exchanges between them.

The social superiority of the hunters' life is implied in Shakespeare's play in the fact that the hunters comprise an aristocratic elite, exiled temporarily in Arden, whereas the shepherds – even Silvius and Phebe – are common people and permanent residents. At the end of the play the hunters, sans Jaques, will return to the world of the court, their social status untouched by exile; they have not become shepherds but have merely exchanged one form of hunting for another. In exile they hunt out of necessity; in power they are privileged to hunt for sport. When they next enter Arden, they may do so to hunt not on foot but *par force*. Although Charles the wrestler likens the Duke's way of life to that of "the old Robin Hood of England" (1.1.116), the carnivalesque potential in that gesture is not fulfilled. Duke Senior does not attack passers-by, does not make incursions into the corrupt society to protect the innocent or fight against injustice, does not engage in sporting contests of prowess, does not, in short, live anything like the traditional life of Robin Hood or do anything to recover his power. Even his hunting, as we shall see, is never connected to poaching. Like many other banished rulers, Duke Senior continues to live in exile the life of a Duke, only in straitened circumstances. He recovers his dukedom only because, in keeping with the play's title, his usurping brother experiences a miraculous conversion.

Rosalind's banishment, not to mention her love for Orlando, forces upon her a rather more adventuresome change in role. She is on the one hand associated with the hunt. The leader of the band of hunters, Duke Senior, is her father, and she enters Arden with a boar spear in her hand (1.3.118). But she is also associated with the shepherd's life, and her social position is thereby compromised in a way that her father's is not. She buys a shepherd's cottage and becomes the confidante of a lovelorn shepherd and the object of a love-sick shepherdess's affections. When she resumes her proper social position at the end of the play, she rejoins the world of hunters. A figure who mediates between both the hunters' and the shepherds' worlds, she quite literally brings them together at the end of the play.

Since Rosalind plays the role of a shepherd in her mock courting with Orlando, their meetings bring together imaginatively the roles of shepherd and forester. Although Orlando seems never to hunt, the role of forester fits well with the "Herculean" qualities that enable him to defeat Charles the wrestler and to kill the lioness that threatens Oliver. Although temporarily besotted with a love-melancholy that Rosalind promises to cure, Orlando is thus associated with "manliness." By disguising Rosalind as a shepherd, Shakespeare creates a delicately gendered difference between the two lovers, even when Rosalind too is "male." She would have no excuse at all for fainting at the sight of Orlando's blood if she were disguised as a hunter. The subversive effects of Rosalind's masculine disguise are thus qualified somewhat not only by its temporary nature but by the specific masculine role she assumes. Although transgressive in her male disguise, Rosalind does not take on the more boisterous and aggressively masculine attributes of a figure like Maid Marian, who often joins Robin Hood in the hunt.

Shakespeare's treatment of the Robin Hood materials is thus by no means socially subversive. Duke Senior is associated with the aristocratic and courtly world of the hunt, and dissociated from the socially compromising world of shepherds or, worse, of genuine outlaws. The disguised Rosalind certainly conveys subversive energies, but even her boar spear yields to a shepherd's staff when she settles in Arden. In bringing together the worlds of hunters and shepherds, Shakespeare subtly perpetuates the divisions within Tudor and Stuart society that kept the two worlds apart. The introduction of hunting into the pastoral world works not so much to make possible a critical perspective on the court but to bring true courtly and country values into harmony with each other.

A similar evasion of social conflict occurs in Shakespeare's treatment of setting. *As You Like It* takes place, for the most part, in the Forest of Arden. Forest settings of virtually any kind would have carried a high political charge for contemporary audiences. Throughout the Elizabethan and Jacobean periods, the forests of England were sites of social, economic, and political conflict. Both the forests themselves and the purlieus around them were often inhabited by poor people, vagabonds and squatters driven off farms elsewhere by the conversion of agricultural land to sheep-grazing. Some were drawn to the forests by the development of mining, which created employment not only in the industry itself but in the cutting of wood to fuel it. The illegal enclosure of forest lands by neighboring landowners, moreover, aroused opposition from those who eked out a living by gathering wood, working in mines, or raising sheep, hogs, or cattle, activities which by tradition provided certain rights of access to forest land. The conflicts that resulted from these competing demands often pitted local commoners against gentry, aristocracy, and monarchy, sometimes in violent protest. To write plays sympathetic to "outlaws" dwelling in the forests of Elizabethan England was thus to enter highly political terrain.[17]

Critics of *As You Like It* commonly assert that Shakespeare's Arden is not a realistic locale but a landscape of the mind. The incongruous flora and fauna of the place lend support to this notion. Arden contains, among other things, an oak tree, a palm tree, olive trees, a lioness, and a green and gilded snake. At some level Shakespeare surely wants to disrupt expectations of social realism and to create a world in which the imagination is given free rein. This said, it must be admitted that the geographical oddities are few and far between, and that the dominant impression of Arden in the play is familiarly local and English, recognizable as a version of Shakespeare's own Warwickshire.[18] The Ardennes of Lodge's *Rosalynde*, in contrast, a place with fountains, groves like arbors, amphitheaters, and lemon trees, bears no resemblance to the actual Ardennes of France.[19]

If Shakespeare intends Arden as a landscape of the imagination, he is curiously insistent about identifying the locale. The word "forest," for example, appears twenty-three times in *As You Like It*, but no more than three times in any other play. The forest is specifically identified as

"Arden," moreover, four times – most provocatively in the exchange between Rosalind and Touchstone upon their first arrival:

> *Ros.* Well, this is the forest of Arden.
> *Touch.* Ay, now am I in Arden, the more fool I.   (2.4.15–16)

The metatheatrical gesture in these lines towards the empty stage as a hopelessly inadequate representation of a forest plays on the notion that Arden, with its palm trees and lionesses, exists essentially in the mind's eye, as the spatial equivalent, perhaps, to Touchstone's pregnant phrase, "much virtue in If" (5.4.103). For some members of Shakespeare's audience, however, this gesture towards the imagination would have taken on yet another dimension. The empty stage is from this point of view a perfect representation of the forest of Arden because in Elizabethan times it was a "Utopia" in the original sense, a "No-place." In the literal and legal meaning of the term, a "forest" of Arden did not exist. In John Manwood's authoritative definition, "A forest is a certaine Territorie of wooddy grounds and fruitfull pastures, priviledged for wild beasts and foules of Forest, Chase and Warren, to rest and abide in, in the safe protection of the King, for his princely delight and pleasure . . ."[20] The so-called forest of Arden had not been a true forest – a royal hunting preserve, subject to the special laws of the forest – from before the time of Henry II.[21] The play is thus rather insistently set in a place that does not exist.

Nor was the area of Arden even heavily wooded in Shakespeare's day. By the early sixteenth century the vast forests of early medieval Arden had yielded to mixed woodland and pasture. The economy was mainly pastoral. In his *Itineraries*, John Leland describes the region as "muche enclosyd, plentifull of gres [grass], but no great plenty of corne."[22] Throughout the century, increased enclosure, the destruction of timber, the conversion of woodland to arable or pasture land, population growth in wooded areas, the development of dairy farming, and the introduction of mining all diminished the woodland available. In 1586 William Camden could still describe the region as mainly woodland, but he noted that it was "not without pastures, corn fields and iron mines."[23] These physical changes in the landscape were both the cause and effect of social and economic transformation. The "rising prices" and "rapid economic change" characteristic of the sixteenth century, notes Ann Hughes, had a "social cost in the Arden, bringing increasing polarisation within local society and the creation of a landless proletariat."[24] The woodlands that remained were under the control of local landowners.

Had Duke Senior and his men been exiled in this region they would probably have lived and hunted in a local nobleman's park.

In his study of five contiguous parishes in Arden during the period 1570 to 1674, V. Skipp provides a picture of the region distinctly at odds with Shakespeare's. Throughout the sixteenth century, the region consisted of about one-third arable land and two-thirds woodland-pasture, so Shakespeare's depiction of a pastoral environment is at least generally accurate. Skipp estimates, however, that as early as 1550 only 9 per cent of the region was common wasteland, with the rest in the possession of private landowners. Skipp's Arden, moreover, increased in population by the astonishing figure of 38 per cent from about 1570 to 1600, many of the immigrants being landless cottagers who eked out a living while the landed husbandmen profited. Shakespeare's Arden, in contrast, is virtually unoccupied and consists of deep forest with the cottages of shepherds on the outskirts. In Shakespeare's Arden life on the land is simple but good. In Skipp's, the food shortages produced mainly by the tremendous influx of population resulted in severe dearth in the 1590s and a genuine crisis, with a sharp drop in population, in the years 1613 to 1619.[25] Against this backdrop of actual life in Arden during the period, Shakespeare's title takes on added meaning.

Shakespeare does allude briefly to this general social context, first in Corin's remarks about his cruel master, a man "of churlish disposition," who "little reaks to find the way to heaven / By doing deeds of hospitality" (2.4.80–82),and secondly, in Orlando's words as he accosts the Duke and his men at their "banquet." When Orlando discovers that he has encountered "civilized" men, he identifies himself as being "inland bred" and therefore knowing "some nurture" (2.7.96–97). He asks pardon for his rudeness by saying, "I thought that all things had been savage here, / And therefore put I on the countenance / Of stern command'ment" (2.7.107–09). What Orlando expects is the rough behavior of the occupants of the squatters' communities that grew up within Elizabethan forests, the kind of people John Norden encountered in the survey he published in 1607. The inhabitants of these scattered hamlets, Norden observes, are "'given to little or no kind of labour, living very hardly with oaten bread, sour whey, and goats' milk, dwelling far from any church or chapel, and are as ignorant of God or of any civil course of life as the very savages amongst the infidels.'"[26] Although Shakespeare evokes a brief image of such a life, the allusion simply marks the absence of the harsh reality it represents. Nor does Corin's master make an appearance.

The economic and social tensions generated by the conflicting forces we have observed created considerable social unrest. Much of the unrest was agricultural, but the forces at work affected both farming and wooded regions. Many counties, among them Warwickshire and Oxfordshire, experienced extensive enclosures during the 1580s and 1590s. In Arden, according to Alasdair Hawkyard, "repeated and sustained efforts by improving landlords to enclose . . . woodland during the Tudor period were bitterly resented by their tenants, and as a result the Forest of Arden was one of the most disaffected agrarian regions in the Midlands, intermittent commissions of enquiry ordered by the Crown providing neither solution nor more than temporary alleviation."[27] In neighboring Oxfordshire, an anti-enclosure rebellion was planned in 1596, for which the chief conspirators were executed for treason. The leader, a carpenter named Bartholomew Steere, who professed devotion to the cause of the common people, had visions of Utopian reform that find no expression in Shakespeare's Arden. Steere is reported to have declared that the world "'would never be well untill some of the gentlemen were knockt downe," that the commoners of Spain had "lyved merrily there" since rising and killing all the gentlemen, and that he cared "not for work, for we shall have a merrier world shortly . . . I will work one day and play the other."[28] Poverty, unrest, rebellion, desperate visions of Cockaigne – these images from Arden and nearby Oxfordshire represent a mode of existence far removed from that of Shakespeare's play.

If Shakespeare's version of Arden is a kind of "no-place," it also exists in a kind of "no-time." Although Charles the Wrestler alludes to the Golden Age, the presence of hunting alone in the play excludes that possibility. More likely is the allusion to Robin Hood and his merry band, for medieval Arden was at least heavily wooded. The mix of woodland and pasture, however, suggests that the Arden of the play is vaguely contemporary, although somehow immune to the social pressures that were transforming its character. In a sense rather broader than Orlando intends, "there's no clock in the forest" (3.2.301). The image of the forest that remains – of babbling brooks, ancient oaks, deer, pastures, and shepherd's cottages – seems an evocation of contemporary Arden as we might like it. In *Poly-Olbion*, published about fifteen years after Shakespeare's play, Michael Drayton treats Arden with nostalgia as a symbol of an England that is being destroyed. Drayton locates Warwickshire in the heart of England, Arden in the heart of Warwickshire, and his muse in the heart of Arden. Although he celebrates the beauty of Arden and its variety of wildlife – he describes the songs of the birds and the majestic tragedy of a stag hunt – Drayton's evocation of the place is suffused with nostalgia. The magnificent forests in which the goddess Diana used to hunt are no longer. "For, when the world found out the fitnesse of my soyle," the Forest herself complains,

> The gripple wretch began immediatly to spoyle
> My tall and goodly woods, and did my grounds inclose:
> By which, in little time my bounds I came to lose.[29]

Drayton responds to Arden with a nostalgia localized in space and in the dim recesses of time, a time before enclosure. The contrast between past and present implies a political judgment. Shakespeare, in contrast, remains more subtly evasive, evoking an Arden that seems to have only one definitive attribute: an exclusion of contemporary social reality. The shadowy allusions to that reality serve as reminders of an absence. Shakespeare's most striking gesture towards social realism is an absentee landlord, Corin's cruel master, who never appears in the play.[30]

Despite his political evasiveness, Shakespeare not only includes but foregrounds the problem of the hunt. The image of the sobbing deer that introduces audiences to the forest of Arden in act 2 scene 1 has proved to be one of the most resonant of the play. The image itself is by no means original with Shakespeare. It appears in the hunting manuals, lending a note of pathos to descriptions of the death of the deer, and has a long poetic and iconographic history. Almost always, the image is strongly anthropomorphic, the actual experience of the deer serving as a mere vehicle for human grief. The *locus classicus* for such treatment is Book 4 of Virgil's *Aeneid*, in which the unhappy Dido, left by Aeneas, rages throughout the town – in Surrey's translation, "like the striken hinde . . . / Amid whose side the mortall arrow stickes." Surrey represents himself by means of the same image in another poem that describes his unhappiness in love:

> Then as the striken dere withdrawes him selfe alone,
> So do I seke some secrete place where I may make my mone.
>   There do my flowing eyes shew forth my melting hart,
> So that the stremes of those two welles right well declare my smart.[31]

Shakespeare's treatment of this convention is so unlike that of his predecessors and contemporaries, and so much more complicated, that it repays considerable attention. In bringing the hunt into the pastoral, Shakespeare achieves a complex and paradoxical effect: on the one hand, he "pastoralizes" hunting based on necessity by suggesting its essential harmony with nature; on the other, however, he reveals the tragic undercurrents within that accommodation. In his treatment of the hunt, as in his treatment of other aspects of the pastoral experience, Shakespeare achieves a measure of pastoral optimism by subjecting that very optimism to skeptical scrutiny. An appreciation of the nature and significance of this achievement requires a rather painstaking analysis of the play's language of the hunt.

The first mention of hunting occurs, as we have seen, in act 2 scene 1, when Duke Senior and the First Lord discuss the reactions of Jaques to a sobbing deer. Although the episode focuses upon Jaques, it is important to recognize that the fact of animal suffering is presented to us through three different characters: Duke Senior, who introduces the topic of the hunt; the First Lord, who develops it by describing the suffering of the deer itself; and, finally and indirectly, Jaques, whose moralizings are reported by the First Lord. Although the three perspectives shade into one another, they are nonetheless distinct. Each represents a different way of coming to terms with the brutal fact that their lives in undeserved exile depend upon the violent death of wild animals.

Duke Senior, who finds "Sermons in stones, and good in every thing" (2.1.17), and whose benign stoicism seems at the moral center of the play, introduces the episode by suggesting a hunt to his companions: "Come, shall we go and kill us venison?" His very next words, however, express reservations:

> And yet it irks me the poor dappled fools,
> Being native burghers of this desert city,
> Should in their own confines with forked heads
> Have their round haunches gor'd.   (2.1.21–25)

This is emphatically a speech of sympathy for the suffering of the deer the Duke is about to hunt, and as such it strikes a note absent completely from Shakespeare's source, Lodge's *Rosalynde*. Duke Senior is saddened that the deer whose forest he occupies should be wounded and killed by the "forked heads" of their arrows.

The complex metaphoric structure of the Duke's lines, however, radically complicates this simple and powerful response. Although its burden is sympathy for the animal, the speech as a whole does not turn the Duke into a vegetarian or prevent the hunt. Instead, it represents a series of strategies, at once rhetorical and psychological, to repress the disturbing consequences of the Duke's twinge of conscience. The Duke begins with the antiseptic desire to "kill" some "venison," ignoring the fact that between killing and venison must come violent death and butchering; to kill a steak is to evade the moral consequences of one's action. The use of the word "venison" is even more evasive in Elizabethan English than it would be in modern English because the word was used of any wild meat and was only gradually coming to be restricted to the meat of deer. To kill venison is not to enact the Duke's own philosophy, in which the cold and winter's wind "feelingly persuade me what I am" (2.1.11).

The Duke's instinctive evasiveness, however, lasts only a moment; he is immediately stricken by the thought of the "poor dappled fools" he is about to pursue. The word "fool" is a term of endearment used often with great emotional power by Shakespeare, as in King Lear's "My poor fool is dead"; the image of deer as fools, as we shall see, recurs throughout the play. In Duke Senior's speech, the image not only humanizes the deer but associates it with the innocence and closeness to God of the "natural" fool, whose motley is hinted at in the dappling of the deer's coat. To pursue the implications of this metaphor, however, would end the hunt altogether: one does not kill helpless and innocent fools. In the space of two lines, it seems, the Duke has veered from a total indifference to the brutalities of the hunt to a sentimentality that threatens hunting itself.

In the next line, however, the Duke re-conceives the image. This time the deer become not fools but "native burghers," a term that subtly works against the incipient sentimentality of "fools," evoking as it does a hint of social condescension: the social, intellectual and emotional relationship between Dukes and fools, who might be their daily companions and critics, is potentially closer than that between Dukes and burghers, who are their distant subjects. To say, moreover, that either burghers or deer live in "their own confines" is to ignore the social realities of the burghers' political dependency upon Dukes and the deers' dependency, in Elizabethan England, upon protected reserves. The metaphoric identification of the deer in their forest with burghers in their native "city" creates a complicated series of overlapping images in the final lines of the Duke's speech. The most obvious way to read the lines, one promoted by most editors, is to interpret the "forked heads" as forked arrows (which were common in the period) and to imagine deer wounded in the haunches – a kind of wounding, as A. Stuart Daley suggests, that would almost inevitably cause a very painful death.[37] Since haunches were never a target in hunting, however, and since they are among the more desirable cuts of venison, it is possible that the Duke is jumping ahead again to the meal itself, envisaging his court using forks to feed themselves on venison. A third possibility, unlikely in the context but recommended by a number of critics, turns the violence against the deer themselves, their antlers goring the haunches of their opponents, as in the rutting season. A final possibility, difficult to justify in relation to the Duke's psychology but linguistically persuasive, is to see in the image a sly and familiar sexual innuendo, whereby the "burghers" become cuckolds, their forked heads produced by the "goring" of their wives' haunches.

The tendency of most editors and critics, of course, is to reduce this proliferation of meanings. At some level, however, they are all evoked by the language of the passage itself. If allowed full scope, the complex resonances that result enable us to appreciate how a sensitive moral being like the Duke can evade the moral consequences of the hunt. If suffering deer cannot be dismissed as venison or sentimentalized as "fools," they can be sympathetically distanced as "burghers." By the alchemy of the metaphor of "forked heads," moreover, Shakespeare implicates both society and nature in a cycle of violence that, although it might "irk" our sensitive spirits, seems inevitable. Deer are gored by hunters' arrows, yet that goring produces sustenance for humans, who use forks to gore them yet again. Burghers' wives are gored by illicit lovers, providing forked heads for the husbands, yet illicit sex is a potentially creative act and an inevitable fact of life. The deer themselves gore each other in the rutting season, an action that joins together the creativity of sex with violent aggression and potential death. To see ourselves feelingly what we are, it seems, is to locate ourselves within these paradoxes – paradoxes that join human with animal life. Although "irked" by animal suffering, in short, the Duke accepts it, as he does the other facts of life that persuade him feelingly what he is.

Jaques, as we shall see, does not accept animal suffering. Before his moralizing is reported, however, the First Lord responds in his own way to Duke Senior's words, painting a picture of a scene that he himself observed. As Jaques was lying beside a brook and underneath an ancient oak, the Lord says,

> a poor sequest'red stag,
> That from the hunter's aim had ta'en a hurt,
> Did come to languish; and indeed, my lord,
> The wretched animal heav'd forth such groans
> That their discharge did stretch his leathern coat
> Almost to bursting, and the big round tears

Cours'd one another down his innocent nose
In piteous chase; and thus the hairy fool,
Much marked of the melancholy Jaques,
Stood on th'extremest verge of the swift brook,
Augmenting it with tears.   (2.1.33–43)

This is the closest one comes in the play, and perhaps in Shakespeare as a whole, to the shock of empathy evoked by Gascoigne's poetic adoption of the voice of a hart in the *Noble Arte of Venerie* or Durer's drawing of the mournful head of a stag, pierced by an arrow.[33] As Linda Woodbridge observes, the passage contains the "seeds of an animal rights argument."[34] The image achieves its emotional effect in part through dramatic shifts in focus. We see first the "hunter's aim" and the generalized languishing it causes. Then we move imaginatively inside the suffering, experiencing it through the minutely observed details of the loud groans, the bursting coat, and the tears coursing down the nose. Finally, we stand back to view the scene as a whole – Jaques' melancholy attention, the swift brook, the weeping deer – as an all-encompassing image of grief.

As in the case of Duke Senior's lines, however, the images of the First Lord evoke a more complex and less potentially sentimental experience than pure empathy for a suffering animal. In some respects, indeed, the First Lord's language works against the elemental experience of an animal's pain at the hands of a hunter, encouraging us to perceive such suffering as an inevitable fact of life, not as the simple result of a violent assault. The First Lord's view of the stag, for example, is anthropomorphic. The stag is first "sequest'red," a word that may mean "removed from office" as well as "cut off from congenial surroundings." Like a man, it wears a "leathern coat" and is likened to a "hairy fool," one that, like Touchstone, is "Much marked of the melancholy Jaques" (2.1.41). The suffering deer thus becomes in certain respects not only a suffering human but, as was the case in Duke Senior's lines, an endearingly innocent human, a fool, and perhaps even a fool wearing an animal skin, as was the custom in folk-dances and folk-plays of the period. The human responsible for the actual grief of the deer, in contrast, is virtually invisible and harmless. It is not that he has wounded the deer, but that the stag has "ta'en a hurt" from "the hunter's aim." The stag itself is therefore complicit in its own wounding, which is occasioned not by the hunter but by his disembodied "aim." Underlying the First Lord's sympathy, then, is an apparent evasion both of human violence and of animal suffering: the "aim" causes wounding, and the pain that results can only be imagined in human terms, as the innocent suffering of a "fool." The sympathy experienced for a deer wounded by an attacking hunter is paradoxically evoked as sympathy for innocent humanity.

The First Lord's sentiments ultimately imply not only the innocence of humanity but the guilt of nature. In "taking" the hunter's aim, as we have seen, the stag itself seems complicit in its own undoing. The deer is "sequest'red," moreover, as the lines later attributed to Jaques make clear, not because it has been singled out by the hunter but because it has been abandoned by the other deer. The grief of the deer itself, moreover, implies a world of inner violence, with groans "discharge[d]" and even tears themselves as hunters: they "Cours'd one another down his innocent nose / In piteous chase." Having pursued each other as dogs pursue a hare, the tears flow into a brook which is not only "swift" but, as depicted earlier by the First Lord, violent: it "brawls along this wood" (32). If we look for the cause of this stag's suffering in human action, then, we look in vain. Its suffering arouses genuine human grief – the First Lord is no hypocrite – but implicit in that grief is a view that paradoxically juxtaposes images of human innocence with natural violence.

The natural violence, however, is also paradoxically human violence. The images we have examined, after all, are human images – of sequestering, of discharging, of coursing, of brawling. So although these images locate violence within the world of nature, they confuse that world with the world of man. In the same way one can say that the image of the fool, especially that of a "hairy" fool, is a liminal image, one that occupies the ambiguous borderland between the human and the animal.

One may be tempted simply to call such thinking anthropomorphic, and to find in it a "colonizing" and assimilationist mentality. In part, this is true. Despite the instinctive sympathy of Duke Senior and the First Lord for the animals that they kill, the language of both shows that they can only feel animal suffering when it is imagined as human suffering, a response that might be said to deny the reality and authenticity of animal experience. The guilt of human violence against innocent nature, moreover, is unconsciously evaded by minimizing human agency and imputing violence to nature itself – in its "brawling" brooks, its "coursing" tears, its "forked heads." The evasion circles back upon itself, however, for the very violence attributed to nature is only capable of articulation in human terms – only humans brawl, course, or make forked implements. The anthropomorphism, in short, has a double effect: on the one hand, it assimilates animal experience into human experience, but on the other, it assimilates human into animal experience. If deer are like humans, humans are also like deer. Both have a capacity for violence, and both have a capacity for suffering.

The central imaginative link between the two realms is provided by the image of the "natural" fool, an image that conveys a mysterious innocence existing at the boundary between man and nature. With the image of the "natural," the tendency to humanize nature becomes indistinguishable from the tendency to naturalize humanity. The figure of the fool defies categorization, calling in question the conventional distinctions between human and animal that neutralize the violence of the hunt. In their focus on the figure of the fool, both passages suggest a new way of thinking about the human relationship with nature, one that, in its paradoxical inclusion of innocence and violence, resists the extremes of indifference or sentimentality. The implied attitude seems similar to that expressed by the modern philosopher, Ortega y Gasset, who observes that "*every good hunter is uneasy in the depths of his conscience when faced with the death he is about to inflict on the enchanting animal*" because "man has never really known exactly what an animal is."[35] The language of Duke Senior and the First Lord captures this indeterminacy.

Whereas the responses of Duke Senior and the First Lord implicitly sanction the very activity that "irks" them by creating a vision of the entire social and natural world as participating in violence, that of Jaques (44–66) is altogether more disturbing. At first, this seems not to be the case. The "moralizings" that the First Lord reports are entirely conventional and emblematic, each image of the deer representing a particular human vice or folly. The deer makes its "testament" as "worldlings" do, bequeathing its tears to a stream that needs no more water. The treatment of a deer's death as a funeral is itself conventional, as P. J. Frankis has shown, citing examples from Drayton and Sidney and the medieval lyric *The testament of the bucke*.[36] The deer's loneliness enacts a familiar proverb: "'thus misery doth part / The flux of company.'" And the sight of a well-fed and "careless herd" passing by indifferently provokes thoughts of those "fat and greasy citizens" who ignore a "poor and broken bankrupt." In one sense, these anthropomorphic images can be said to work reciprocally, as do those of Duke Senior and the First Lord: if the deer are imbued with human motivations and behavior, such as the indifference to suffering of "fat and greasy citizens," then these same citizens are acting like deer. Jaques' emphasis on folly and vice might be said to complement and extend the emphasis on physical violence provided by Duke Senior and the First Lord. The interwining of society and nature implied in each of these visions is captured in the

First Lord's comment that Jaques' moralizings "pierceth through / The body of [the] country, city, court, / Yea, and of this our life." For Jaques, it seems, there are no distinctions: folly, vice, and misery unite the entire body of our life.

Despite its tendency to complement and extend the vision of Duke Senior and the First Lord, Jaques' moralizing is as a whole more paradoxical and disturbing than the compassion of the other two. Although the implications of his emblems are potentially reciprocal, as we have seen, characterizing both the human and the natural world in the same terms, their conventional quality distracts attention from the animal itself. In contrast to Duke Senior and the First Lord, whose images rely on precise observation of nature and a mysterious and vital likeness between animal and human experience, Jaques seems not to see the animals at all but to look through them at the underlying folly and misery of human experience. The deer serve merely as emblems for human behavior. His moralizing does not break out of the tradition of the beast fables or the emblem books. Such detachment is itself implicated in violence by the language of the First Lord, who notes that "most invectively" Jaques "pierceth through . . . the body . . . of this our life." Like the forked arrows of the hunters, Jaques' invectives work to destroy their targets.

One may see in Jaques' conventional moralizing, then, tendencies noted by many critics in general interpretations of his character – tendencies towards conventional posturing, indifference to genuine suffering, and a reductive and aggressive cynicism. His melancholy moralizing can thus be dismissed as mere self-indulgence. The First Lord's description of this melancholy scene does not end with Jaques' moralizings, however, but with his final assault on humanity and a final image of his behavior. The climax of the episode comes with Jaques' attack on the tyranny of their own life in the wilderness. In the report of the First Lord, Jaques swears

> that we
> Are mere usurpers, tyrants, and what's worse,
> To fright the animals and to kill them up
> In their assign'd and native dwelling-place. (60–63)

If Jaques' conventional emblems distract from animal suffering, focusing instead upon the follies of human life in society, this final statement confronts us not only with the reality of animal suffering but with the fact of human responsibility. The evasiveness in the responses of Duke

Senior and the First Lord is here replaced by an unequivocal moral judgment.

This judgment, moreover, is joined with feeling. Our final image of Jaques is of him "weeping and commenting / Upon the sobbing deer" (65–66). Although there is much in Jaques' behavior throughout the play that suggests self-indulgent posturing, in his contemplation of the stag, as the First Lord makes clear, Jaques believes himself to be alone. Overall, then, Jaques' response to the sobbing deer seems contradictory. On the one hand his conventional moralizing seems to reflect at best an indifference to animal suffering, as such, or at worst a cynicism that unites the whole world, humans and animals, in folly, vice, and misery; empathy for the animal is precluded in either case. On the other hand, his unequivocal attack on human tyranny and his own weeping upon the sobbing deer suggest a deep emotional identification with the animal, based upon a split between human evil and animal innocence.

With this final and disturbing image of the stag as innocent victim of human tyranny, the episode comes to an end. The implications of Jaques' moralizing and weeping are left suspended. Instead of pursuing the questions raised by Jaques' emotional attack on human tyranny, the Duke merely dismisses them as amusing symptoms of his melancholy. "I love to cope him in these sullen fits," he says, "For then he's full of matter" (68–69). The Duke is thus distracted from his earlier desire to "go and kill us venison," but only because he prefers the amusement of the melancholy Jaques. He is utterly unmoved by the scene that the First Lord has painted before him. The violence of the hunt will continue to "irk" him, presumably, but not enough to abandon hunting or to think deeply about its human significance. Duke Senior, like Jaques, has a fondness for moralizing. Unlike Jaques, however, he not only finds "tongues in trees, books in the running brooks," and "sermons in stones," but "good in every thing" (16–17).

Amiens admires Duke Senior's optimism. "Happy is your Grace," he says, "That can translate the stubbornness of fortune / Into so quiet and so sweet a style" (18–20). The lines are richly evocative and might be taken as a comment on the action of the play itself – Shakespeare translating the misfortunes of his characters into the quiet and sweet style of a redemptive pastoral. The peculiar dangers of this kind of translation are evasiveness and sentimentality, just as those of Jaques' translations are cynicism and self-indulgence. If in writing *As You Like It* Shakespeare set about translating the stubbornness of fortune into the quiet and sweet style of redemptive pastoral, he deliberately complicated his task

not by including villains – they are easily converted – but by including
Jaques and Touchstone, who resist conversion and are neither quiet nor
sweet. Neither character appears in Shakespeare's source, Lodge's
Rosalynde. He also complicated his vision of pastoral, as we have seen in
the image of the sobbing deer, not only by including the hunt but by
highlighting through Jaques its violation of the bond between humans
and nature. The resonance of Jaques' image of tyranny never quite goes
away – Shakespeare admits the untranslatable – but for the most part
Shakespeare's treatment of the hunt follows that of Duke Senior
himself. He translates the violence of the hunt into a quiet and sweet
style of pastoral. Shakespeare's treatment of hunting throughout the
play can be seen as a complex series of negotiations to overcome indirectly the irreconcilable conflict that Jaques depicts between human
morality and the hunt. In one sense, we may say that these constitute a
series of evasions, strategies that render the culpable innocuous. If they
are evasions, however, they are knowing evasions, for they are prompted
by Shakespeare's own decision to thrust the issue of the hunt into the
limelight. Neither Jaques nor an anti-hunting perspective exists in his
source, Lodge's *Rosalynde.* These evasions characterize not only
Shakespeare's treatment of the elemental violence of the hunt itself but
of the controversies surrounding the hunt in the period.

Perhaps the most obvious way in which Shakespeare counteracts
Jaques' conviction of human tyranny is by representing the Duke's
hunting as a necessity, forced upon him and his men by their exile in
Arden. Despite the Duke's rather suspicious zest – "Come, shall we go
and kill us venison?" – he and his men kill not for pleasure but to live.
And yet it still "irks" them. In the dominant hunting culture in the
period, of course, hunting "for the pot" was treated with contempt.
Hunting was a recreation, a sport, to be justified for its promotion of
warlike virtues. Its aristocratic and noble character, indeed, could only
be justified if it were divorced from any contact with mercenary or
domestic gain. From the perspective of the royal and aristocratic sport
of hunting, Jaques' critique is difficult to answer, and the humanist tradition of opposition to aristocratic hunting as leading to war and tyranny
depended upon that difficulty. From the perspective of simple human
survival, however, Jaques' anti-hunting sentiments seem merely silly and
Duke Senior's hunting easily defensible, with or without the moral
qualms that continue to "irk" him. Whether Duke Senior will resume
hunting for pleasure once restored to his dukedom is a question
Shakespeare leaves unanswered.

For Elizabethans sensitive to the controversies surrounding hunting, Shakespeare's portrait of aristocrats hunting for necessity would have had a special impact. His allusions to hunting throughout the play, indeed, seem calculated to remind his audience of the conventions of aristocratic hunting by overturning them. As Daley has shown, for example, the Duke does not engage in aristocratic *par force* hunting, associated with the recreational and "military" hunt, but in stalking with the bow and arrow, a humbler kind of hunting, necessary in exile.[37]

The same ironic inversion of hunting conventions underlies Shakespeare's representation of the Duke's "banquet." In Lodge, this is an opulent affair. The banished King, Gerismond, "that day in honour of his Birth made a Feast to all his bolde yeomen, and frolickt it with store of wine and venison, sitting all at a long table under the shadowe of lymon trees."[38] In Shakespeare the proximity of the "banquet" to the discussion of the hunt links it to the customary "assembly" held at the beginning of a hunt, celebrated in hunting manuals such as Gascoigne's *Noble Arte of Venerie* and in tapestries such as *Les Chasses de Maximilien*. The feasting at such assemblies, as depicted in these works, was astonishingly opulent and required the immense logistical support necessary to bring tables, viands, cooking implements, and wines into a forest glade. The depiction in the *Arte of Venerie* of Queen Elizabeth attending such a picnic captures the ambiance of such events (fig. 2). Although such affairs may seem "pastoral" in design, they connote less a harmony between civilization and nature than an invasion of nature by civilization. In *As You Like It*, in contrast, the word "banquet" is ironically intended, and the simple repast of fruit stands in opposition to the elaborate picnics conventionally associated with the culture of the hunt. The contrasting significance of the two kinds of banquet is also apparent in their social function. The traditional assembly joins the hunters together to select their prey and to plan the method of pursuit. For Orlando, however, the Duke's "banquet" is a means of nurturing Adam, and his language calls attention to the difference between such banqueting and the traditional hunters' feast:

> Then but forbear your food a little while,
> Whiles, like a doe, I go to find my fawn,
> And give it food.   (2.7.127–29)

This same tendency to soften or "pastoralize" the customs of the contemporary hunt characterizes the brief depiction of a return from the hunt in act 4 scene 2. The procession that takes place in this scene is

based upon the actual practice of the hunt, which traditionally culminated in a ceremonial return to the home or lodge of the chief lord. The
leader of the procession would have been the lord of the hunt or a surrogate. The head of the deer would have been carried at the front of the
procession, the deer's carcass, in sections, carried behind. Although
there is no conclusive evidence to show that songs were sung, the practice is highly likely, and one can assume as well an atmosphere of festive
merriment; whether the chief hunter would have worn the skin of the
deer, as is done in this case and in many of the folk customs, is uncertain. The arrival home was announced by the sound of the hunters'
horns, and the day was ended, traditionally, with a feast. Jaques' characterization of the event as a triumphal procession seems to capture its
spirit. In Munday's *The Death of Robert, Earl of Huntington,* Friar Tuck
carries "*a Stag's head, dauncing,*" as part of a procession returning from a
hunt in which a stag wearing Caesar's collar has been killed.[39] Although
both Shakespeare and Munday allude to actual hunting behavior, both
episodes may also incorporate closely related folk customs, such as the
Horn Dance of Abbots Bromley, or the festive procession led by a buck's
head to honor the feast of St. Paul at St. Paul's Cathedral.[40]

   In transposing the return from the hunt to the stage in act 4 scene 2,
Shakespeare retains its processional and festive nature, yet evokes
complex overtones that almost certainly go beyond the original custom.
For one thing, the event is directed by Jaques, who has not participated
in the hunt and who has been described earlier, as we have seen, weeping
over the fate of a wounded deer. Jaques' comments, therefore, although
not opposed to the celebration, place it in an ironical framework. The
irony is extended by an apparent allusion to Elyot's treatment of hunting
in *The Governor.* Elyot recommends only the kind of hunting that comes
closest to imitating war. In this spirit, he urges upon hunters a ceremony
imitating that of the Roman conquerors. Those who "show most prowess
and activity" in such warlike hunting, he says, should be given "a garland
or some other like token . . . in sign of victory, and with a joyful manner
. . . be brought in the presence of him that is chief in the company; there
to receive condign praise for their good endeavour."[41] Jaques' directions
mock this attitude. He instructs the hunters that the forester who killed
the deer be presented "to the Duke like a Roman conqueror," with the
"deer's horns [set] upon his head, for a branch of victory." The conventional view of the hunt as a training ground for the skills of war is thus
undermined by Jaques in the bathetic contrast between Roman conqueror and killer of deer. The inescapable association of the deer's horns

with those of the cuckold, moreover, convert this image of conquest into an image of sexual impotence. Jaques' final subversive gesture is to dismiss the hunters' song as mere noise: "Sing it. 'Tis no matter how it be in tune, so it make noise enough" (8–9). The celebration of the hunt is thus framed by a sardonic debunking of the whole endeavor. Although he does not weep over the body of this deer, Jaques remains deeply alienated from the idea of the hunt and contemptuous of the hunters themselves. For audiences, Jaques' framing comments are difficult to reconcile, emotionally or intellectually, with the festive spectacle that ensues.

The representation of the hunters' song depends upon an existing custom, as is made clear by Jaques' request, "Have you no song, forester, for this purpose?" No songs of this type survive, however, and extensive work by editors and musicologists has failed to identify a source for the one performed on stage. The song may well be Shakespeare's invention. In the First Folio, it reads as follows:

> What shall he have that kild the Deare?
> His Leather skin, and hornes to weare:
> Then sing him home, the rest shall beare this burthen;
> Take thou no scorne to weare the horne,
> It was a crest ere thou wast borne,
> Thy fathers father wore it,
> And thy father bore it,
> The horne, the horne, the lusty horne,
> Is not a thing to laugh to scorne. (4.2)

I quote the version in the First Folio because there has been considerable debate among editors about the clause "the rest shall beare this burthen" in the third line. Some take it as part of the song, an implied stage direction indicating that, while the victorious hunter wears the horns, the rest will carry the burden of the slaughtered deer. Others, including the Riverside editors, detach it from the text of the song, treating it as a stage direction requiring the rest of the hunters to sing the ensuing "burden," or refrain. Whichever meaning one chooses, the total context of the scene suggests a single action: the victorious hunter, wearing the horns of the deer, and even its skin, leads a triumphant and merry procession of hunters singing a traditional song.

Although the song centers upon the inevitable joke on cuckoldry, the performance as a whole works against Jaques' corrosive debunkery of the hunt in several ways. In the song's version of the triumph, the victorious hunter is given not only the horns to wear but the "leather skin."

Such a costume works against Jaques' mockery of the "Roman conqueror," evoking instead the popular festivities, such as the charivari or
horn dance, in which the figure of the deer can represent not only cuckoldry but virility. This image of the deer, indeed, might be said to reconcile Jaques' conflicting images of contempt, the Roman conqueror and
the cuckold, bringing the two paradoxically together in a festive assertion of man's union with nature: in his identification with the deer, the
hero is at once conqueror and victim, cuckolder and cuckold. The horns
of the cuckold themselves enact this paradox, of course, for they represent both the phallic power of the seducer and the impotency of the
deceived husband. The allusion to the "leather skin," moreover, suggests
the material necessity that underlies this particular hunt; the skin worn
in dance as a costume will be eventually worn as clothing, perhaps even
as the "leathern coat" alluded to earlier in the First Lord's image of the
wounded stag:

> The wretched animal heav'd forth such groans
> That their discharge did stretch his leathern coat
> Almost to bursting . . .   (2.1.36–38)

The costume of the skin, moreover, relates the episode to such folk traditions as the Plough Plays, in which the Fool figure was often a leader
and wore a coat of skins. As we have already seen, in the earlier description of the wounded deer this "leathern coat" links the deer to the figure
of the fool. The image of the leader cavorting as a deer thus implies not
only the triumph of the hunt but a sympathetic identification with the
animal itself. Both hunter and deer are "fools" in "leathern coats."

Similarly, the equivocal directions, "the rest shall beare this burthen,"
can be seen as a gesture of reconciliation. If read as printed in the First
Folio, as part of the song rather than as a separable stage direction, the
clause can fulfill both of the functions that editors usually treat as mutu-
ally exclusive alternatives. The opening singer, the Second Lord, can
direct the message to the rest of the Lords, who both carry the carcass
of the deer and join in the refrain that follows. In such a case, the physical burden – and perhaps even the moral burden – imposed upon the
hunters by the kill is relieved by the singing of the song, as is customary
in work-songs. Music, then, becomes another reconciler of conflict – the
reality of the deer's death and the burden it imposes translated into
harmony. In this sense the ritual progression of the hunt achieves the
same effect as the ritual progression of the couples at the end of the play:

in both cases tensions and discords are momentarily suspended in the reconciling medium of music.

The words of the "burden" are themselves devoted to reconciliation and acceptance of one's place in nature. The hunter who wears the deer's horn, along with men in general, is offered the consolation that it is "no scorn to wear the horn," a sentiment that answers Jaques' earlier contempt. The horn is an emblem of the male condition, a "crest" that is passed down through each patriarchal generation and must be accepted and worn with grace; it makes men a part of nature. Even in these lines, which focus so insistently on the lamentable fact of cuckoldry, the alternative symbolism of the horn emerges at the end: "the lusty horn / Is not a thing to laugh to scorn." The "crest" is thus an ambiguous one, representing both impotency and sexual virility. It is worn by the best hunter of the day.

As already mentioned, it is difficult to relate this scene precisely to the custom of the procession homeward because the social evidence is so scanty. Examined in its own terms, the dramatic episode might be said to continue the evasive strategies outlined earlier, and to continue to place them in irreconcilable conflict with Jaques' anti-hunting perspective. The entire thrust of the song and procession, one might say, is to harmonize man and nature, to "pastoralize" the hunt, even at a moment which celebrates the bloody triumph of man over nature. The "burden" of guilt is lifted in song. The carcass of the deer is in full view, its skin and horns worn as trophies of victory. Yet these trophies are not for mere display but for use; in the context of exile, they fulfill essential human needs. And they are worn not merely as emblems of victory but as acknowledgments of a union between man and animal – one that encompasses both sexual power and sexual powerlessness. The entire thrust of the song and procession, in short, is to convert what for Jaques is discordant "noise" into harmony. Although the Duke is not present at the song, he is the ultimate goal of the procession, and its spirit seems to capture his own response to the natural elements, as forces that "'feelingly persuade me what I am'" (2.1.11). In this "pastoralizing" of the hunt, it seems to me, Shakespeare avoids sentimentality but continuously evades, even while representing it, the radical threat embodied in Jaques' alternative vision. This is not hunting without blood, but it is nonetheless hunting "as you like it."

In representing life as we like it, then, Shakespeare slides away from the social and political conflict that the inclusion of hunting within the pastoral invited. The only way in which he engages in the contemporary controversies surrounding hunting and the forests is through the Duke's discomfort with and Jaques' emotional protest against the killing of deer. Including hunting within the pastoral is most tellingly difficult for Shakespeare because it evokes the essential problem in the human relationship with nature, a problem evaded by conventional pastoral, that of violent and murderous conflict. The dilemma for the pastoral represented by this conflict is left unresolved, insofar as Jaques remains unchanged and unsocialized at the end of the play, determined merely to seek wisdom of an old hermit who lives in Arden rather than to return to the court.

Although Shakespeare allows Jaques' pessimistic vision of the tyranny of man over nature to haunt the play, he nonetheless, through Duke Senior, the First Lord, the song of the huntsmen, and, implicitly, through Orlando, presents a vision of the hunt that ties human and animal life together in bonds that include both violence and kindness. As we have seen, this unsentimental but tolerant and accepting vision of reciprocity is expressed in a number of different ways in the representation of the hunt. Perhaps its most significant emblem, however, is that of Orlando's heroic action both in putting aside his desire for vengeance against his wicked brother, Oliver, and in killing the lioness that threatens his brother's life (4.3.104–32). As Richard Knowles has shown, the episode almost certainly alludes to Hercules's killing of the Nemean lion, and in this sense celebrates the heroism of Orlando.[42] The contrast between the Nemean lion, however, and the beast that threatens Oliver, is striking: the one is large, violently aggressive, and male; the other is a "sucked and hungry lioness" (126), with "udders all drawn dry" (114) – a female that needs food because it has been suckling its cubs. In this small episode Shakespeare achieves a complex and unsentimental awareness of the animal and human worlds as implicated in both nurturing and killing.

Both Orlando and the lioness are engaged in a protective and nurturing action – the one to save the life of his brother, the other to save the life of its cubs. Yet for both creatures this benign and "kindly" purpose requires killing. Orlando, we might say, saves his brother through exalted reason, whereas the animal tries to feed its young through mere instinct. But the two actions are balanced in such a way that distinguishing them becomes difficult. Even Oliver, who has been saved from the lioness, refers not to its murderous instinct but to the "royal disposition" that leads it to "prey on nothing that doth seem as dead" (117–18). We might apply to the episode Montaigne's challenge to human arrogance in the

Apology for Raymond Sebond: "there is no likely-hood, we should imagine, that beastes doe the very same things by a naturall inclination, and forced genuitie, which we doe of our owne free-wil and industrie. Of the very same effects we must conclude alike faculties; and by the richest effects infer the noblest faculties, and consequently acknowledge, that the same discourse and way, wee hold in working, the very same, or per-happes some other better, doe beasts hold."[43] Even the "green and gilded snake" of this scene suggests, in its union of natural and courtly symbols, a commingling of human and natural life that includes on both sides beauty and danger.

The breaking down of boundaries between human and animal life implied in Shakespeare's language of the hunt throughout *As You Like It* may derive in part from Shakespeare's continuing fascination with Ovid, whose descriptions of metamorphoses embody a materialist conception of the underlying unity of all of nature. The "recurring materialist theme of the *Metamorphoses*," as Robert Pogue Harrison observes, is the "preformal kinship of all creation, which enables human beings to be transformed into animals, trees, flowers, and other forest phenomena."[44] Whether Shakespeare's vision is materialist in any but a superficial sense is of course doubtful. But the depth and intricacy of his metaphoric rela-tions between animals and humans in *As You Like It* can hardly be explained in merely linguistic terms. The metaphoric relations between human and animal in Shakespeare are also metamorphic. A deer is like a man in wearing a leathern coat, and a man is like a deer in wearing one as well, and in folk festivals a man may become a deer by wearing the deer's leathern coat, which is no more than a skin. Even Jaques' opposition to hunting has an Ovidean precedent, for in Book 15 of the *Metamorphoses* Pythagoras inveighs at length against the killing and eating of animals.

Although Shakespeare shies away from the political and social conflict potentially embodied in the hunt, he thus engages directly the debate about man's relation to nature as it figured in conceptions of the hunt. He uses the image of the hunt to challenge the sentimental idealism that often characterizes conventional pastoral and the greenworld motif. He uses it as well to challenge implicitly the notion of hunting for sport. More subtly and ambivalently, he uses it to underline, through Jaques' sentimental extremism, the moral dilemma posed by the human depen-dence upon animal food. Although the play as a whole implies an accep-tance of man's role as a killer, it does so, as we have seen, by implying a mutuality in the relationship between man and nature. In so doing,

Shakespeare breaks down the boundaries erected between human and animal life by the conventional Christianity of his day, which easily justified animal suffering and death, even in sport, on the ground that the Bible gives humans lordship over the animals, and that God provides only humans with immortal souls. Shakespeare's blurring of these boundaries carries to an extreme tendencies implicit in the metaphoric linkage of animal and human life that runs throughout the Western tradition. Although Shakespeare does not give the deer a literal voice, as does Gascoigne in the *Arte of Venerie*, his metaphors imply a community among humans and animals rarely to be found in conventional Elizabethan Christianity.

This new attitude towards animal suffering bears a remarkable affinity to that expressed by Montaigne in the essay "Of Cruelty." "As for me," Montaigne remarks, "I could never so much as endure, without remorce and griefe, to see a poore, silly, and innocent beast pursued and killed, which is harmeles and voide of defence, and of whom we receive no offence at all." The example he uses to illustrate his distress is, as in Shakespeare, a weeping deer – a stag that, exhausted from the chase, "findes his strength to faile-him," and, "having no other remedie left him, doth yeelde and bequeath himself unto us that pursue him, with teares suing to us for mercie." When he considers "the neere resemblance betweene us and beastes," he says, "truely I abate much of our presumption, and am easily removed from that imaginary Soveraigntie, that some give and ascribe unto us above all other creatures." "*Unto men we owe Justice,*" he concludes, "*and to all other creatures, that are capable of it, grace and benignitie.* There is a kinde of enter-changeable commerce, and mutuall bond betweene them and us."[45]

In its depiction of hunting, *As You Like It* may be called a politically evasive play, subversive only in the offhand dismissiveness of its title, which suggests that the playwright offers us the evasions we enjoy, knowing full well that real forests offer other visions. In contrast, however, it may be called an ecologically progressive play, one that by introducing the hunt into the pastoral world implicitly criticizes hunting for sport, and accepts hunting for necessity only if it involves a reverence for life and recognition of all the bonds that tie animals and humans together. The complex metaphoric relationships between humans and animals that characterize Shakespeare's treatment of the hunt throughout the play provide an experiential grounding for Montaigne's belief in "a kinde of enter-changeable commerce, and mutuall bond betweene them and us." Although progressive in its own time, this belief would be undermined in the late seventeenth century by Cartesian rationalism, which denied not only reason to animals but feelings and sensations.[46]

In his treatment of what might be called the ecology of pastoral hunting, Shakespeare develops a hard-edged or unsentimental vision of the hunt by creating images of harmony between the human and natural world that implicate both in the destructive and creative paradoxes of mortal experience. Such a vision of the hunt carries with it an implicit social critique. In *As You Like It*, pastoral hunting implies not only opposition to the culture of hunting for sport but, as in Montaigne, the need for a new attitude of sympathy and respect for wild nature. In Jaques' uncompromising extremism, furthermore, Shakespeare provides a haunting reminder that even such a benign and progressive attitude as Montaigne's cannot disguise the fundamental and always disturbing fact that humans kill in order to live. By challenging the traditional culture of the hunt and the attitude towards nature that sustained it, Shakespeare achieves a measure of social disturbance even while offering a vision of the world as we like it.

CHAPTER SEVEN

Political hunting: Prospero and James I

In act 4 scene 1 of *The Tempest* Prospero celebrates the betrothal of
Ferdinand and Miranda with "some vanity" of his "art" (41), a masque
presided over by Juno, the goddess of marriage, and Ceres, the goddess
of the harvest. In the middle of the performance, however, he suddenly
remembers the threat posed by Caliban, Stephano, and Trinculo, who
are at this moment on their way to assassinate him and make themselves
lords of the island. He abruptly breaks off the masque and, deeply troubled, tries to reassure Ferdinand and Miranda, who wonder at his altered
state of mind. He then directs Ariel to trap the conspirators by tempting
them with "*glistering apparel*" (193.s.d.), a ruse that easily distracts
Stephano and Trinculo, much to Caliban's dismay. As they start to carry
away their loot, the three conspirators are set upon by spirits, who, urged
on by Prospero and Ariel, chase them away. The scene concludes at this
point, with Prospero assuring Ariel that their labors are nearly at an end
and that his promised freedom is imminent. At the beginning of the next
scene, prompted by Ariel's sympathy for the suffering of his enemies,
Prospero announces that he will turn away from vengeance, forgive his
enemies, and renounce his magical art.

   Prospero's chase of the conspirators is Shakespeare's final representation of the hunt:

   *A noise of hunters heard. Enter divers SPIRITS in shape of dogs and hounds, hunting
them about; Prospero and Ariel setting them on.*
Pros. Hey, Mountain, hey!
Ari. Silver! there it goes, Silver!
Pros. Fury, Fury! there, Tyrant, there! hark, hark!
   [*Caliban, Stephano, and Trinculo are driven out.*]
Go, charge my goblins that they grind their joints
With dry convulsions, shorten up their sinews
With aged cramps, and more pinch-spotted make them
Than pard or cat o'mountain.

Ari   Hark, they roar!
Pros. Let them be hunted soundly. At this hour
Lies at my mercy all mine enemies.   (4.1.254–63)

Prospero orders the attack, with Ariel as chief huntsman. The lesser spirits are dogs, each with a distinctive name. The *"noise of hunters"* presumably includes the sound of the horn, the barking of the dogs, and the hallowing of the hunters themselves. Although the fierce confusion of the hunt is evoked in sound, language, and action, its ultimate goal, the death of the hunted, is in this instance deflected. Prospero orders the conspirators to be "hunted soundly," a phrase that suggests thrashing more than killing. His directions, moreover, extend to physical torment but not to death. While this restriction insulates the audience somewhat from the full implications of the action, it can have no such effect on Caliban, Stephano, and Trinculo, who hear behind them as they run the terrifying sound of dogs, horns, and hunters.

The masque scene in which this hunt occurs has received much attention from critics, as have the other obviously allegorical episodes in the play, such as the opening storm, the appearance of the harpies, and the game of chess played by Ferdinand and Miranda. For the most part, however, the significance of the hunt itself has been ignored. Why, we might ask, at this climactic moment in the play, should Prospero's final attack upon his enemies take the symbolic form of a hunt? Potential answers to this question will lead us in many directions – into the dynamics of the play itself, into Shakespeare's previous representations of the hunt, into conventional humanist attitudes towards the hunt, and into the politics of the hunt in the court of James I. Exploration of each of these contexts should ultimately convince us that Prospero's hunting of the conspirators is as rich and complex a symbol as any other that the play provides.

The most startling feature of Prospero's response to the threat posed by Caliban and his cohorts is its extremity. As soon as he remembers their plot, Prospero becomes so deeply moved that Miranda herself remarks, "Never till this day / Saw I him touch'd with anger, so distemper'd" (4.1.144–45). The melancholy vision of the "revels" speech leaves him unconsoled, his "old brain troubled" (159). And as he attends to Caliban, he thinks bitterly of his slave's degenerate and degenerating nature:

> A devil, a born devil, on whose nature
> Nurture can never stick; on whom my pains,

> Humanely taken, all, all lost, quite lost;
> And as with age his body uglier grows,
> So his mind cankers.   (188–92)

Prospero's response to such hopelessness is not despair but violent revenge: "I will plague them all, / Even to roaring" (192–93). The hunt, then, is presented not as a methodical plan, a corrective punishment, but as a spontaneous invention, a symptom of inner rage.

The violence of Prospero's reaction to the threat represented by the conspirators cannot be explained or justified in relation to the seriousness of the threat itself. Prospero is a great magician; Caliban, Stephano, and Trinculo are mere playthings of his art. Given Prospero's power, the rebellion should be a mere nuisance. If we are to explain Prospero's rage, therefore, we must consider not who these figures are but what their action represents. They are potential assassins and usurpers, and their attempt to seize power is the fourth such attempt to which the play alludes. Before the play begins, two usurpations have taken place: in Milan, Antonio usurped Prospero's position as Duke, and on the island, Prospero usurped Caliban's rightful title, at least according to Caliban. As the play proceeds, Prospero himself tempts Antonio and Sebastian into another plot of usurpation against Alonzo. The action of the conspirators, then, is part of the play's continuing exploration of the quest for political power. In the light of what seems an endless cycle of attempted usurpations, Prospero's rage against Caliban and his cohorts suggests his still unsuppressed fury against Antonio, whose usurpation initiated the cycle. In this sense it is less Caliban who angers him than the reality of usurpation itself, an implication that seems present in Prospero's juxtaposition of his punishment of Caliban with that of his other enemies: "Let them be hunted soundly. At this hour / Lies at my mercy all mine enemies."

Prospero's rage, however, is more deeply self-directed than this analysis suggests. The masque episode, as has often been observed, recapitulates symbolically the original action that caused the loss of Prospero's dukedom. In Milan, having devoted himself to the liberal arts, and having grown careless of his political role, Prospero made himself vulnerable to usurpation. For this he blames himself. By dedicating himself to the "bettering" of his mind, he tells Miranda, he "awak'd" in his "false brother . . . an evil nature" (1.2.90–93). Now, thirteen years later, having withdrawn again from his political responsibilities into "some vanity" of his "art" (4.1.41), an idealistic celebration of the future of Miranda and Ferdinand, he jeopardizes both them and himself by neglecting the danger of assassination and usurpation. Prospero's anger, then, is the anger of disillusionment, not only with Caliban, and by extension Antonio, but with himself. The price of political power, it seems, is constant vigilance, which he finds it impossible to maintain. Although Prospero recovers himself in time to avert the danger, the play's conclusion is sufficiently realistic to suggest the ongoing nature of the problem.

Such a reading of the masque scene as a whole can be accommodated to many of the various discourses within which the play has been interpreted. Prospero's dangerous tendency to lose himself in a world of art, to project upon experience his own conceptions, and to respond with impatience or vengeful rage when the world does not answer to his desires – this dynamic may be articulated in the language of art, of theater, of magic, of politics, of colonialism, and of paternity, to mention only the more common interpretative contexts. The multivalency of the play's language, indeed, creates a layering of complementary discourses, not all of which can be sustained by even the most expansive critical or theatrical interpretation.

Central to this interpretative complexity, and to any interpretation of the hunt, is Caliban, the history of whose representations suggests both the inevitability and falsity of reducing the play's proliferation of meanings. The figure has been as much constrained by critics and directors as by Prospero. Both on stage and in criticism he has been seen as, among other things, a native American, a monster, an animal, a devil, and a projection of the instinctual drives of Prospero himself.[1] Each of the above images has a certain validity, responds to something within the text, yet if applied consistently oversimplifies the role. Many of the discourses within which Caliban is defined are complementary, but not all: he cannot be played as both a native American and an animal, for example, yet the language of the play alludes to both roles. By its very nature, critical or theatrical interpretation tends to dissolve the essential mystery of the character.

The play invites us to imagine Caliban not in a fixed role but as a being who resists categorization, who inhabits the liminal realm between the human and bestial, both within the mind and in the world at large. As a liminal creature, he remains forever beyond our grasp: we cannot know who or what he is. He is at once essential to human survival and dangerous. He is both a human product and an autonomous being. He is responsive to beauty yet brutish in his instincts and behavior. He is capable of language but incapable, it seems, of "civilization." To hunt Caliban, then, is to hunt that which is irredeemably "other," beyond even Prospero's self-interested imaginings. To hunt Caliban, however, is also to hunt Stephano and Trinculo, who are refreshingly familiar and simply human. Any interpretation of Prospero's hunting, therefore, must begin with the fact that, whatever the identity of Caliban, the hunting is directed towards human subjects. The blurring of categories introduced by the figure of Caliban extends the gesture into the wider context of varying kinds and degrees of bestiality. To hunt the conspirators, it seems, is to hunt not only men but certain elements in both human and external nature.

To see in Prospero's rage against the conspirators not only an immediate response to the threat that they represent but a reflection of his rage towards Antonio, towards himself, towards all that resists the fulfillment of his imaginative desires, does not explain the particular image of the hunt. Prospero's desires for retribution take different symbolic forms throughout the play: he creates elsewhere a tempest, for example, and a banquet that vanishes in an onslaught of harpies. Why does his rage against Caliban and his confederates take the particular symbolic form of a hunt?

One obvious place to look for an answer to this question is in Shakespeare's own mythology of the hunt, a mythology that had evolved over a lifetime in the theater. As we have seen throughout this study, Shakespeare routinely links hunting to violence against humans, especially the violence of war, and most of his allusions to hunting in this context focus on savage and vengeful fury. Richard of Gloucester's furious desire to "hunt" young Clifford during the battle of Towton is typical: "Nay, Warwick, single out some other chase, / For I myself will hunt this wolf to death" (*3 Henry VI.* 2.4.12–13). Richard's gesture, of course, is not the same as Prospero's. Richard merely invokes an expressive metaphor, for one thing, whereas Prospero literalizes the metaphor by imitating an actual hunt. The goal of "hunters" such as Richard, moreover, is straightforward and literal: they seek to kill the human that they have redefined as prey. Prospero's response to Caliban may be similarly violent and furious, but he stops short of killing, seeking only to torment his victim. In this sense, there are no literal or exact precedents in Shakespeare for Prospero's action. Nonetheless, his hunt participates in a linkage of hunting, anger, and violence that runs throughout the plays.

Shakespeare uses hunting imagery not only to express the perspective of the hunter but of the prey. Sometimes such imagery connotes the rape of injured innocence, as in the case of Lucrece, Lavinia, and Lady

Macduff and her children. In others, it simply evokes the pathos of the helpless victim, whether innocent of wrongdoing or guilty: Julius Caesar, Falstaff, and Talbot are all like bayed stags when surrounded by those who want to kill or punish them. Even the hunting of vermin can occasion a flash of sympathetic identification, as when Lear tells Cordelia that "He that parts us shall bring a brand from heaven, / And fire us hence like foxes" (5.3.22–23). In view of the frequency of such images in Shakespeare, it is remarkable that there are no counter-examples, no instances in which the hunt is used simply as a metaphor of righteous pursuit, without an undercurrent of sympathy for the hunted that compromises the notion of just punishment.

In its association of the hunter with rage and violent assault, then, and with the hunted as a sympathetic victim, the chase of the conspirators in *The Tempest* might be considered a culmination of Shakespeare's negative representations of the sport. Prospero's attack is partly justified, of course, since the conspirators seek to kill him, but his anger propels him beyond rational justice into the sphere of violent revenge. In this regard the names of his dogs take on a precise significance – the one is Fury, the other Tyrant. As a symptom of Prospero's potentially dangerous aspirations towards transcendent power, the hunting episode is comparable to the speech in which he renounces his magic, which, by virtue of its allusions to the witchcraft of Medea, hints at the diabolic potential within his magic. The significance of both dramatic moments is not to undermine the value of Prospero's magic or, in the case of the hunting episode, to legitimize Caliban's desire to kill Prospero, but to call attention to Prospero's own inner potential to do harm. His renunciation of his magic follows upon his renunciation of revenge, which in turn follows upon the furious hunt of the conspirators. Before he returns to Milan, Prospero not only renounces his magic but acknowledges, if grudgingly, a bond with Caliban: "this thing of darkness I / Acknowledge mine" (5.1.275–76).

Shakespeare's treatment of the hunt in *The Tempest* is not merely self-referential; as in the case of the many other allegorical episodes in the play, it carries a wealth of conventional meaning. As we have seen in previous chapters, certain strands in both Reformation and humanist thought provide powerful critiques of hunting. One of these critiques focuses on the tendency of hunting to fuel violent behavior, to turn the very hunters themselves, as Erasmus's Folly observes, into savage beasts.[2] Such fury is often politicized, linking hunting to tyranny. In his commentaries on the Book of Genesis, for example, Calvin couples the notions of bestiality and tyranny and associates both with the Old Testament figure of Nimrod, "a mighty hunter before the Lord" (Genesis.10.9).[3] Both Sidney – in Philiside's song, "Ister Bank" – and Agrippa attack hunting as the historical origin of tyranny.[4] For Agrippa, contemporary kings, princes, and even prelates "doo seeke daily, to have some thinge to conquere, and hunte," turning their destructive instincts against both defenseless animals and humans.[5]

Agrippa's diatribe seems particularly relevant to *The Tempest* because of his unusual concern with hunting as an attack upon nature itself. Most writers in the anti-hunting tradition focus on the negative effect that hunting has upon humans: either upon the commoners who are victimized by the practice or upon the hunters who are brutalized. For Agrippa, however, to hunt is not merely to persecute humans but to "exercise tyranny againste beastes." It is "a cruell Arte, and altogeather tragicall, whose pleasure is in deathe, and bloude . . ." Many hunters, he observes, "have runne into so greate madnesse, that they became enimies to nature."[6] Agrippa's advocacy of respect for nature, even bestial nature, provides a useful perspective on the role of Caliban and on the "rough magic" with which Prospero attempts to control nature.

At the end of his discourse on hunting, Agrippa recalls the condition of Eden, when humans and animals lived in tranquillity, disharmony beginning only with original sin: "And so, togeather with sinne, the anoyaunce, the persecution, and the flighte of livinge creatures entred in, and the Artes of Huntinge were devised."[7] This contrast between a brief age of innocence and a long and continuing history of hunting is also found in authors, like Ovid, who portray the degeneration of human history from the Golden to the Iron Age. Underlying both Agrippa's and Ovid's versions of the cruelty of the hunt is a notion of kinship between all living things, a kinship that has been violated historically in the falling away from a Golden Age or an Eden. A similar contrast between a peaceable kingdom and perpetual conflict also underlies the sudden shift in *The Tempest* away from the idealized vision of natural harmony represented by Iris, Ceres, and Juno to the fury of Prospero's hunt. It is as if we plunge in one moment from a golden to an iron age. And in the same moment we replace an image of Prospero as a benign and even godlike ruler with Prospero as a furious tyrant.

Given our inevitable anthropocentrism, the image of Prospero hunting the conspirators is particularly disturbing because it reduces humans to the status of animals. The anti-hunting literature we have been exploring, however, suggests that even if one interprets Caliban as other than human the image should also disturb. From this perspective the hunt evokes Prospero's destructive impatience with nature as it is, an impatience that characterizes his relationships throughout the play not only with Caliban but with Ariel, who also yearns for freedom. As a magician, Prospero aspires towards the absolute domination of nature, an impulse that becomes most clearly apparent in the speech in which he glories in his dangerous powers before renouncing them forever. At the end of the play this renunciation is accompanied by the freeing of Ariel into the air and, probably, the release of Caliban to the freedom of the island. When Prospero acknowledges Caliban as his own – "this thing of darkness I / Acknowledge mine" – he thus suggests a begrudging acceptance of that which he finds unregenerate in all nature, to which he himself is inevitably bound.

The association of hunting with cruelty is central to Montaigne's essay "Of Cruelty." Montaigne's views on the hunt are particularly significant in relation to *The Tempest* because two of his essays – "Of Cannibals," and "Of Cruelty" – are clearly echoed in the play. The former allusion, appearing in Gonzalo's naive attempt to imagine a golden age, has been much studied; the latter, however, has received little attention. This allusion is unmistakable, however, as Eleanor Prosser has demonstrated, and occurs at what might be considered the climax of the play, the point at which Prospero turns from vengeance to forgiveness:

> Though with their high wrongs I am strook to th' quick,
> Yet with my nobler reason, 'gainst my fury
> Do I take part. The rarer action is
> In virtue than in vengeance. (5.1.25–28)

Montaigne's passage, which contains many verbal echoes, ranks virtue as *"much more noble"* than mere "inclinations unto goodnesse."[8] Virtue is demonstrated not by those whose good nature shields them from the temptation of revenge, but by those who feel injury, desire revenge, and yet control their passion through reason.

The event that immediately precedes Prospero's renunciation of vengeance, and by less than thirty lines in the text, is his furious hunt of Caliban, Stephano, and Trinculo. Despite the proximity of Prospero's wild chase to the passage in question, however, neither Prosser nor other scholars who cite "Of Cruelty" as a source mention the importance of hunting to the essay.[9] Montaigne's most telling example of uncontrollable and irrational fury in "Of Cruelty" is the hunt. Admitting his own complicity in the irresistible appeal of the chase – the "showting, jubeting and hallowing, still ringing in our eares" – Montaigne goes on to deplore the various kinds of torture Roman tyrants and other rulers have inflicted upon criminals, urging that if such inhuman outrages must take place for deterrent effect they should be visited not upon the living bodies but upon the corpses of the offenders. [10] The topic of cruelty to humans leads him to that of cruelty to beasts, which he also finds abhorrent. His conclusion, which has served as a touchstone for Shakespearean values throughout this study, seems implicit in the ending of *The Tempest*:

there [is] a kinde of respect, and a general duty of humanitie, which tieth us, not only unto brute beasts that have life and sense, and are Sensitives, but unto trees and plants, which are but Vegetatives. *Unto men we owe Justice, and to all other creatures, that are capable of it, grace and benignitie* [Florio's italics]. There is a kinde of enter-changeable commerce, and mutuall bond betweene them and us. [11]

In Montaigne's essay "Of Cruelty," then, Shakespeare found not only the notion that the "rarer action" lies in a virtue that proceeds from struggle rather than in one that proceeds from mere innocence. He found there an image of the hunt used as an example of tempestuous passion, irrational and uncontrollable. He found a protest against cruel punishments of men, even of men guilty of the most heinous crimes. He found a protest against cruelty to animals that focuses on the hunt. And he found a notion of a "mutuall bond" joining human, animal and vegetative nature. It is even possible that Shakespeare found in Montaigne's essay the germ of Caliban's final desire to "be wise hereafter, / And seek for grace" (5.1.295–96), for the ambiguity of the word "grace" seems to echo "*Unto men we owe Justice, and to all other creatures, that are capable of it, grace and benignitie.*" Montaigne's "Of Cruelty" thus implies not only a powerful endorsement of the bonds that tie humans to one another in sympathy but an unconventional endorsement of the bonds between the human and the natural world. In Prospero's struggle to forgive Antonio, to release Ariel, and to accept Caliban, we may perhaps see the glimmering of both of those ideas.

Thus far the context we have explored in attempting to understand the hunting episode in *The Tempest* has been strictly literary: Shakespeare's own depictions of hunter and hunted, and the anti-hunting tradition represented in writers such as Agrippa and Montaigne. There is another and at least equally immediate context for the episode, however, that of the politics surrounding the hunt in the court of James I. The king was an obsessive hunter, and his hunting occasioned considerable protest both within and outside the court. Since any association

between James I and Prospero at his most tyrannical seems unlikely on
the face of it, however, for reasons of censorship if for no other, one must
proceed cautiously. I shall therefore turn first to broad questions of the
play's relationship to court politics, and then to the particular question
of James's hunting and its political implications, focusing on those features that seem most relevant to Prospero's hunt in *The Tempest*.

As Stephen Orgel observes, despite the fact that *The Tempest* was performed at court both in 1611 and in 1613, there is no evidence to suggest
that the play was written or modified for court performance.[12] There is
little doubt, however, that it is deeply implicated in court issues, as
numerous critics have made clear. The play's concern with the union of
kingdoms, peaceful succession, appropriate diplomatic marriages of
children, the need for discipline in promising heirs – these and other
topics have been traced plausibly to the court environment surrounding
the play. Recent studies have also shown the relevance to the play of
more overtly subversive and popular discourses, such as those of treason,
both domestic and political, and colonialism.[13] One cannot read criticism of the play or accounts of James I, moreover, without being struck
by the startling resemblances between Prospero and the king, both of
whom share, in addition to absolute political authority, a preoccupation
with the occult, a delight in masques, a tendency to neglect their duties,
a concern with the political marriages of progeny, and a proneness to fits
of rage. While much of this contextual criticism has been illuminating,
the sheer proliferation of relevant perspectives has not resulted in substantial agreement about those that are most significant or about the
overall political positioning of the play. The more we learn about the
immediate context, it seems, the more complicated both the history and
the play become.

To understand the political significance of Prospero's furious hunt, we
must consider the threat of royal absolutism as it was embodied in both
the Parliamentary crisis of 1610 and in James's obsession with hunting.
The Parliamentary crisis arose out of continuing debates over supply
and the royal prerogative.[14] The debates of 1610 took place in the
context of the "great contract," by which the king had agreed to forfeit
certain claims upon his subjects in exchange for a grant of annual
revenue. From the viewpoint of the Crown, desperately in need of
money, the main purpose of the session was to secure a grant of subsi-
dies. From the viewpoint of many members of the Commons, however,
the main purpose, as Elizabeth Read Foster puts it, was "the expression
and preparation of grievances, ecclesiastical and temporal."[15]

The question of the royal prerogative that dominated the Parliament of 1610 emerged from the king's attempt to enhance his revenues by increasing impositions on imported and exported goods. Since such impositions had traditionally served mainly a regulatory purpose, the king's desire to treat them as royal revenue aroused much opposition in the Commons. Such a move was treated as an illegitimate extension of the royal prerogative. The king was therefore called upon to defend his prerogative, which he did with the absolutist theories that he had enunciated over a lifetime. The Commons defended its position, with various members making provocative statements that challenged the prerogative. The recalcitrance of the Commons precipitated a major debate: could the Crown levy additional customs duties without the consent of Parliament? Because the king tried at one point to silence the arguments against him, on the ground that the debate itself undermined his prerogative, the conflict raised the further and fundamental question of the right to free speech in the Commons. The problem of the levy was left unresolved, the great contract collapsed, and the king dissolved Parliament in February 1611. The great contract failed, according to Elizabeth Read Foster, mainly because of the Commons' distrust of the Crown. "The King will not acknowledge his prerogative to be inferior to law," commented the Earl of Huntingdon, "'and therefore no good assurance and tie can be made but his prerogative will be above it."[16]

The anxious question that ran throughout the entire session, from the viewpoint of the Commons, is whether the king's absolutist inclinations could be contained. On this score the arguments put forward by the crown, including those made by the king in person, were not reassuring. In two major speeches the king enunciated his prerogative in language that took the absolutist position to extremes. On 21 March 1610, in a speech later published in his *Works,* James addressed directly what he took to be the major question posed by the Commons, whether he intended to continue ruling "according to the ancient forme of this State, and the Lawes of this Kingdome" or whether he intended not to limit himself "within those bounds, but to alter the same when [he] thought convenient, by the absolute power of a King." To many, his answer was not reassuring. "The State of MONARCHIE," James had declared, "is the supremest thing upon earth: For Kings are not onely GODS Lieutenants upon earth, and sit upon GODS throne, but even by GOD himselfe they are called Gods."[17] In his speech of 21 May he took the absolutist position to its logical conclusion: "If a king be resolute to be a tyrant, all you can do will not hinder him. You may pray to God that he may be good and thank God if he be."[18] As both the king's words and the reaction of auditors such as John Chamberlain make clear, the shadow under which the 1610 debate was conducted was that of future tyranny.[19]

In the midst of the debates, shortly after 14 May, the news arrived that the French king, Henri IV, had been assassinated. James, like his subjects, was stunned by the news, and he reacted with fear and horror at the prospect of his own death in a like manner. Immediate precautions were taken to protect the king, and especially to guard him carefully while hunting. A few days after the assassination he was seen riding through London with an armed guard.[20] In Parliament, fears for the king's safety became intertwined with conflicts over his prerogative.

The 1610 debates in Parliament thus provide an illuminating context within which to view the potential for tyranny implicit in Prospero's attack upon Caliban, Stephano, and Trinculo. In both instances, a ruler is beset by internal dissension and by disputes over prerogative; Caliban's position, after all, is that the island belongs to him. In both instances, a ruler is subject to fits of rage when challenged and to hyperbolic assertions of supreme authority. In both instances, a ruler is fearful of assassination. In both instances, finally, a ruler defines his power in relation to hunting. The intertwining of hunting with potential tyranny that characterizes Shakespeare's treatment of Prospero, as we shall see, is also to be found in the person and politics of King James.

At the age of eighteen James had already established his reputation as an obsessive hunter, the French envoy, M. de Fontenay, observing that "he loves the chase above all the pleasures of this world, living in the saddle for six hours on end." Later in the same letter, Fontenay criticizes James in a way that was to become familiar throughout his entire reign, noting that he was "too idle and too little concerned about business, too addicted to his pleasure, principally that of the chase."[21] In his first progress after his coronation as King of England, laments Francis Osborne in his memoirs, James was wearing a garment "as greene as the grasse he trod on, with a fether in his cap, and a horne instead of a sword by his side: how sutable to his age, calling, or person, I leave to others to judge from his pictures . . ."[22]

James hunted throughout his career – in middle and old age, in sickness and in health. He hunted en route to the estates of his nobles while on progress and was entertained with hunting when he arrived. He hunted at his own vast parks and forests, such as Royston and Newmarket, and even established formal procedures to be followed by his government while he was away from court and in the field.[23] Hunting was intertwined with nearly all his private and public activities. He conducted court business and wrote letters in the midst of hunting trips. He cheered sick nobles with the prospects of hearing once again the "wild hallow" of the hunt. When his daughter Princess Mary died of a fever in 1607, he sent the Earl of Salisbury to console the Queen while he went hunting at Cheshunt Park.[24] James himself died, appropriately, after catching a tertian ague, according to Sir Anthony Weldon, on the last hunt of the year "as wel as of his life."[25]

James's voluminous correspondence records his obsession with hunting, most revealingly in his metaphoric identification of the sport with politics. This identification occurs most consistently in his letters to his first minister, Robert Cecil, between 1604 and 1610. Perhaps the most striking feature of this correspondence is the salutation with which James begins every letter: "my little beagle." Whether James alludes to hunting in such letters or not, their imaginative framework, whatever the political topic, is that of the hunt: James's chief minister, responsible for implementing his political will, is his favorite hunting dog, his little beagle. The metaphor, moreover, is often carried beyond the salutation, as in the following letter, in which James orders Cecil to prepare Theobalds for his hunting while on progress:

My little beagle,
It is now time that ye prepare the woods and park of Theobalds for me. Your part thereof will only be to harbour me good stags, for I know ye mind to provide for no other entertainment for me there than as many stags as I shall kill with my own hunting. Yet ye have that advantage that I trust so much to your nose that when I hear you cry it I will halloo to you as freely as to the deepest-mouthed hound in all the kennel. And since ye have been so much used these three months past to hunt cold scents through the dry beaten ways of London, ye need not doubt but it will be easy for you to harbour a great stag amongst the sweet groves about your house. Only beware of drawing too greedily in the lyam, for ye know how that trick hath already galled your neck.[26]

The psychology and tone of this letter are typical. The nickname "beagle" is affectionate, and the letter captures James's pleasure in both Cecil and the hunting he will provide. There is no mistaking the implications of the metaphor, however: James is master, Cecil a favorite dog. Cecil "hunts" the king's prey in London and harbours stags for him at Theobalds, but he must never forget that he is on a leash, which will "gall" his neck if he shows signs of pursuing his own will rather than the king's. The metaphor thus captures implicitly James's absolutist notions of kingship: he is the hunter, his enemies the prey, and his agents his hounds, trained in obedience to his will. Even the Council as a whole is praised in a later letter as a "good kennel that all run well."[27]

Although most of James's metaphoric identifications of hunting with political affairs focus on tracking and pursuing, on one occasion the end latent in the metaphor, that of violent death, is actually pronounced. Presumably alluding to an episode involving witches and prophets at Hinchingbrooke in January of 1605, James informs his "little beagle" that he has been "out of privy intelligence" with him since they last parted because he has been "kept so busy with hunting of witches, prophets, Puritans, dead cats, and hares."[28] In view of James's harsh attitudes and policies towards witches and Puritans, the use of the hunting metaphor in this instance is genuinely ominous. The leveling effect created by James's syntax is also disturbingly suggestive, for it reduces all of the items to the value of dead cats, an allusion so absurd in context that it must hint at some meaning now lost. In the privacy of his correspondence, then, James saw his political affairs in general through the eyes of a hunter and his enemies in particular as prey, sometimes as prey to be literally destroyed.

By the time of the Parliamentary crisis of 1610, James had become notorious for his personal obsession with hunting, his lavish expenditures on the sport, and his incessant efforts to limit it and punish illegal hunting through royal proclamations and the Game Acts. Although the Parliamentary debates of that year did not explicitly include the issue of hunting, James himself was driven to include it as yet another potential threat to his prerogative. In the same speech in which he declared that the state of monarchy was "the supremest thing upon earth," and that kings were "not onely Gods Lieutenants upon earth" but were called "Gods" even by "God himselfe,"[29] James exhorted Parliament to attend to the protection of the forests and game. He chided the members for their casting out of a bill for the preservation of woods in the last session, accusing them of "frowardnesse" and reminding them of the general need for fuel, and timber for the navy, and of his own pleasure in the hunt: "yee know my delight in Hunting and Hawking, and many of your selves are of the same minde." He rebuked them too for unsatisfactory bills passed in the previous session, 1605–06, regarding the preservation of pheasant and partridge and the unlawful hunting of deer and conies.[30]

Hunting was of course only one of several issues touched upon in this speech. Given the nature of Parliament's grievances and his own desperate need for the grant of funds, however, it is remarkable that he gave the issue any attention at all. Even more remarkable is the aggressive and hectoring tone of his remarks, which reveal a good deal of tension surrounding the subject, even among those who might seem predisposed in its favor. The tone of the king's remarks lends support to Francis Osborne's bitter comment, in his memoirs, that in James's reign "one man might with more safety have killed another, than a raskall-deare, . . . [so] tragicall was this sylvan prince against dear-killers, and indulgent to man-slayers."[31] James's pursuit of protection for his favorite recreation, in short, was as vigorous and uncompromising in this speech as his defence of the royal prerogative in general. For James, it seems, kings were both Gods and hunters.

James's passion for the hunt aroused controversy at all levels of society. At the heart of the matter was the same problem that we have encountered in the Parliamentary conflict of 1610: fears of James's extension of the royal prerogative. In reacting against the neglect of the game laws by his predecessors, as Chester and Ethyn Kirby have demonstrated, James sought to restore a "moribund prerogative, a claim to the personal control of the game everywhere in England and to the right of hunting wherever the king pleased."[32] According to Roger B. Manning, "the increased emphasis on the prosecution of hunting offences in Star Chamber and other equity courts certainly represented a revival of the royal prerogative in ways that the Tudor monarchs had never contemplated . . ."[33]

James's son, Charles I, was also a hunter. Although far less obsessive about the sport than his father, he was at least as committed to the royal prerogative, and he continued his father's aggressive policies: restricting hunting to a privileged elite, prosecuting unlawful hunting, and maintaining and extending royal parks and forests. The forces set in motion by James I, in short, accelerated under Charles I, and the results were disastrous. In September 1641 there were popular attacks against Windsor Forest, attacks which Manning notes displayed "a distinct antimonarchical bias," and which continued for several years. Throughout the Civil Wars, moreover, parks and forests were routinely destroyed and deer slaughtered, at least in part as protests against the monarchy and noble privilege. Manning concludes that "James I and Charles I had made the royal hunting reserves a symbol of royal tyranny."[34]

When Prospero first hunted Caliban, Stephano and Trinculo on stage in 1611, then, he did so in a political atmosphere in which hunting and the threat of tyranny were intertwined. In this sense the hunting scene in *The Tempest* might be said to crystallize a deep cultural anxiety about James's rule, with Prospero's regression to the primitive tyranny of the hunt as a means of "punishing" his conspirators playing out fears of a hunter-king that were being expressed in Parliament, in letters, and on the streets of London. From this perspective, Prospero's decision to renounce vengeance, abjure his magic, and release Ariel and (probably) Caliban to their natural elements might provide a wish-fulfillment fantasy of personal reformation and social reconciliation. If so, the fantasy seems seriously qualified by the many irresolutions of the play's ending, which include hints of Prospero's own pessimism and recalcitrance.

If conceived as an indirect comment on James's rule, the hunting scene may seem difficult to reconcile with the political realities of state censorship and court performance. On 29 March 1608, for example, the French ambassador reported that because two plays had offended the king all the London theaters were shut down and threatened with permanent closure. In one of the plays, the ambassador observes, James himself had been represented cursing and swearing because he had been robbed of a bird and beaten a gentleman who had called off his hounds from the scent.[35] The episode shows that in 1608 James's hunting was a likely topic for satire, but its message on censorship is more difficult to extract. On the one hand, it reveals the vulnerability of actors to immediate and arbitrary political reprisals; on the other, it suggests that even the most flagrant mockery of the king could escape prosecution (and attract audiences).

In addressing the question of censorship, it is important to keep in mind that we are dealing not only with scripts but with performances before both a courtly and popular audience. Both modes of representation are open to alteration of various kinds – ranging from subtle nuance to complete inversion of meaning. It is easy to imagine, for example, radically different treatments of the hunting episode in a court and a popular setting: in the former the episode could have been omitted, or truncated, or treated as farce; in the latter it could have been used to insinuate satirical possibilities. The scene itself, of course, is rich enough to support various interpretations, theatrical or critical, ranging from sympathetic approval of Prospero's firmness against usurpation to anxious horror at his anger and cruelty. Given James's attitudes and susceptibility to drink, it is even arguable that the king at least might not have found anything offensive even in the most forbidding of theatrical realizations of the scene. The many variables in performance, then, can be seen to multiply the variables in textual interpretation. In this respect the hunting episode more than meets the test of "functional ambiguity" developed by Annabel Patterson in her study of censorship in the period.[36]

Ambiguity is different from overt subversiveness of the kind that Curt Breight finds, for example, in his article on the discourse of treason in the play. Although Breight's insistence on "the theatre's wide range of ideological possibilities" provides a useful corrective to the more influential view of conservative ideological containment, his attempt to read the play as "a politically radical intervention in a dominant contemporary discourse" is not very persuasive.[37] More in keeping with the realities of censorship and the complexities of Shakespeare's dramatic methods are interpretations that recognize the ideological containment implied in Shakespeare's dramatic form, a form that begins and ends with Prospero in authority but at the same time enables the expression of doubts, anxieties, and criticism. Critics as far apart as Donna B. Hamilton and Paul Brown, for example, have in this respect come to similar conclusions. For Hamilton, Shakespeare's overall strategy in the representation of Prospero, and by implication, James, is epideictic, a mode of praise that contains within itself the possibility of criticism and instruction. For Brown, the play expresses the tensions within the ideology of early colonialism but without resolving them. In Hamilton's argument, the play functions much as one of Jonson's masques was intended to function, as an idealized but instructive portrait of the king and court. In this sense, Shakespeare might have represented the potential within the king, and within absolute rule in general, for acts of tyranny, but represented as well the overcoming of that temptation, in the disciplined decision to seek virtue rather than vengeance. Although plausible enough, I find this line of argument less convincing than that of functional ambiguity because it implies a strong degree of didacticism on the part of the author and the centrality of James and the court as an intended audience.

The most plausible position, it seems to me, is to assert not only Shakespeare's immersion in the culture of his day, including the culture of the hunt and the Jacobean court, but to allow him a measure of independence as a playwright. The story told in *The Tempest* includes far more than Jacobean political issues, and even those issues are broadly framed. Illuminating contexts for the "hunting" of Prospero may thus be found in Agrippa's attacks on hunting; in the "hunting" of King James in sport and politics; in the proverbial role of Nimrod as great hunter; in myths of the Iron Age; in the use of dogs against natives by Spaniards in the new world; in the persecution of native peoples, in Scotland, Ireland, or the New World; and in the persecution of "masterless men" in Elizabethan England. A local reading need not be reductive. Given the working conditions of an Elizabethan dramatist, in fact, one begins to suspect that, whether by accident or design, the habit of functional ambiguity was in large part responsible for the endlessly widening ripples of meaning that we associate with Shakespeare's art in particular. In this sense, his very immersion in the immediate particulars of cultural experience, and the threats that such immersion entailed, might be in part responsible for the very "universality" that has been traditionally claimed for his works.

Although Shakespeare develops Prospero's hunt primarily as a political symbol, moreover, it is well to remember that the implications of the episode extend beyond a narrow conception of politics. The liminal status of one of the conspirators, Caliban, as we have observed, aligns Shakespeare's treatment of the hunt at least partly with that of Agrippa and Montaigne, both of whom are concerned with the welfare of animals in a literal sense. The very liminality of Caliban, his apparent position at the boundaries of the human and the animal world, opens up the possibility of literalizing the metaphor of the hunt and extending the question of cruelty into the realm of nature itself. As Jonathan Bate reminds us, *The Tempest* is not only a political play but a play about the relationship of culture to nature.[38] At the end of the play Prospero renounces his power over nature as dangerous, frees Ariel to the elements, and probably leaves Caliban to his island. However one interprets these actions, they do not imply a tyrannical attitude towards nature. Nor is it easy to reconcile them with the passion of the hunt.

Prospero's begrudging acceptance of Caliban and his final release of both Caliban and Ariel challenge the conventional notion of man's right to absolute dominion over nature. Shakespeare's treatment of Caliban and Ariel is curiously reminiscent of his treatment of the weeping deer in *As You Like It*. In both cases he blurs the boundaries between the natural and the human world, suggesting that they are parts of a continuum, not separate and unbridgeable categories. Ariel exists at the boundaries between spirit and matter, Caliban at the boundaries between the human and bestial. They both possess an external reality, as objective beings, but also an internal reality, as capacities within Prospero himself. Ariel is "my spirit," the means by which Prospero executes his magic; Caliban is "mine," the means by which he caters to his bodily needs. The acknowledgment of the ultimate freedom and autonomy of these creatures at the end of the play suggests a heightened emphasis on the kinship between living things that stretches the traditional conception of man's relationship to nature. In this kinship lies Prospero's redefinition of his "so potent art" as a "rough magic" that must be renounced (5.1.50). The "vanity" of Prospero's art leads to a furious and tyrannical hunt.

James I, ironically, can be called an early conservationist. He enlarged the forests and parks of England, protected and increased the wildlife, even sometimes in opposition to his own officers, for whom the collection of revenues through timber was the highest priority. As is true of some modern hunters, however, his passion for environmentalism derived from the simple desire to kill; nowhere does he ever express a need to preserve and protect the natural environment for the sake of nature itself. For him, forests existed to serve the recreation of the king. This kind of "tyranny" was not in Shakespeare's day a significant political issue; opposition to James's forest policies was not based on the innate value of wild nature. Shakespeare's play, however, at least hints towards a more modern attitude, one that was shortly to be undermined, ironically, by the development of Baconian science and Cartesian rationalism. To release Ariel to the air and Caliban to his island is to give up a coercive power over elemental nature, to recognize its own autonomy. This is not to sentimentalize nature, for both Ariel and Caliban can only be left to their own devices if left in their own sphere; in society, both must be controlled. Nor does the gesture towards release sentimentalize Prospero or the play. The release is hard earned, reluctant, and, like the play's other hopeful gestures towards a "brave new world," carries with it a skepticism born of tragic experience.

The Tempest thus participates in the Jacobean culture of the hunt in many ways. It crystallizes in a single, powerful symbol Shakespeare's continuing preoccupation with the violence of the hunt. It situates Prospero's furious chase of the conspirators within a long tradition of thought linking the origins of the hunt with the origins of tyranny. It alludes to contemporary anxieties about tyranny in the court of King James, anxieties that were deeply intertwined with the various manifestations of the king's obsession with the hunt as a symbol of royal power. Drawing on Montaigne's novel and progressive feelings of sympathy for brute creation, moreover, the play implies a need to return Caliban and Ariel to their natural elements, to resist the human desire to tyrannize over nature itself. In this sense the play poses, but does not resolve, the very modern conundrum, that human purposes require subordinating a wild nature that is better off left alone.

CHAPTER EIGHT

Conclusion: Shakespeare on the culture of the hunt

Both the absence of an intellectual biography and the elusiveness of the plays make it difficult to write convincingly about Shakespeare's attitudes or opinions. One is tempted to resort to Keats's conception of "negative capability" or to Barthes' denial of the very concept of authorship and to abandon the quest altogether. The theme of hunting poses a particular challenge, since none of the works is centrally "about" hunting, and the allusions to and representations of the hunt are therefore incidental to broader questions of human experience. Even when the plays give prominence to the sport, moreover, as does *Love's Labor's Lost*, they do not express a specific agenda or a didactic point of view: Shakespeare is not G. B. Shaw.

Given the elusiveness of Shakespearean dramatic form, it becomes not only difficult to extrapolate authorial views but seductively easy to impose our own. It is not surprising, therefore, that two impressive scholars of the hunt, D. H. Madden and Matt Cartmill, find in Shakespeare confirmation of their own views. Madden, impressed by Shakespeare's easy technical mastery of the hunt, concludes that he was "beyond doubt a sportsman, with the rare skill in the mysteries of woodcraft, loving to recall the very names of the hounds with which he was wont to hunt"; Cartmill, noting that Shakespeare consistently links hunting to rape and murder, observes that among his characters, "a distaste for the hunt is a sign of common decency."[1] The quest to discover the recurrent themes and patterns of language through which implied authorial attitudes are revealed is inevitably subjective.

It should be clear already, from our detailed exploration of Shakespeare's many allusions to the hunt, that my own view inclines strongly towards Cartmill's. Individually, each of the works implies a critique of the culture of the hunt; collectively, the recurrent patterns of the critique imply a coherent authorial point of view. In *Venus and Adonis*, hunting is a metaphor for both destructive male aggression, as an initiation into war, and for destructive female aggression, as an initiation into sexuality. The same themes recur in *Titus Andronicus*, where rape, mutilation and murder comprise the sport of a hunting party. In both *Titus Andronicus* and *Julius Caesar*, moreover, the attempt to ritualize killing, as in the hunt, serves only to heighten the ironic gap between the aspiration towards sacrifice and the reality of savage butchery. In the comic world of *Merry Wives*, predation also serves as a metaphor for human experience, although with more benign, if not wholly innocuous, effect; as a poacher of deer and women, Falstaff is finally hunted down himself, the victim of the social violence of the charivari. In *Love's Labor's Lost*, the cruelty of the hunt is acknowledged by the hunter herself, the Princess of France, and serves as a touchstone for the unfeeling sportfulness of an aristocratic court. In *As You Like It*, a play that does more to foreground the plight of hunted animals than any other in the canon, Duke Senior's regrets and Jaques' tears for a dying deer accentuate the paradoxes in the notion of pastoral hunting. In *The Taming of the Shrew* a hunting lord and a falconer embody the male braggadocio in patriarchal rule, with the falcon Kate providing a wish-fulfillment fantasy of successful taming. In *The Tempest*, finally, the hunting of Caliban, Stephano, and Trinculo becomes a metaphor for the tyrannical potential of Prospero's art.

The most powerful challenge to the notion that Shakespeare's conception of the hunt is negative, it seems to me, comes from the brief hunting episode in *A Midsummer Night's Dream*, an episode that has so far escaped our attention. Surely, we might argue, at least here we find a festive hunt, a moment that replicates the positive ideology that resonates through the handbooks on hunting and the remarks of James I. As would have been common in the Elizabethan period, Theseus and Hippolyta celebrate their wedding with a hunt. They take delight in the beauty of the morning and admire together the music of the hounds. The event seems entirely joyful and decorous: the participants are warriors but in love; the dogs are beasts but disciplined and musical. In this brief moment, the hunt seems to become a positive symbol of social order, uniting man and woman, human and beast, and prefiguring the harmonious resolutions that characterize the ending of the play. Is it possible that in this single episode Shakespeare allows his audience to revel in the conventional pleasures of the hunt?

Before considering the episode in detail, it might be helpful to consider a benchmark for festive representations of the hunt, a speech that occurs at the beginning of Greene's *Friar Bacon and Friar Bungay*. In this speech, Prince Edward's friend Lacy describes the joy of a hunt that the two men have just completed:

> Alate we ran the deer, and through the lawns
> Stripp'd with our nags the lofty frolic bucks
> That scudded 'fore the teasers like the wind.
> Ne'er was the deer of merry Fressingfield
> So lustily pull'd down by jolly mates,
> Nor shar'd the farmers such fat venison,
> So frankly dealt, this hundred years before . . .[2]

"Frolic" is the governing word in this description. The hunt is a festive game, shared with equal delight by the nags, the bucks themselves, the teasers (the hounds that rouse the game), the mates, and even the farmers, whose trampled fields are more than compensated by the gift of venison. In such a portrait the hunt becomes a festive rite, expressing the social and natural communion in which Fressingfield manifests its true and "merry" identity. This is an idealized version of the positive attitudes towards the hunt popularized by the handbooks on the sport. Lacy's description is utterly without irony and contains no recognition of the various kinds of opposition to hunting – social, religious, political, ethical – that we have considered throughout this study.

The hunting episode in *A Midsummer Night's Dream* evokes a general atmosphere reminiscent of Lacy's celebration. The focus is not the kill but the delightful music of the hounds. Theseus begins by expressing his desire to hear the "musical confusion / Of hounds and echo in conjunction" (4.1.110–11). His words bring memories of her own hunting to Hippolyta's mind, and she tells of accompanying Hercules and Cadmus once when, in "a wood of Crete they bay'd the bear / With hounds of Sparta" (113–14). The sound of these hounds, she says, was incomparable: "I never heard / So musical a discord, such sweet thunder" (117–18). In reply, Theseus asserts the superiority of his hounds to any she has yet heard; they are "bred out of the Spartan kind" (119), and are "match'd in mouth like bells, / Each under each" (123–24). "A cry more tuneable," he assures her,

> Was never hollow'd to, nor cheer'd with horn,
> In Crete, in Sparta, nor in Thessaly.
> Judge when you hear.   (124–27)

Before Hippolyta can judge, however, they discover the sleeping lovers and "set aside" their "purpos'd hunting" so that all of the couples, "three and three," may return to Athens to hold "a feast in great solemnity"

(183–85). As in *Friar Bacon and Friar Bungay*, it seems, the characters are sympathetic and the context is ceremonial, joyful, and comic; the hunt becomes an emblem not of violence but of social and natural concord.

Qualifying the comic delight of this scene, however, are several underlying sources of tension. The relationship between Theseus and Hippolyta, for example, seems appropriately symbolized by the paradox of festive hunting. Both are powerful and aggressive figures, linked to the energetic and "masculine" activity of the hunt; Hippolyta is literally an Amazon. Their conversation about hunting is subtly competitive – both characters see hunting as a symbol of personal power – and hints at the likelihood of continuing tension in a relationship that began with wooing by the sword. Theseus is proud of his hounds, yet Hippolyta counters that pride with her own evocations of hunting with figures superior to Theseus: Hercules and Cadmus, whose prey was not the relatively harmless deer but the more deadly and challenging bear. Having won Hippolyta with the sword, Theseus must continue to woo her with heroic assertions of masculine prowess; she resists, but with a self-assertiveness muted to accord with her new marital role. For both characters the violence of the battlefield seems merely sublimated in the sporting competition of the hunt. In this sense their relationship prefigures that of Petruchio and Katherine in *The Taming of the Shrew*.

Theseus's delight in the music of his hounds might be taken as an emblem of this sublimation, for it transforms violent discord into a source of esthetic pleasure. Yet even the magic of this transformation is shadowed by a hint of satire. In his pride in the music of his hounds, Theseus plays the role of a familiar social type. To the dismay of Puritans, hunters in the period lavished great sums on the breeding and care of their dogs, and, like Theseus, they often had voices more in mind than speed or scenting ability. In *Country Contentments*, for example, Gervase Markham gives directions for creating a consort of hounds:

If you would have your Kennell for sweetnesse of cry, then you must compound it of some large dogges, that have deepe solempe mouthes . . .,which must as it were beare the base in the consort, then a double number of roaring, and loud ringing mouthes, which must beare the counter tenor, then som hollow plaine sweete mouthes, which must beare the meane or middle part: and so with these three parts of musique you shall make your cry perfect . . .[3]

Theseus himself recognizes one negative effect of breeding hounds for music when he notes that, although his hounds are "match'd in mouth like bells," they are "slow in pursuit" (123).

The concord of these slow hounds, like the harmony created within

A Midsummer Night's Dream as a whole, is deeply paradoxical. It marks a high civilization – Theseus delights in the music of the hunt rather than in the kill – but a fragile one, in which naturally opposed forces are poised momentarily in delicate equilibrium. Theseus's pride in his dominion over nature is itself ironic, given the instability of the fairy world that lies beyond his control. The beauty he achieves through his hounds, moreover, like the concord of his own marriage, masks underlying violence; the song of the hounds, no matter how delightful, as the eighteenth-century poet William Somervile later observed, is ultimately the sound of the beast, "Op'ning in concerts of harmonious joy, / But breathing death."[4]

The mythological subtexts underlying the roles of Theseus and Hippolyta also hint at a latent violence associated with hunting that shadows the festive nature of the moment. Hippolyta's account of hunting with Hercules and Cadmus seems to have been Shakespeare's own invention. In the context of the hunt, allusions to both characters are ironic: Hercules, the slayer of the Nemean lion, is also, in at least one account, the slayer of Hippolyta herself; Cadmus is the grandfather of Actaeon, a hunter who is destroyed by his own hounds. Theseus himself is celebrated as a hunter in mythology. He participates, for example, in Meleager's hunt of the Calydonian boar in the *Metamorphoses*.[5] More significantly, he and Hippolyta will later have a son, Hippolytus, who achieves fame as a hunter and worshipper of the goddess of the hunt, Artemis. Through the treachery of his stepmother, Phaedra, however, Hippolytus will be cursed and banished by his own father. One might argue, of course, that Shakespeare excludes these ominous subtexts from the play, but the centrality of the hunt to the episode in question surely pulls them towards the surface. For audiences with a knowledge of the mythology behind the characters, Theseus's wedding hunt has subtle tragic overtones.

The comic paradox of a festive hunt holds together in this scene because of an absence: the event that would unravel the paradox, the kill, never takes place. The hunt is interrupted by the discovery of the young lovers lying asleep on the ground. The movement from hunting to awakening the lovers represents a kind of modulation or metamorphosis whereby the latent violence of the hunt becomes transformed into life-giving love. The lovers are themselves awakened by the hunting horns; they have become Theseus's prey. This is truly a festive hunt, then. But its festivity depends upon an interruption of the true end of the hunt, death, and its replacement by marriage and social renewal.

Unlike Greene, who creates a stereotypically perfect scene of hunting, a joyful communion of man and nature in which even the prey participates, Shakespeare creates a festive hunt that is shadowed by reminders of violence and death. Within the comic contours of the episode, in short, lie the major hunting themes that Shakespeare was to explore in tragic, ironic, and satirical contexts throughout his career: sexual violence, war, patriarchal power, and the domination of nature. To underline these themes, of course, as the present line of argument has required, is to destroy the delicate comic balance of the scene. But their presence shows that even Shakespeare's most benign representation of the hunt carries critical and potentially tragic overtones.

As a poet and dramatist who moved between the worlds of Stratford and London, and whose audiences ranged from commoners to monarchs, Shakespeare would have been highly sensitive to the social and political implications of the topic of hunting. In general, as we have seen, the Elizabethan and Jacobean gentry, aristocracy, and monarchy were emotionally and intellectually committed to a positive ideology of the hunt. One would expect this fact to register upon any writer with social and economic ambitions. In this regard, Ben Jonson provides a useful foil to Shakespeare. Jonson's tendency to idealize the hunt is apparent in at least two plays – *Cynthia's Revels* and *The Sad Shepherd* – and throughout the poems and masques.

As the name implies, *Cynthia's Revels* celebrates Cynthia, or Diana, the goddess of the moon and the hunt, a figure who represents an idealized conception of Queen Elizabeth. The play also celebrates an idealized image of Jonson himself, as Crites the poet and masque-maker, and seems to have been designed to enable Jonson to offer the Queen "his services as a maker of court entertainments."[6] Not surprisingly, the play's few allusions to the hunt are favorable. Although the Diana of the play is accused of injustice in her punishment of Actaeon (the Earl of Essex in the allegory behind the play), she defends herself as appropriately "austere." This "austerity" is captured in images that celebrate the just power of the huntress. As "Queen and huntress, chaste and fair," she is asked to "give unto the flying hart / Space to breathe, how short soever," forgoing her proper role as huntress only for the temporary occasion of her revels. One of the four cardinal properties of her court, moreover, is "Good Audacity," whose symbol is *divae viragini* [divine female warrior], which expresses her "hardy courage in chase of savage beasts, which harbour in woods and wilderness."[7] Although Jonson's treatment of Elizabeth's role as huntress is symbolic, the symbolism carries with it an acceptance and promotion of the ideology of the royal hunt.

Jonson's plays occasionally include satiric thrusts at hunters, but they never attack the sport itself – merely the social pretensions and eccentricities of contemporary social types. Master Stephen, the country gull in *Every Man In His Humour*, wants to learn the "hawking and hunting languages" because they "are more studied than the Greek or the Latin" and provide access to the company of gallants. Puntarvolo, in *Every Man Out of His Humour*, a hunter devoted to "singularity," loves his dogs, hawks and wife equally and "has dialogues and discourses between his horse, himself, and his dog."[8] His is a harmless eccentricity, not one that threatens the true ethos of the sport.

An idealization of the hunt runs throughout the poems, particularly in those that, like "To Penshurst" and "To Sir Robert Wroth," praise the country life. "Penshurst" describes the King's impromptu visit to the estate while out hunting, a visit that celebrates the King's graciousness and the readiness of his hosts to receive him. In "To Sir Robert Wroth," the country estate conjures up visions of the Golden Age, a notion that for Jonson and Wroth, unlike Ovid, includes the joys of hunting. The aristocratic bias of the latter poem is revealed in the dissociation of hunting from any need for food: the true nobility of Wroth and his friends is demonstrated by the fact that they hunt "more for the exercise, then fare."[9] In this, they align themselves not only with the aristocratic ideology of the hunt but with the views of James I, who time and again stressed his need to hunt for the sake of his health.

In the masque *Time Vindicated*, the role of Diana, originally appearing as goddess of the hunt in *Cynthia's Revels*, reappears. When she is forced to defend her favors to the two hunters, Hippolytus and Cephalus, against Love's report to Time, Diana says that she has brought the youths forth

> To make them fitter so to serve the Time
> By labor, riding, and those ancient arts
> That first enabled men unto the wars.

Saturn yields to this assertion of her chaste purpose, and the Chorus celebrates hunting as the noblest exercise, one that promotes health, aids the faculties, chases away ill habits, and, as long as hunters follow the example of King James, protects Peace.[10] In developing his theme in this masque, Jonson interestingly attempts to reconcile James's commitment to pacifism with the traditional view of the sport as a training ground for

war. One can see in this maneuver, by which peace becomes paradoxically the end of an activity that promotes war, an anticipation of later
defenses of the hunt, which find in it less a preparation for war than a
surrogate, deflecting energies that might otherwise kill men. In his poem
The Chase (1735), for example, William Somervile praises the hunt as "the
sport of kings; / Image of war, without its guilt."[11]

Jonson, in short, was wedded to the courtly ideology of the hunt in
ways that Shakespeare was not. In contrast, Shakespeare's treatment of
the courtly ethos of the hunt, as we have seen, is deftly ironic. In the
reign of Elizabeth, he writes not of a "Queen and huntress, chaste and
fair," but of a Princess of France, whose ambivalence about hunting is
displayed in a setting distinctly reminiscent of Elizabeth's own progresses. In the reign of James I, he writes not of a King who pursues the
hunt only for the sake of his health but of a Duke who vents his rage at
rebellious subjects by symbolically hunting them. In neither case is
Shakespeare's flirtation with satire of the monarch necessarily dangerous. The allusions are oblique, tonally complex, and easily deflected in
the dynamics of stage representation. But their presence suggests, in a
small but focused way, the broad differences between Jonson and
Shakespeare in their orientation towards the world of the court. As a city
boy of modest means and, later, a masque writer for the Jacobean court,
Ben Jonson lacked Shakespeare's familiarity with hunting, his potential
access to it economically, and his ability to insulate himself from the
courtly ideology that sustained it. Shakespeare, unlike Jonson, wrote no
country-house poems or masques idealizing the world of the hunt; nor
are his occasional satiric thrusts against this world centered upon the
pretensions of those who, without the aristocratic credentials, yearn to
be part of it. Shakespeare's critical energies go to the heart of the courtly
ideology itself.

Central to Shakespeare's treatment of the hunt is its affinity with the
violence of war. In this sense, his imagery of hunting seems to grow out
of the humanist opposition to the sport, articulated most powerfully, as
we have seen, by writers such as More, Erasmus, and Agrippa.
Throughout the canon the link between hunting and war tends to
appear more directly in metaphors than in full scenes, metaphors that
focus not on positive qualities, such as military virtue or prowess, but on
savage, murderous violence. Caroline Spurgeon, for example, discovered that in only one out of thirty-nine hunting images was the sport
"pictured as a gay and joyous pastime, and described from the point of
view of the sportsman."[12] Her single positive image comes from the

English herald in *King John* as he attempts to persuade the citizens of Angiers to open their gates to the English army:

> And like a jolly troop of huntsmen come
> Our lusty English, all with purpled hands,
> Dy'd in the dying slaughter of their foes.
> Open your gates and give the victors way.   (2.1.321–24)

Although the image identifies the exultation of military victory with that of successful hunters, whose "purpled hands" are emblems of conquest, the thrust of the passage as a whole is rather heavily ironic. In the context of the herald's rhetoric, the image of "purpled hands" is not "jolly" at all but savagely ominous, conveying the implied threat that these hunters are now likely to dip their hands in the blood of the people of Angiers.

Most of Shakespeare's metaphoric links between hunting and war emphasize the murderous violence of individual combat. In such instances, the discipline imposed by the ceremonial hunt, with its elaborate etiquette, is not transferred to military action, despite the fact that both the hunt and battle were subject to elaborate chivalric codes. Instead, the image connotes unfettered violence and murderous blood-lust. And there are many such images, so many that they might be said to represent a Shakespearean convention in the depiction of war. In *2 Henry VI* York seeks vengeance against old Clifford on the battlefield, telling Warwick to seek out "some other chase, / For I myself must hunt this deer to death" (5.2.14–15). In *3 Henry VI* Richard of Gloucester uses virtually the same phrase in relation to young Clifford, who is now the object of revenge for having killed both York and young Rutland. "Nay, Warwick," Richard says as Clifford runs off, "single out some other chase, / For I myself will hunt this wolf to death" (2.4.12–13). The substitution of wolf for deer suggests the increasing brutality of the civil wars and of the men who pursue them. In *Troilus and Cressida*, Ulysses's treatment of the enemy as an animal to be hunted is rather more dispassionate, respectfully chivalric, and understated: "There is no tarrying here, the hart Achilles / Keeps thicket" (2.3.258–59). In the same play, however, Hector pursues an unnamed Greek warrior for the sake of his armor: "Wilt thou not, beast, abide? / Why then fly on, I'll hunt thee for thy hide" (5.6.30–31). In this instance, the chivalric and hunting codes intersect, with both the pursuit of armor and the pursuit of a hide being ignoble motives. In contrast to this venal conception of the hunt is that of Coriolanus, whose hatred of his enemy, Aufidius, acknowledges his worth as a warrior: "He is a lion / That I am proud to hunt" (1.1.235–36). Coriolanus is later betrayed by Aufidius, ironically, and dies encircled by assassins in a manner suggestive of the baying of a stag.

The impulse to kill in battle, then, is repeatedly associated with the hunt. The nuances of the comparison vary greatly, ranging from murderous revenge to chivalric acknowledgment of the worth of an adversary, suggesting the diversity of motives that might also characterize the hunt itself. In each case, however, the metaphors suggest the centrality in both hunting and warfare of a powerful drive to kill. In that sense, the use of hunting metaphors undermines the chivalric ideology so often used to sustain both warfare and hunting. From this vantage point neither activity can be called truly recreational or sporting. Although one cannot conclude that Shakespeare followed the humanists in deploring hunting as a cause of war, one can conclude that he implied a deep affinity between the two, not only in the centrality of death to both activities but in the motivations of the hunter-warriors.

Perhaps the only truly sympathetic association of hunting with warfare in Shakespeare occurs, ironically, in the comparison made by the encircled Talbot in *1 Henry VI* between his plight and that of an English stag. Here the hunt is seen not from the vantage point of the attacking hunter but from that of the desperate prey:

> How are we park'd and bounded in a pale,
> A little herd of England's timorous deer,
> Maz'd with a yelping kennel of French curs!
> If we be English deer, be then in blood,
> Not rascal-like, to fall down with a pinch,
> But rather, moody-mad; and desperate stags,
> Turn on the bloody hounds with heads of steel,
> And make the cowards stand aloof at bay.   (4.2.45–52)

The powerful effect of this passage depends upon the way in which Talbot converts an image suggestive of bow and stable hunting – that of a herd of fallow deer being driven within a park – into an image suggestive of *par force* hunting, with the magnificent bayed stag turning on its attackers. In so doing he not only demeans the French as attacking curs but converts the initial English mood of bewildered fright into one of enraged and desperate aggression. This image of a helpless animal surrounded by attacking predators haunts Shakespeare's imagination and recurs throughout the plays; helplessness of this kind can become transformed into a desperate moral power, as happens in the taunting of York in *3 Henry VI* or in the blinding of Gloucester in *King Lear*.

The closest Shakespeare comes to direct engagement with the conventional argument that hunting prepares young men for war is in *Cymbeline*, which features a hunting scene involving Belarius and his two "sons," Guiderius and Arviragus. As outlaws, the three men hunt out of necessity, so that their hunting is of a more primitive kind than would be customary among Elizabethan aristocrats. Since the boys eventually prove themselves as valiant warriors in battle against the Romans, one might expect their success to be attributed not merely to their noble blood but to their youthful training in the hunt; this is the convention that Spenser follows in his praise of Sidney in "Astrophel." Curiously, however, the opposite seems true. Arviragus, for example, has nothing but contempt for their life as hunters:

> We have seen nothing.
> We are beastly: subtle as the fox for prey,
> Like warlike as the wolf for what we eat;
> Our valor is to chase what flies.   (3.3.39–42)

When confronted for the first time with war itself, Arviragus is drawn instinctively to battle by his noble blood but dismisses the value of his training as a hunter:

> What thing is't that I never
> Did see man die, scarce ever look'd on blood,
> But that of coward hares, hot goats, and venison!   (4.4.35–37)

One might attribute these anti-hunting sentiments to Arviragus's youthful impatience for actual combat and to his innate nobility, which causes him to excel in warfare instinctively, without the need for any training that the hunt might provide. Such a viewpoint, however, would have been unconventional in the period. Spenser provides an instructive contrast in the *Faerie Queene*. In Book VI, Canto ii, the noble youth Tristram, having been forced to grow up in the forest and having therefore learned the ways of the hunt, puts his skills to good use by killing a discourteous knight, a deed that brings him to the attention of Calidore, who rewards him by making him his squire. Like Sidney in Spenser's "Astrophel," Tristram prepares himself for the role of warrior by pursuing the hunt as a young man. Whereas Spenser stays within the convention, Shakespeare works against it. In *Cymbeline* certain virtues of the warrior are celebrated through the characters of Guiderius and Arviragus, but the origin of these virtues is seen to rest in innate nobility alone. In the totality of the play, this unconventional dissociation of hunting from military prowess is a minor matter, but it is worth noting that the dissociation was also un-Jacobean; in *Basilicon Doron*, King James himself had proclaimed in print the military value of the hunt. In *Cymbeline*, as in *The Tempest*, Shakespeare seems to have missed an obvious opportunity to align his play with prominent royal views in support of hunting.

Common to the humanist argument against the hunt is the paradox that pursuing beasts ultimately bestializes men. In view of Shakespeare's repeated analogies between hunting and war, one might assume an underlying sympathy for this Erasmian position. As is usually the case in Shakespeare, however, the issue is dealt with indirectly; no character expresses a view on the subject. Characters who exhibit what might be called bestial tendencies in war are associated with the hunt – the language of the chase comes naturally to their lips on the battlefield – but the drama leaves open the question as to whether they have become violent warriors because they are hunters or whether innate tendencies towards violence simply find expression in both activities.

The closest Shakespeare comes to commentary on the psychological effect of repeated acts of violence is in *Henry V*. Encouraging his troops during the siege of Harfleur, Henry urges the nobles to "imitate the action of the tiger; / Stiffen the sinews, [conjure] up the blood, / Disguise fair nature with hard-favor'd rage" (3.1.6–8). At the end of this speech the yeomen are also included and the entire attack becomes metaphorically a hunt:

> I see you stand like greyhounds in the slips,
> [Straining] upon the start. The game's afoot!
> Follow your spirit; and upon this charge
> Cry, 'God for Harry, England, and Saint George!'   (31–34)

The exhortation is rhetorically complex, with Henry attempting to ennoble his troops by paradoxically bestializing them. The nobles become tigers; the yeomen, who are given "noble lustre" (30) in their eyes, become noble dogs, greyhounds. The image of tigerish hunting with which the speech begins is ultimately transformed into an English hunt, with the king and his mounted nobles letting slip the dogs of war.

In the present context, the most significant image in the address is that of imitating the action of the tiger, an image that suggests that savage violence is a mask, to be put on or off at will. The apparent implication of such an image is that violent action does not become habitual, that hunting and war are in a sense theatrical activities, in which humans may play temporarily the role of beasts and escape morally and psychologically unscathed. This is precisely the view of the hunt offered by the most important modern philosopher of hunting, Ortega y Gasset, who defines the sport as a conscious and artificial re-enactment of the primitive confrontation of man and beast, which depends upon "an imitation of the animal."[13] Ortega y Gasset does not explore the question as to whether such acts of imitation have the capacity to brutalize the actor. In *Henry V*, however, an argument for the brutalizing effect of war – and by extension, the hunt – appears in the long and eloquent speech by the Duke of Burgundy, in which he laments the destruction of France. The land has become wild, he says, and the people, even children, have grown "like savages – as soldiers will / That nothing do but meditate on blood – / To swearing and stern looks, defus'd attire, / And everything that seems unnatural" (5.2.59–62). Characteristically, Shakespeare does not resolve the discordant views implied by Henry V and the Duke of Burgundy; nor does he engage them in direct debate. That he mixes the language of hunting and war to frame the issue, however, suggests an imaginative awareness of the contemporary debate.

In sum, Shakespeare's representation of war is deeply affected by the traditional association of war with the hunt. His representation of the contemporary debate surrounding the hunt, however, is oblique. Whether hunting prepares men for war is left an open question, although the examples of Arviragus and Guiderius in *Cymbeline* suggest a skeptical response. Whether hunting causes cruelty or merely expresses it is also left an open question, although there is no doubt that Shakespeare identifies the two in representations of war. Hunting metaphors abound in battle, and not usually in chivalric contexts, where the formality and discipline of the hunt might carry over into the etiquette of chivalric war, but in contexts accentuating violent bloodshed and confusion. Although the contemporary ideology of both hunting and war treated them as highly ritualized activities, Shakespeare's allusions to hunting occur most often when war loses its ritualism and degenerates into anarchic violence.

In promoting the courtly ideology of the hunt, Ben Jonson was ironically led to promote an aggressive and powerful role for women. Under Elizabeth, who hunted throughout her reign, Jonson created the role of "Queen and huntress, chaste and fair." Under James, whose Queen was painted in hunting attire, with horse and leashed dogs by her side, he created a second Diana, who appears in the masque *Time Vindicated*, and who, like the Diana of *Cynthia's Revels*, promotes the values of the hunt.

Under Charles I, whose Queen, Henrietta Maria, was painted at least twice in readiness for the hunt, Jonson created the role of Maid Marian in the *Sad Shepherd*, who delights in the hunt *par force*.[14] By treating his female hunters within the aristocratic ideology of the court, the Jonson who seems almost misogynistic in such plays as *Volpone* or *Epicoene* appears to move towards a celebration of female power.

The implications of Shakespeare's treatment of female hunters is difficult to assess. The aristocratic ethos of the sport, as we have seen, is strongly "masculine," both in Shakespeare and Elizabethan society. Virility, military prowess, sexual aggression, bravado – these are the stereotypical qualities that tend to be linked to the hunt. At their most benign, they appear in such characters as Theseus and Petruchio, whose swagger has a kind of charm; at their most savage, they appear in such characters as Tamora's sons in *Titus Andronicus*, or, far more subtly, Brutus in *Julius Caesar*, for whom the ritual of the hunt justifies the suppression of human feeling. Shakespeare's skeptical and satiric treatment of the hunt is in many respects a skeptical and satiric treatment of the stereo-typical male ethos.

While the satiric undercurrents in the treatment of male hunters are relatively straightforward, the implications of the roles of the few female hunters are less clear. Shakespeare follows Elizabethan custom in showing females as aggressive hunters. In this sense, he can be said to challenge, as the custom itself challenged, at least for aristocratic women, the stereotypical dichotomy between hard, unfeeling males and soft, tender females. In the context of Shakespearean hunting, however, female aggression is not a sign of liberation. In the case of Tamora, for example, hunting is a figure for human depravity. In the case of the more benign hunting female, Hippolyta, her Amazonian status does not protect her from being defeated in war by Theseus, the male hunter overcoming the female. Although Katherine in *Taming of the Shrew* is not portrayed as a hunter, her metaphoric role as haggard falcon makes her a hunter too, one ultimately tamed to do her master's will. Shakespeare's female hunters may seem aggressive and powerful, for good or ill, but in either case their power is ultimately constrained by patriarchal control.

The most interesting and problematic example of the female hunter in Shakespeare is that of the Princess in *Love's Labor's Lost*, whose reluc-tance to hunt springs from a tender compassion for the deer's plight. Although such sensitivity is stereotypically female, it is shared, in *As You Like It*, by both Duke Senior and Jaques. The Princess's sensitivity, more-over, is not translated into action. She pauses to reflect, but she goes on to kill. And in her case Duke Senior's justification for hunting, the need for food, provides no excuse: the hunt is mere sport, and the sport, park hunting, notoriously easy and effete. As we have seen, the Princess's suppression of her "natural" instincts in the interest of deadly social sport becomes a figure for life in the aristocratic court of Navarre. Since the young men are also suppressing their natural instincts, however, in attempting to rise above love, the general problem is shared by both male and female.

Insofar as Shakespeare's few hunting females are characterized in relation to the hunt, then, they are brought within the governing male ethos of the sport. If they are hunters, they exemplify, "naturally" or through the suppression of compassion, the stereotypically male attributes of aggression and dominance; this is true even of metaphoric hunters such as Venus. At their worst these attributes make the women monsters of depravity (Tamora); at their best, as in the case of Hippolyta or the falcon Kate, they give them a strong-willed independence that stretches but does not break the limits of patriarchal marriage. Even Tamora is ultimately undone by the male hunter, Titus, who serves up her sons as a venison pasty. In this sense all of Shakespeare's female hunters are ultimately subject to male domination, whether benign or merciless. Lavinia, raped and mutilated as a defenseless "deer" in *Titus Andronicus*, is thus not unique in being victimized by the hunting ethos; her fate merely stands at the grimly absurdist end of the spectrum. The only huntress whose power seems unchallenged is Venus, and she is a goddess.

In his allusions to hunting, as we have seen throughout this study, Shakespeare tends to draw upon the cultural critique of the hunt found in such writers as Erasmus, More, Agrippa, and Montaigne. As we saw in chapter 1, another mode of opposition was available to Shakespeare, that of the Puritans, exemplified by such writers as Philip Stubbes, who objected to hunting in part because of its cruelty to animals but mainly because of its disastrous social effects upon the poor, whose lands were destroyed and whose incomes were depleted so that hounds could live in heated kennels. This kind of social protest towards the sport seems almost invisible in Shakespeare. The testing of the hunt that runs throughout *As You Like It* includes no reference to the protests of the poor against landlords eager to expand their hunting parks at the expense of forest or common land. Nathaniel in *Love's Labor's Lost* is an Anglican curate, devoted to the hunt as a "reverent sport," not a Puritan preacher; nor is Dull a simple farmer whose crops are destroyed by deer who forage outside Navarre's park. The commoners of *Love's Labor's Lost* are as enamored of the hunt as their social superiors and, although excluded from direct participation in the sport, are as keen to compete vicariously. Their vicarious enjoyment of the pursuits of their betters evokes a subtle satiric irony rather than direct social protest. Shakespeare's satiric energy, if we can call it that, is focused more on the internal dynamics of the court world than on potential opposition from outside and below.

Ironically, discordant voices muted or unheard in Shakespeare were to have a major impact on the development of the hunt within a few short years of his death. To some extent, these voices may be detected in the brief moments of Prospero's hunt, where the latent threat of tyranny crystallizes negative views towards the royal hunt that later found expressions in the Civil Wars. But other, more impersonal forces were also at work in Jacobean society to alter profoundly the culture of the hunt: among them, wide-scale destruction or enclosure of forest land, dislocation and repression of the woodland poor, quarrels between gentry and monarchy over the control of forest land, increasing restrictions on the right to hunt, and glaring inequities in the distribution of wealth, symbolized in the expenditures on parks, horses, and dogs. By the end of the seventeenth century, these social tensions, stretched to the breaking point in the Civil Wars, had radically altered the culture of the hunt.

The historical moment in which Shakespeare's images of the hunt resonated with deep cultural meaning was thus a brief one. Within fifty years of his death the forests and parks of England were in such a parlous state that writers like Pepys struggled to renew them through campaigns of planting – more for shipbuilding and industry, however, than for the king's recreation. The parks, their fences destroyed and their deer slaughtered in the Civil Wars, were rebuilt and re-stocked with foreign animals during the Restoration, but with disappointing results; despite these efforts, as E. P. Thompson shows, in Windsor Forest alone the deer population declined from 3066 in 1607 to 461 in 1697.[15] Though it lingered on at court, the hunt, like the monarchy itself, had lost much of its royal potency. Formerly a ritual of kingship, the hunt became increasingly a sport of the squirearchy. Even the prey became less royal, the scarcity of deer, especially the traditional symbol of royalty, the red deer, encouraging the substitution of the verminous and once contemptible fox. The image of the poacher, formerly that of a member of a wild band of night hunters, slaughtering deer not out of need but out of social vengeance, became increasingly that of the isolated and poor countryman, eking out his living with an occasional rabbit for the pot. And the sympathy for the deer itself, which flickers momentarily in writers like Montaigne, Agrippa, and Shakespeare, was eventually reduced to a sentimental fantasy by the harsh philosophy of Descartes, which made of living animals insentient machines.

Although the Elizabethan culture of the hunt was soon swallowed up by history, Shakespeare's images of hunting raise questions that continue to perplex contemporary Western societies – societies in which, like his own only more so, the practical necessity for the hunt is long gone, and in which a once meaningful ritual has become mere sport. At the center of Shakespeare's evocations of the hunt lie questions about the origins and cultivation of violence, about sexuality, about male and female identity, about social bonding and political power, about ritual and emotion, and about human ties to nature. Although Shakespeare does not answer these questions – his very elusiveness seems one secret of his continuing theatrical life – he probes them energetically, forcing us to consider, even in the flash of a metaphor, what it is to be a hunter and what to be a hunter's prey.

Notes

I INTRODUCTION: THE CULTURE OF THE HUNT AND SHAKESPEARE

1 Two versions of this painting exist: the original, reproduced here, painted in 1603 by Robert Peake, featuring as the prince's companion the young John, 2nd Lord Harington, and a copy, painted probably in 1606–07, replacing Lord Harington with the young Robert Devereux, 3rd Earl of Essex. Both young men were educated in the company of the prince and became his close companions. Both portraits are reproduced in Oliver Millar, *The Tudor, Stuart and Early Georgian Pictures in the Collection of Her Majesty the Queen*, 2 vols. (London: Phaidon, 1963); see vol. I, plate 6, and vol. II, plate 36. Although Millar and other art historians refer to the deer as a stag (a fully mature red deer), it has some characteristics of the fallow deer and was probably not painted from life. As Julius S. Held argues, a bloody gash on the deer's neck indicates that the Prince is not preparing to administer the *coup de grâce*, as has often been claimed, but sheathing his sword after having tested its edge and the strength of his arm in the manner recommended in [George Gascoigne's] *The Noble Arte of Venerie or Hunting* (1575), p. 134; the severing of the head will be left to others. See Held's "Le Roi à la Ciasse," *The Art Bulletin* 40 (1958): 144–45.
2 Quoted in Keith Thomas, *Man and the Natural World* (London: Allen Lane, 1983), 184.
3 Frederick Chamberlain, *The Private Character of Henry the Eighth* (New York: Ives Washburn, 1931), 140.
4 Joseph Strutt, *The Sports and Pastimes of the People of England*, ed. J. Charles Cox (London: Methuen, 1903), 9.
5 Charles Carlton, *Charles I* (London: Routledge and Kegan Paul, 1983), 3, 129.
6 Antonia Fraser, *King Charles II* (London: Weidenfeld and Nicolson, 1979), 292, 420.
7 E. P. Thompson, *Whigs and Hunters: The Origin of the Black Act* (London: Allen Lane, 1975), 40. For a useful survey of the changes to forests, chases, and parks in England, see Leonard Cantor, *The Changing English Countryside, 1400–1700* (London: Routledge and Kegan Paul, 1987), 96–118.
8 John Nichols, *The Progresses and Public Processions of Queen Elizabeth*, 3 vols.(London: 1823), 1: 74n.

9 *The Noble Arte of Venerie or Hunting* (1575) has been ascribed to George Turbervile, but Charles and Ruth Prouty show conclusively that the work is Gascoigne's; see "George Gascoigne, *The Noble Arte of Venerie*, and Queen Elizabeth at Kenilworth," in *Joseph Quincy Adams Memorial Studies*, ed. James G. McManaway, Giles E. Dawson, and Edwin E. Willoughby (Washington[DC]: 1948), 650–55. Although a few sections of the work are original with Gascoigne, *The Noble Arte of Venerie* is essentially a translation of the 1573 edition of Jacques du Fouilloux, *La Venérie*, itself a compendium of earlier French hunting manuals. For reviews of the most important English manuals in the period, see D. H. Madden, *The Diary of Master William Silence* (London: Longmans, Green, 1907), 364–71, and Marcia Vale, ed., *The Gentleman's Recreations* (Cambridge: D. S. Brewer, 1977), 30–33.

10 John Manwood, *A Treatise of the Lawes of the Forest* (1615; facs. rpt. Amsterdam: Walter J. Johnson, 1976), 18–18v. Manwood's definition is not entirely accurate: forests were unenclosed game preserves but were not necessarily wooded. For a useful discussion of the forest and game laws and the controversies surrounding them, see Roger B. Manning, *Hunters and Poachers* (Oxford: Clarendon Press, 1993), 57–82.

11 Manwood, *Lawes of the Forest*, 25v–26.

12 Manning, *Hunters and Poachers*, 59.

13 For a discussion of Stuart attempts to expand the royal prerogative through the game laws, see Chester and Ethyn Kirby, "The Stuart Game Prerogative," *English Historical Review* 46 (1931): 239–54.

14 Quoted in P. B. Munsche, *Gentlemen and Poachers: The English Game Laws 1671–1831* (Cambridge: Cambridge University Press, 1981), 14; Munsche provides a useful account of the development of the laws surrounding the hunt.

15 [Gascoigne], *Arte of Venerie*, A4v.

16 For accounts of Gascoigne's life, see C. T. Prouty, *George Gascoigne* (1942; rpt. New York: Benjamin Blom, 1966) and Ronald C. Johnson, *George Gascoigne* (New York: Twayne, 1972).

17 [Gascoigne], *Arte of Venerie*, 236.

18 G. A. Wilkes, ed., *The Complete Plays of Ben Jonson*, 4 vols. (Oxford: Clarendon Press, 1981), I: 185.

19 Manning, *Hunters and Poachers*, 60. The law dates from the reign of Richard II; see *Statutes of the Realm*, 9 vols. (1810–22), II, 65, 13 Rich. II, st. 1, c. 13.

20 S. Schoenbaum, *William Shakespeare: A Documentary Life* (Oxford: Clarendon Press, 1975), 137, 167.

21 Manning, *Hunters and Poachers*, 60.

22 Schoenbaum, *William Shakespeare*, 188, 173.

23 Manning, *Hunters and Poachers*, 60. See *Statutes of the Realm*, IV, 1055, 1 Jac. I c. 27; IV, 1088, 3 Jac. I c. 13; and IV, 1167, 7 Jac. I c. 11.

24 Madden, *Diary of Master William Silence*, vii; Madden provides no evidence to show that Shakespeare would have been legally entitled to hunt.

25 Caroline F. E. Spurgeon, *Shakespeare's Imagery* (Cambridge: Cambridge University Press, 1968), 30–33, 100 03; Matt Cartmill, *A View to a Death in the*

Morning: Hunting and Nature through History (Cambridge, Mass.: Harvard University Press, 1993), 78–79.

26 Nigel Nicolson and Alasdair Hawkyard, *The Counties of Britain: A Tudor Atlas by John Speed* (London: Pavilion Books, 1988), 61.

27 Susan Lasdun, *The English Park: Royal, Private and Public* (London: 1991), 32–33.

28 William Harrison, *The Description of England*, ed. Georges Edelen (Ithaca, N.Y.: Cornell University Press, 1968), 254, 256.

29 Cited in Vale, ed., *The Gentleman's Recreations*, 29.

30 See, for example, T. S., *A Jewell for Gentrie* (1614; rpt. Amsterdam: Walter J. Johnson, 1977), F3v. This author, depending upon William Twiti's *The Art of Hunting* (1327), asserts that the hare is not only the king of all beasts of venery but the best sport.

31 For useful descriptions of all of these methods of hunting, see John Cummins, *The Hound and the Hawk: The Art of Medieval Hunting* (London: Weidenfeld and Nicolson, 1988), 32–67; although Cummins describes medieval customs, the essential nature of the hunt remained unchanged in the sixteenth and seventeenth centuries. The terminology used to describe the various kinds of hunting is vague in Shakespeare's period. Cummins' term "bow and stable" is not used, as far as I can tell, and "*par force*," when used, is often translated as "at force." The term "stable," Cummins suggests, probably refers not to the line of awaiting hunters but to the line of beaters whose job it was to herd the deer in the right direction (50–51). For additional descriptions of Elizabethan deer hunting, see Madden, *Diary of Master William Silence*, 11–65, 221–40.

32 *The Workes* (1616; rpt. Hildesheim: Georg Olms Verlag, 1971), 185–86.

33 Jean Wilson, *Entertainments for Elizabeth I* (Woodbridge, England: D. S. Brewer, 1980), 89–90.

34 For a lively survey of the use of parks in Shakespearean and Restoration drama, see Anne Barton, "Parks and Ardens," *Proceedings of the British Academy* 80 (1993): 13–104.

35 Sir Thomas Elyot, *The Book Named the Governor*, ed. S. E. Lehmberg (London: Dent, 1962), 68.

36 W. A. Baillie-Grohman and F. Baillie-Grohman, eds., *The Master of Game* (New York: Duffield, 1909), xxiii.

37 Chamberlain, *Henry the Eighth*, 181.

38 Manning, *Hunters and Poachers*, 194.

39 Ibid., 41.

40 Quoted from Schoenbaum, *Shakespeare's Lives* (Oxford: Clarendon Press, 1970), 109; Schoenbaum provides a detailed account of the various versions of the story, 108–14.

41 Ibid., 110.

42 Ibid., 111.

43 Ibid., 114, 716–17; E. K. Chambers, *William Shakespeare: A Study of Facts and Problems*, 2 vols. (Oxford: Clarendon Press, 1930), 1: 18–21.

44 Manning, *Hunters and Poachers*, 183.

45 Ibid., 10.
46 Richard Blome, *Gentleman's Recreation* (1686), 67.
47 Elizabeth Read Foster, ed., *Proceedings in Parliament 1610*, 2 vols. (New Haven: Yale University Press, 1966), 1: 51.
48 John Evelyn, *Sylva* (1664; rpt. Menston, England: Scolar Press, 1972), 115.
49 G. P. V. Akrigg, ed., *Letters of King James VI and I* (Berkeley: University of California Press, 1984), 246.
50 Thomas, *Man and the Natural World*, 153, 160–61.
51 Nichols, *Progresses*, 1: 17; the report notes that "Sir Thomas Pope had the *devising* of this show."
52 Manning, *Hunters and Poachers*, 19.
53 See *Annalia Dubrensia* (1636; rpt. Menston, Yorkshire, England: Scolar Press, 1973). In his introductory note, Bent Juel-Jensen indicates that Robert Dover "took over and revived" the games in about 1611; their date of origin is uncertain.
54 Sir Thomas Cockaine, *A Short Treatise of Hunting (1591)*, Shakespeare Association Facsimiles No.5 (Oxford University Press, 1932), A3–A3v.
55 Niccolò Machiavelli, *The Prince*, ed. and trans., Robert M. Adams, 2nd edn.(New York: W. W. Norton, 1992), 41.
56 Elyot, *Governor*, 66–67.
57 James I, *The Workes* (1616; rpt. Hildesheim: Georg Olms Verlag, 1971), 185–86. Praise for the martial hunt is also to be found in Plato's *Laws*, in which the noblest hunting is "the hunting of four-footed prey that employs horses, dogs, and the bodies of the hunters themselves. In this type the hunters use running, blows, and missiles thrown by their own hands to prevail over all their prey, and this is the type that should be practiced by whoever cultivates the courage that is divine" (Trans. Thomas L. Pangle [Basic Books: New York, 1980]), 217.
58 José Ortega y Gasset, *Meditations on Hunting*, trans. Howard B. Wescott (New York: Charles Scribners, 1972), 135.
59 Robert P. Adams, *The Better Part of Valor* (Seattle: University of Washington Press, 1962), 15, 45–47, 145–46. See also Claus Uhlig, "'The Sobbing Deer': *As You Like It*, ii.i.21–66 and the Historical Context," *Renaissance Drama* 3 (1970): 79–109; Uhlig sketches the development of this humanist tradition from its origin in John of Salisbury's *Policraticus* to Pope's *Windsor Forest*.
60 Thomas More, *Utopia*, trans. Ralph Robinson (1551; facs. rpt. Amsterdam: Da Capo Press, 1969), M2–M2v.
61 Desiderius Erasmus, *Chaloner: The Praise of Folie*, ed. Clarence H. Miller, *Early English Text Society* (London: Oxford University Press, 1965), 54.
62 Henry Cornelius Agrippa, *Of the Vanitie and Uncertaintie of Artes and Sciences*, ed. Catherine M. Dunn (Northridge: California State University, 1974), 260–63.
63 Sir Philip Sidney, *The Countess of Pembroke's Arcadia (The Old Arcadia)*, ed. Jean Robertson (Oxford: Clarendon Press, 1973), 259.
64 Ovid, *Metamorphoses*, trans. Mary M. Innes (Baltimore: Penguin Books, 1955), 31 33, 337.

65 Ortega y Gasset, *Meditations on Hunting*, 89.
66 Cavendish's poem is printed in *Kissing the Rod: An Anthology of Seventeenth-Century Women's Verse*, ed. Germaine Greer, et. al. (London: Virago Press, 1988), 168–72.
67 Cartmill, *A View to a Death*, 82–83; Cartmill identifies the author erroneously as Turbervile. Gascoigne's ambivalence is supported by the fact that three of the four subversive poems – those of the hare, fox, and badger – do not appear in the French original, and the fourth, that of the hart, is expanded from 99 to 133 lines (see *Arte of Venerie*, 135–40).
68 Thomas, *Man and the Natural World*, 154.
69 Philip Stubbes, *The Anatomie of Abuses* (1583; facs. rpt. Amsterdam: Da Capo Press, 1972), P5.
70 [Gascoigne], *Arte of Venerie*, chapter 76, p. 358 (the text's pagination is erroneous).
71 Thompson, *Whigs and Hunters*, 56.
72 Harrison, *Description*, 253–63, 326–29. For a useful treatment of Harrison's religious inclinations, see Annabel Patterson, *Reading Holinshed's Chronicles* (Chicago: University of Chicago Press, 1994), 26–27, 58–70.
73 Harrison, *Description*, 259.
74 *Hunters and Poachers*, 224.
75 *The Field* 3(1853): 342.
76 For Nonsuch, see Nichols, *Progresses*, I: 74n; for Cowdray, see Wilson, *Entertainments for Elizabeth I*, 89–90.
77 John Stevens, *Music and Poetry in the Early Tudor Court* (Cambridge: Cambridge University Press, 1979), 401.
78 [Gascoigne], *Arte of Venerie*, 140.
79 These are common to the hunting manuals. In the *Arte of Venerie*, for example, George Gascoigne cites the bone in the heart of the hart as a cure for trembling of the heart; the pizzle as a cure for the bloody flux; the head as an antidote to poisons; the horn as a cure for worms; and the marrow or grease as a cure for the gout (39–40).
80 For the medieval traditions behind this version of the hunt of love, see Marcelle Thiébaux, *The Stag of Love* (Ithaca, NY: Cornell University Press, 1974); Thiébaux cites Orsino's speech on p. 245.

2 HUNTRESSES IN *VENUS AND ADONIS* AND *LOVE'S LABOR'S LOST*

1 See *Kissing the Rod: An Anthology of Seventeenth-Century Women's Verse*, ed. Germaine Greer, et. al. (London: Virago Press, 1988), 172.
2 *Calendar of State Papers, Venetian*, 15 (10 July, 1618), 260.
3 Desiderius Erasmus, *Chaloner: The Praise of Folie*, ed. Clarence H. Miller, *Early English Text Society* (London: Oxford University Press, 1965), 54.
4 For a useful anthology of criticism on the poem, which includes a wide-ranging introductory survey, see Philip C. Kolin, ed., *Venus and Adonis: Critical Essays* (New York: Garland Publishing, 1997).

5 William Shakespeare, *The Poems*, ed. John Roe (Cambridge: Cambridge University Press, 1992), 135n. 1122.

6 Coppélia Kahn, for example, in *Man's Estate* (Berkeley: University of California Press, 1981), sees Adonis's claim that he is too young to love as merely a mask for his refusal to love at all (29); for her, Adonis is fatally narcissistic and his tragedy represents the idea that "for a man, sexual love of woman is vital to masculinity"(42). Although Adonis's adolescent narcissism is important to the poem, Kahn's formulation, as I hope will become clear, oversimplifies the characters of Adonis and Venus and the conception of love developed throughout.

7 In *Hunting in Middle English Literature* (Woodbridge, Suffolk: Boydell Press, 1993), Anne Rooney discusses the medieval tradition of the chaste hunter in ways that are suggestive for Adonis. She cites, in particular, a story curiously like that of Adonis, Marie de France's *Guigemar*, in which the hero, who spurns love but loves to hunt, wounds a mysterious white hind, only to have the arrow rebound and pierce his thigh. When Guigemar later falls in love, he leaves the hunt behind. In this story, as in others, according to Rooney, love of the hunt is linked to sexual immaturity (50–51).

8 G. P. V. Akrigg, ed., *Letters of King James VI and I* (Berkeley: University of California Press, 1984), 8. The portrait, by Arnold Bronckorst and dated *c.* 1580, is in the Scottish National Portrait Gallery, Edinburgh.

9 Charles Carlton, *Charles I* (London: Routledge and Kegan Paul, 1983), 3.

10 Ronald Hutton, *Charles the Second* (Oxford: Clarendon Press, 1989), 3.

11 For an account of the relationship between Shakespeare and the Earl, see G. P. V. Akrigg, *Shakespeare and the Earl of Southampton* (London: Hamish Hamilton, 1968). See also the provocative but unconvincingly abstract attempt by Patrick M. Murphy to read *Venus and Adonis* as a critique of the custom of wardship under which Southampton suffered: "Wriothesley's Resistance: Wardship Practices, and Ovidian Narratives in Shakespeare's *Venus and Adonis*," in *Venus and Adonis*, ed. Kolin, 323–43.

12 Quoted in Shakespeare, *The Poems*, ed. Roe, 13n.

13 Charlotte Carmichael Stopes, *The Life of Henry, Third Earl of Southampton, Shakespeare's Patron* (Cambridge: Cambridge University Press, 1922), 27.

14 *Calendar of State Papers, Domestic*. Edward VI. vol. II: 1581–90, 680 (14 July 1590); Akrigg, *Southampton*, 27.

15 B. W. Beckingsale, *Burghley, Tudor Statesman* (London: Macmillan, 1967), 276–77.

16 Akrigg, *Southampton*, 66, 136, 144.

17 For a brief review of Elizabethan adolescent and courtship customs, see Edward Berry, *Shakespeare's Comic Rites* (Cambridge: Cambridge University Press, 1984), 26–32.

18 *Berkeley Manuscripts: Abstracts and Extracts of Smyth's Lives of the Berkeleys*, ed. Thomas Dudley Fosbroke (London: John Nichols, 1821), 113, 186.

19 If, as a recent study of *Les Chasses* tentatively suggests, the young man is the young Ferdinand I, he would have been about thirty when the work was

being done. Both the identification and dates, however, are subject to doubt; see Arnout Balis, et al., *Les Chasses de Maximilien* (Paris: Editions de la Réunion des musées nationaux, 1993), 122.

20 Evidence of boar hunting is difficult to find and ambiguous. If the sport existed at all, it was certainly rare. See Joseph Strutt, *The Sports and Pastimes of the People of England*, ed. J. Charles Cox (London: Methuen, 1903), 14, and William Harrison, *The Description of England*, ed. Georges Edelen (Ithaca, N.Y.: Cornell University Press, 1968), 328. Roger B. Manning observes that if James I hunted a wild boar in Windsor Forest in 1617, it must have been put there for his pleasure; see *Hunters and Poachers* (Oxford: Clarendon Press, 1993), 23.

21 Quoted in John Cummins, *The Hound and the Hawk: The Art of Medieval Hunting* (London: Weidenfeld and Nicolson, 1988), 97. Cummins's book includes a useful survey of the nature of the medieval boar hunt and its symbolism (96–108). See also Rooney, *Hunting in Middle English Literature*, 78–85; Rooney argues that the "boar-hunter is a paragon of military prowess"(85).

22 [George Gascoigne], *The Noble Arte of Venerie or Hunting* (1575), 149.

23 Sir Thomas Elyot, *The Book Named the Governor*, ed. S. E. Lehmberg (London: Dent, 1962), 37.

24 For a brief review of interpretations of the boar, see Philip C. Kolin, "Venus and/or Adonis Among the Critics," in *Venus and Adonis*, ed. Kolin, 45–50.

25 Edward Topsell, *The Historie of the Foure-Footed Beastes* (1607; facs. rpt. Amsterdam: Da Capo Press, 1973), 697.

26 A. T. Hatto, "'Venus and Adonis' – and the Boar," *Modern Language Review* 41 (1946): 353–61.

27 Douglas Bush, *Mythology and the Renaissance Tradition in English Poetry* (1932; rpt. New York: Pageant Book Co., 1957), 138n.

28 William Keach, *Elizabethan Erotic Narratives* (New Brunswick, N.J.: Rutgers University Press, 1977), 81.

29 Don Cameron Allen, "On *Venus and Adonis*," in *Elizabethan and Jacobean Studies Presented to Frank Percy Wilson*, ed. Herbert Davis and Helen Gardner (Oxford: Clarendon Press, 1959), 100–11. W. R. Streitberger qualifies and extends Allen's argument usefully by placing Adonis's development in the context of Elizabethan adolescence. He, too, however, ignores the erotic implications of Adonis's love of the hunt, which he interprets as a desire for a healthy and moral life, as defined by such writers as Thomas Elyot. See W. R. Streitberger, "Ideal Conduct in *Venus and Adonis*," in *Venus and Adonis*, ed. Kolin, 171–79.

30 Marcelle Thiébaux notes that the medieval *Ovide Moralisé* treats Adonis's death as "a self-induced punishment for his excessive indulgence in hunting, a wicked pastime anyway which, taken allegorically, represents his lechery"(296); see "The Mouth of the Boar as a Symbol in Medieval Literature," *Romance Philology* 22 (1969): 281–99. There is no evidence that this interpretation influenced Shakespeare's.

31 Matt Cartmill, *A View to a Death in the Morning: Hunting and Nature through History* (Cambridge, Mass.: Harvard University Press, 1993), 238.

32 Jonathan Bate, *Shakespeare and Ovid* (Oxford: Clarendon Press, 1993), 60–65.

33 Bruce R. Smith, *Homosexual Desire in Shakespeare's England* (Chicago: University of Chicago Press, 1991), 136.

34 Harrison, *Description of England*, 254.

35 In an article confirming the identity of the portrait's subject as Elizabeth of Bohemia, Mark Weiss suggests that it was executed in conjunction with the painting of Prince Henry and Sir John Harington at the ritual death of the deer. Sir John was a close friend of Prince Henry's, and Elizabeth was sent to live with Lord and Lady Harington in Warwickshire. According to Weiss, close inspection of the two paintings reveals, in addition, that they represent the same deer, hound, and horse. See Mark Weiss, "Elizabeth of Bohemia by Robert Peake," *Apollo* 132 (1990): 407–10.

36 Jean Wilson, *Entertainments for Elizabeth I* (Woodbridge, England: D. S. Brewer, 1980), 89–90.

37 Elyot, *Governor*, 68.

38 James I, *The Workes* (1616; rpt. Hildesheim: Georg Olms Verlag, 1971), 185–86.

39 For brief but useful reviews of the traditions surrounding the hare, see Cummins, *Hound and the Hawk*, 110–19, and Beryl Rowland, *Animals with Human Faces* (Knoxville: University of Tennessee Press, 1973), 88–93.

40 See, for example, Allen, "On *Venus and Adonis*," 109.

41 Margaret Cavendish's "The Hunting of the Hare," which presents the hunt from the terrified hare's point of view, echoes Venus's description; see *Kissing the Rod*, 171.

42 [Gascoigne], *Arte of Venerie*, A4v.

43 Michel de Montaigne, *The Essays*, trans. John Florio (1603; facs. rpt. Menston, England: Scolar Press, 1969), 247, 249 (the latter page has been numbered erroneously as 237).

44 Keach, *Elizabethan Erotic Narratives*, 65.

45 Heather Dubrow, *Captive Victors: Shakespeare's Narrative Poems and Sonnets* (Ithaca, New York: Cornell University Press, 1987), 25–26.

46 Bate, *Shakespeare and Ovid*, 58.

47 Dubrow, *Captive Victors*, 42.

48 Keach, *Elizabethan Erotic Narratives*, 84.

49 See, however, Louis Adrian Montrose, *"Curious-Knotted Garden": The Form, Themes, and Contexts of Shakespeare's* Love's Labour's Lost (Salzburg: University of Salzburg, 1977), 109–12. Montrose's approach to the hunt complements my own, I believe, although he restricts himself to brief comments on its symbolic and metaphoric significance and does not develop its relationship to criticisms of hunting in Elizabethan society.

50 Ibid., 110.

51 Miriam Gilbert, *Love's Labour's Lost* (Manchester: Manchester University Press, 1993), 99; if I understand Gilbert correctly, this production also

represented the Princess as deciding not to hunt, an interpretation for which I can find no support in the text.

52 Graham Holderness, Nick Potter, and John Turner, *Shakespeare: Out of Court* (London: Macmillan, 1990), 19–48.

53 *The Geneva Bible*, ed. Lloyd E. Berry (1560; facs. rpt. Madison: University of Wisconsin Press, 1969), 2 *Corinthians*: i. 12.

54 William C. Carroll, *The Great Feast of Language in* Love's Labour's Lost (Princeton: Princeton University Press, 1976), 39.

55 Desiderius Erasmus, *Chaloner: The Praise of Folie*, ed. Clarence H. Miller, *Early English Text Society* (London: Oxford University Press, 1965), 54.

56 William C. Carroll discusses the speech as "choric commentary"; see *Great Feast of Language*, 91.

57 In a useful article that links Queen Elizabeth in detail to the Princess of France, Maurice Hunt suggests that the Princess's reluctance to hunt is "stereotypically feminine"(183). Hunt fails to consider the broad anti-hunting context within which the Princess's remarks are made; nor is he able to associate Elizabeth herself with such a negative view of hunting. See "The Double Figure of Elizabeth in *Love's Labor's Lost*," *Essays in Literature* 19 (1992): 173–92.

58 Patricia Parker, "Preposterous Reversals: *Love's Labor's Lost*," *Modern Language Quarterly* 54 (1993): 435–82. Parker demonstrates the ways in which the highbrow verbal comedy of the play is repeatedly "contaminated or brought low by the 'low matter' of the bodily and sexual"(437).

59 The terminology is conventional. John Manwood names a buck of the first year, a "Fawne"; of the second, a "Pricket"; of the third, a "Sorell"; of the fourth, a "Sore"; of the fifth, a "Bucke of the first head"; and of the sixth, a "Bucke, or, a great Bucke"(*Lawes of the Forest*, 43v).

60 Montrose, "*Curious-Knotted Garden*," 67–90.

61 David Bevington, "'Jack Hath Not Jill': Failed Courtship in Lyly and Shakespeare," *Shakespeare Survey* 42(1989): 6.

62 Montaigne, *Essays*, 251.

3 "SOLEMN" HUNTING IN *TITUS ANDRONICUS* AND *JULIUS CAESAR*

1 Geoffrey Bullough, ed., *Narrative and Dramatic Sources of Shakespeare*, 8 vols. (London: Routledge and Kegan Paul, 1957),VI: 40, 42. For a review of the debate on sources, see *Titus Andronicus*, ed. Alan Hughes (Cambridge: Cambridge University Press, 1994), 6–9.

2 Bullough, *Narrative and Dramatic Sources*, V:86.

3 The words "hart" and "stag" tend to be used interchangeably in descriptions of the hunt, since both were highly respected and hunted in the same ceremonial manner. The author of one handbook, for example, advises that "in the hunting of the Hart or Stag, being of all the most princely and royal chase, it giveth an exceeding grace unto a huntsman to use the tearmes fit and proper unto the same" (T. S., *A Jewell for Gentrie* [1614; rpt. Amsterdam:

Walter J. Johnson, 1977], F2). Technically, the hart was the larger and nobler of the two. John Manwood observes that "of all other beasts of venery, the Hart is the most noblest, and the most worthiest beast, and taketh the first place"(*A Treatise of the Lawes of the Forest* [1615; facs. rpt. Amsterdam: Walter J. Johnson, 1976], 41v).

4 "The Ceremonies of *Titus Andronicus*," in *Mirror Up To Shakespeare*, ed. J. C. Gray (Toronto: University of Toronto Press, 1984), 160; see also Stephen X. Mead, "The Crisis of Ritual in *Titus Andronicus*," *Exemplaria* 6 (1994): 459–79; Mead reads the play as "a crisis of community-binding ritual"(463).

5 For an illuminating study of the importance of this feast to the ritualism of the play, see Naomi Conn Liebler, *Shakespeare's Festive Tragedy* (London: Routledge, 1995), 85–111; Liebler sees in the Rome of the play a conflict between a traditional religious order and an emerging secular and political one.

6 For insightful accounts of both plays in relation to the commonplace Elizabethan horror of human sacrifice, which was intensified both by Reformation debates about the Mass and by colonial encounters abroad, see Richard Marienstras, *New Perspectives on the Shakespearean World*, trans. Janet Lloyd (Cambridge: Cambridge University Press, 1985), 40–72.

7 Walter Burkert, *Homo Necans: The Anthropology of Ancient Greek Sacrificial Ritual and Myth*, trans. Peter Bing (Berkeley: University of California Press, 1983), 38.

8 See Arnold Van Gennep, *The Rites of Passage*, trans. Monika B. Vizedom and Gabrielle L. Caffee (Chicago: University of Chicago Press, 1960).

9 See [George Gascoigne], *The Noble Arte of Venerie or Hunting* (1575), 90, 95.

10 [Gascoigne], *Arte of Venerie*, 126–35; further citations to this edition are indicated parenthetically.

11 William Twiti, *The Art of Hunting (1327)*, ed. Bror Danielsson, *Stockholm Studies in English 37* (Stockholm: Almqvist and Wiksell, 1977), 51. Stage representations of this event suggest that it was widespread in the period; see my treatment of the procession homeward in *As You Like It* (p. 181).

12 See Keith Thomas, *Man and the Natural World* (London: Allen Lane, 1983), 17–50.

13 *Countrey Contentments* (1615; facs. rpt. Amsterdam: Theatrum Orbis Terrarum, 1973), 3.

14 Michel De Montaigne, *The Essays*, trans. John Florio (1603; facs. rpt. Menston, England: Scolar Press, 1969), 248. See also Richard Marienstras's insightful treatment of the ritual of the hunt in *New Perspectives*, 11–39.

15 *Lawes of the Forest*, 18–18v.

16 *Chaloner: The Praise of Folie*, ed. Clarence H. Miller, *Early English Text Society* (London: Oxford University Press, 1965), 54.

17 As Anne Barton observes, both the setting and nature of this hunt are ambiguous; see "Parks and Ardens," *Proceedings of the British Academy* 80 (1993): 55–56. At different times, the hunt seems to take place in a forest, chase, and park; to some characters, the place is cheerful, to some, ominous.

The sport combines, oddly, the pursuit of a panther into a pit and the *par force* pursuit of a stag. The confusion seems appropriate in a play that dissolves the boundaries between the civilized and barbarian.

18 For the custom of the *reveille*, see John Brand, *Observations on Popular Antiquities* (London: Chatto and Windus, 1877), 403–05. For a description of making a bay, see [Gascoigne], *Arte of Venerie*, 124–27.

19 For an enlightening discussion of the displacement of the Virgilian by the Ovidian myth throughout the play, see Heather James, "Cultural Disintegration in *Titus Andronicus*: Mutilating Titus, Vergil and Rome," *Themes in Drama* 13 (1991): 123–40.

20 Ovid, *Metamorphoses*, trans. Mary M. Innes (Baltimore: Penguin Books, 1955), 152.

21 William Harrison, *The Description of England*, ed. Georges Edelen (Ithaca, N.Y.: Cornell University Press, 1968), 132.

22 The most influential study of *Julius Caesar* from this perspective is that of Brents Stirling in *Unity in Shakespearian Tragedy* (New York: Columbia University Press, 1956), 40–54.

23 The image of a carcass hewn and thrown to the hounds probably refers to the fox, marten or gray; see D. H. Madden, *The Diary of Master William Silence* (London: Longmans, Green, 1907), 63.

24 René Girard, *A Theater of Envy: William Shakespeare* (New York: Oxford University Press, 1991), 213. Girard's theory of the sacrificial crisis fits *Julius Caesar* unusually well; in his view, Cassius's mimetic envy of Caesar precipitates an act of foundational violence, which fails because it does not encompass the total community (185–226). Girard's conception of the origin of sacrifice is interestingly juxtaposed with Burkert's in Robert G. Hamerton-Kelly, ed., *Violent Origins* (Stanford: Stanford University Press, 1987).

25 Arthur Humphreys notes that the word "spoil" was a "hunting term for the cutting up of the quarry, from Old French *espoille*, Latin *spolium*, the skin stripped from the dead animal." His commentary on the passage as a whole is helpful; see *Julius Caesar*, ed. Arthur Humphreys, *The World's Classics* (Oxford: Oxford University Press, 1994), 170n.206.

26 Allusions to the tradition occur in Wyatt's sonnet, "Whoso List to Hunt" and in [Gascoigne], *Arte of Venerie*, 43. For a richly documented study of the tradition, see Michael Bath, *The Image of the Stag: Iconographic Themes in Western Art* (Baden-Baden: Verlag Valentin Koerner, 1992), 23–64.

27 For an account of the importance of blood to the spectacle of the play, see Leo Kirschbaum, "Shakespeare's Stage Blood," in *Shakespeare: Julius Caesar*, ed. Peter Ure (London: Macmillan, 1969), 152–59; Kirschbaum's article was originally published in *PMLA* 64(1949).

28 For the rite of "blooding," see above, pp. 39–41. The account of bathing occurs in a letter of 12 June, 1619 from Nathaniel Brent to Sir Thomas Edmondes; see *Calendar of State Papers, Domestic, 1619–23* (London: 1858), x: 53. Reports of the medicinal and cosmetic value of bathing in deer's blood are common in the hunting manuals; Gervase Markham, for example, says

that the blood of the stag is "excellent for all kinde of Fluxes, and to make the skin white and smooth"; see *Countrey Contentments*, 28.

29 Who actually kills the stag is not described in most of the manuals. They tend to imply, however, that the killing is done by a single individual. The *Noble Arte* illustrates the event with a woodcut showing a hart at bay and a single huntsman, sword drawn; see chapter 41. It is quite possible, of course, that the dogs themselves would often kill the animal. Sir Thomas Cockaine seems to imply as much in his description of the death: "When you have killed the Stagge with your hounds . . ."(c3); see *A Short Treatise of Hunting (1591)*, Shakespeare Association Facsimiles *No.5* (Oxford University Press, 1932). Antony's use of the word "princes" would become doubly ironic in such a case.

30 *Arte of Venerie*, 124–25. The French original includes the story of the Emperor and a general moral on the variability of fortune but lacks any acknowledgment of the moral difficulty that disturbs Gascoigne; see Jaques Du Fouilloux, *La Venerie de Jaques du Fouilloux* (Paris: Abel l'Angelier, 1606), 52.

31 *Hunters and Poachers*, 48.

32 John Smyth, *The Lives of the Berkeleys*, ed. John Maclean, 3 vols. (Gloucester: John Bellows, 1883–85), II: 378–79.

33 Manning, *Hunters and Poachers*, 137.

34 For an account of the complex mixture of politics, religion, and economics in a massacre of deer in 1642, see Dan Beaver, "The Great Deer Massacre: Animals, Honor, and Communication in Early Modern England," *Journal of British Studies* 38 (1999): 187–216.

35 Madden, *Diary of Master William Silence*, 31–32.

4 THE "MANNING" OF KATHERINE: FALCONRY IN *THE TAMING OF THE SHREW*

1 Edwin Wilson, ed., *Shaw on Shakespeare* (New York: E. P. Dutton, 1961), 188.

2 Lynda E. Boose, "Scolding Brides and Bridling Scolds: Taming the Woman's Unruly Member," *Shakespeare Quarterly* 42 (1991): 181n. Boose's own essay powerfully challenges this consensus by placing the play in the context of the barbaric custom of bridling scolds. For reasons that should become clear, although I much admire Boose's essay, I find that the taming of falcons provides a more immediate context for the play than the bridling of scolds. Boose provides a helpful list of criticism dealing with issues of gender. For a more recent and more general survey of criticism, and a helpful contextual guide, see Frances E. Dolan, *William Shakespeare, The Taming of the Shrew: Texts and Contexts* (New York: St. Martin's Press, 1996). The most thorough survey of the theatrical tradition is to be found in Tori Haring-Smith, *From Farce to Metadrama: A Stage History of 'The Taming of the Shrew,' 1594–1983* (Westport, Conn.: Greenwood Press, 1985); see also Graham Holderness, *The Taming of the Shrew* (Manchester: Manchester University Press), 1989.

3 Robert B. Heilman, "The 'Taming' Untamed, or the Return of the Shrew," *Modern Language Quarterly* 27 (1966): 157.

4 Peter Saccio, "Shrewd and Kindly Farce," *Shakespeare Survey* 37 (1984): 33–40.

5 John C. Bean, "Comic Structure and the Humanizing of Kate in *The Taming of the Shrew*," in *The Woman's Part: Feminist Criticism of Shakespeare*, ed. Carolyn Ruth Swift Lenz et al. (1980), 74.

6 Joel Fineman, "The Turn of the Shrew," in *Shakespeare and the Question of Theory*, ed. Patricia Parker and Geoffrey Hartman (New York: Methuen, 1985), 141.

7 Saccio, "Shrewd and Kindly Farce," 37.

8 Marianne Novy, *Love's Argument* (Chapel Hill: University of North Carolina Press, 1984), 62.

9 *The Geneva Bible*, ed. Lloyd E. Berry (1560; facs. rpt. Madison: University of Wisconsin Press, 1969), 1.28.

10 Gervase Markham, *Countrey Contentments* (1615; facs. rpt. Amsterdam: Da Capo Press, 1973), 2–3.

11 George Turbervile, *The Booke of Faulconrie or Hauking* (1575; facs. rpt. Amsterdam: Theatrum Orbis Terrarum, 1969), 6.

12 Anne Barton, "Introduction" to *The Taming of the Shrew*, in *The Riverside Shakespeare*, ed. G. Blakemore Evans (Boston: Houghton Mifflin, 1974), 106.

13 Fredson Bowers, ed., *The Dramatic Works in the Beaumont and Fletcher Canon*, vol. IV (Cambridge: Cambridge University Press, 1979), 1.2.147–57.

14 The definition is from the very useful glossary provided in Frederick II of Hohenstaufen, *The Art of Falconry*, ed. and trans., Casey A. Wood and F. Marjorie Fyfe (Stanford: Stanford University Press, 1943).

15 Ibid.

16 Symon Latham, *Lathams Falconry* (1615; facs. rpt. Amsterdam: Theatrum Orbis Terrarum, 1976), 4; for a useful survey of Shakespeare's treatment of falconry, see Maurice Pope, "Shakespeare's Falconry," *Shakespeare Survey* 44 (1991): 131–43.

17 Edmund Bert, *An Approved Treatise of Hawkes and Hawking* (1619; facs. rpt. Amsterdam: Theatrum Orbis Terrarum, 1968), 3.

18 Bert, *Hawkes and Hawking*, 7.

19 Frederick II of Hohenstaufen, *Art of Falconry*, 157.

20 Markham, *Countrey Contentments*, 88–89. The word "broaking," if such it is (the "b" is difficult to decipher) presumably comes from the verb "to broke," which means to negotiate or bargain; or perhaps the word is "stroaking." George R. Hibbard quotes the passage, with the word as "stroaking," in "*The Taming of the Shrew*: A Social Comedy," *Tennessee Studies in Literature*, Special Issue No. 2 (1964): 15–28; Hibbard's insightful article focuses on the play as a realistic and satiric depiction of the marriage market in Elizabethan England.

21 T. H. White, *The Goshawk* (London: Jonathan Cape, 1951), 16. White's account of his own, ultimately unsuccessful, attempt to train a hawk by

Elizabethan methods conveys forcefully the complex and intense relationship between man and bird.

22 Bert, *Hawkes and Hawking*, 41, 49.

23 Laurie E. Maguire makes this point in her insightful discussion of Shakespeare's several Kates: "'Household Kates': Chez Petruchio, Percy and Plantagenet," in *Gloriana's Face*, ed. S. P. Cerasano and Marion Wynne-Davies (Detroit: Wayne State University Press, 1992), 133.

24 *The Geneva Bible*, Genesis 2.20.

25 Turbervile, *Booke of Faulconrie or Hauking*, 130, 142.

26 Bert, *Hawkes and Hawking*, 52.

27 Wilson, ed., *Shaw on Shakespeare*, 186. The stage tradition of the whip seems to have originated with Garrick in the nineteenth century; see Haring-Smith, *From Farce to Metadrama*, 29. A delightful variation on the whip motif occurs in the 1929 film of the play featuring Douglas Fairbanks, Jr. and Mary Pickford: Petruchio carries a big whip but is eventually cowed by Katherine, who carries a small one.

28 White, *Goshawk*, 102.

29 Camille Wells Slights, "The Raw and the Cooked in *The Taming of the Shrew*," *Journal of English and Germanic Philology* 88 (1989): 180; although I am not finally persuaded by Slights's article, she presents a thoughtful case for Petruchio as teaching Katherine "that she can create her own identity"(181).

30 In the Arden edition of the play, Brian Morris also sees this episode in relation to the training of a falcon. For Morris, however, it is merely one of a series of tests of obedience that culminates in Katherine's final speech; he does not distinguish between the process of training and the practice of the sport itself, which occurs in the final scene of the play (see *The Taming of the Shrew* [London: Methuen, 1981], 127–28).

31 Latham, *Lathams Falconry*, 24–25.

32 See *Annalia Dubrensia. Upon the yeerely celebration of Mr. Robert Dovers Olimpick Games upon Cotswold-Hills* (London: 1636).

33 This is the gloss provided by H. J. Oliver; see *The Taming of the Shrew* (Oxford: Oxford University Press, 1994), 223n.33. In *The Noble Arte of Venerie or Hunting* (1575), George Gascoigne directs the hunters to start the chase of a "harbored" deer by crying "To him, to him, thats he thats he"(106).

34 For further development of connections between the induction and the ending, see Dorothea Kehler, "Echoes of the Induction in *The Taming of the Shrew*," *Renaissance Papers* (1986): 31–42.

35 Margaret Loftus Ranald, *Shakespeare and His Social Context* (New York: AMS Press, 1987), 117.

36 Ibid., 119.

37 Ibid., 132.

38 Turbervile, *Booke of Faulconrie*, 6.

39 Dolan, The Taming of the Shrew: *Texts and Contexts*, 307–08; Dolan provides a brief discussion of the role of falconry in the play and excerpts from the books on falconry by Turbervile and Latham (304–12).

40 Morris, ed., *The Taming of the Shrew*, 128, 133, 143.
41 Bean, "Comic Structure," 65–78.
42 See William and Malleville Haller, "The Puritan Art of Love," *Huntington Library Quarterly* 5 (1942), 250–51.
43 Thomas, *Man and the Natural World*, 32–33.
44 Quoted in Matt Cartmill, *A View to a Death in the Morning: Hunting and Nature through History* (Cambridge, Mass.: Harvard University Press, 1993), 51.
45 Latham, *Lathams Falconry*, 35.
46 For a radically different reading of this episode, see P. J. Gabriner, "Hierarchy, Harmony and Happiness: Another Look at the Hunting Dogs in the 'Induction' to *The Taming of the Shrew*," in *Reclamations of Shakespeare*, ed. A. J. Hoenselaars (Amsterdam: Rodopi, 1994), 201–10. Gabriner interprets the dogs as "an emblem of the comic ideal, in which individual voices are neither eliminated nor merged into one, but are rather so ranged within a natural order that mutual harmony and social happiness become possible"; they therefore represent the natural hierarchical order into which Katherine is "liberated" by Petruchio (210).
47 [Gascoigne], *Arte of Venerie*, 32–38.
48 Thomas, *Man and the Natural World* (London: Allen Lane, 1983), 103.
49 [Gascoigne], *Arte of Venerie*, 34, 30.
50 Coppélia Kahn, *Man's Estate* (Berkeley: University of California Press, 1981), 104, 117.
51 Holderness, *The Taming of the Shrew*, 26–48; for the earlier stage history, see Haring-Smith, *From Farce to Metadrama*.
52 Leah Marcus, "The Shakespearean Editor as Shrew-Tamer," *English Literary Renaissance* 22 (1992): 178, 198–99.
53 John Smyth was born in 1567 and joined the household of Lord Henry Berkeley in 1584 to attend upon the son and heir, Thomas, then nine years old. He joined William Ligon and young Thomas for studies at Magdalen College, Oxford, for three years and then studied at the Middle Temple. He rejoined the household in 1596, serving in various capacities, and died in 1640. Although the title-page indicates that his history ends in 1618, Smyth must have added to it after that date, for in some instances it extends to 1628. I use the following edition of the work throughout this chapter, citing page references to volume II (1883) parenthetically: John Smyth, *The Lives of the Berkeleys*, ed. John Maclean, 3 vols. (Gloucester: John Bellows, 1883–85). For a summary of Smyth's life, see the preface to volume I. Smyth's account of the family, including the members for whom he worked, is remarkably candid and lends credence to his dedicatory statement of purpose: "In a playne and home-bred stile cleere from passion or partiallity, Ile freely write the truth I know."
54 Most editors now consider the mysterious play entitled *The Taming of A Shrew* to be dependent upon Shakespeare's *The Taming of the Shrew*. If they are correct, then *The Shrew* must have been written before 1594, when *A Shrew* was published; generally, editors suggest 1592 or somewhat earlier for

Shakespeare's work. For an excellent introduction to the play, including the question of date, see the edition of Ann Thompson (Cambridge: Cambridge University Press, 1984). The argument for the Berkeleys as a "source" does not depend upon a specific date for Shakespeare's play or a specific relationship between it and *A Shrew*.

55 See H. R. Woudhuysen, *Sir Philip Sidney and the Circulation of Manuscripts 1558–1640* (Oxford: Clarendon Press, 1996); Woudhuysen argues that the Queen's College copy of the *Old Arcadia* was probably made for Henry Berkeley, whose connections to the Sidney family were close enough to allow some talk of marriage between his daughters and Philip and Robert Sidney in 1573. Woudhuysen suggests "that few would call a bird Stella unless they had a particular interest in Sidney and his literary works"(326).

56 Manning, *Hunters and Poachers*, 141; see also 139–43.

57 E. K. Chambers, *The Elizabethan Stage*, 4 vols. (Oxford: Clarendon Press, 1923), II: 103–04.

58 Mark Eccles, *Shakespeare in Warwickshire* (Madison: University of Wisconsin Press, 1961), 116–17. The first to provide a detailed account of Thomas Russell was Leslie Hotson; see *I, William Shakespeare* (New York: Oxford University Press, 1938).

59 See the Arden edition of *A Midsummer Night's Dream*, ed. Harold F. Brooks (Bristol: Methuen, 1979), liii–lvii.

60 For discussions of the sources, see Geoffrey Bullough, ed., *Narrative and Dramatic Sources of Shakespeare*, 8 vols. (London: Routledge and Kegan Paul, 1957), II: 57–68, and Thompson, *Shrew*, 9–17.

61 Ibid., 11, 13.

5 THE "RASCAL" FALSTAFF IN WINDSOR

1 The pun is clear from Holoferne's lines in *Love's Labor's Lost* describing the deer the Princess has killed: "The deer was (as you know) *sanguis*, in blood, ripe as the pomewater . . ."(4.2.3–4).

2 Although the *Oxford English Dictionary* places the first appearance of the latter meaning of "embossed" no earlier than 1641, it is used in this sense in reference to a stag hunt by Florio in Montaigne's essay, "Of Cruelty," published in 1603; see *The Essays*, trans. John Florio (1603; facs. rpt. Menston, England: Scolar Press, 1969), 249 (the page is marked erroneously, 237).

3 The most influential treatment of Falstaff's resurrection from this perspective has been C. L. Barber's; see *Shakespeare's Festive Comedy* (1959; rpt. Cleveland: World Publishing Company, 1968), 205–13. For an account of the folk-plays, see E. K. Chambers, *The English Folk-Play* (1933; rpt. New York: Russell and Russell, 1964), and Alan Brody, *The English Mummers and Their Plays* (Philadelphia: University of Pennsylvania Press, 1970); Brody includes photographs of the Bromley horn dancers (figs. 5, 6).

4 J. Dover Wilson, *The Fortunes of Falstaff* (Cambridge: Cambridge University Press, 1964), 25–31.

5 See Roger B. Manning, *Hunters and Poachers* (Oxford: Clarendon Press, 1993), 10, and William Harrison, *The Description of England*, ed. Georges Edelen (Ithaca, N.Y.: Cornell University Press, 1968), 132. Harrison notes that if "the inferior sort of artificers and husbandmen" come upon a piece of venison and a cup of wine" at a feast, they imagine themselves to have "fared so well as the Lord Mayor of London."

6 Katherine Duncan-Jones and Jan Van Dorsten, eds., *Miscellaneous Prose of Sir Philip Sidney* (Oxford: Clarendon Press, 1973), 97; a crowder is a fiddler.

7 John E. Housman, ed., *British Popular Ballads* (New York: Barnes and Noble,1952), 177; further citations to this edition are indicated parenthetically by stanza.

8 It is possible that the ballad is also echoed in the witches' prophecy in *Macbeth*. The witches tell Macbeth that "none of woman born" shall "harm" him (4.1.80–81). In the ballad, Percy meets Douglas's challenge with the assertion that he has never feared single combat with any man: "Nethar in Ynglonde, Skottlonde, nar France, / nor for no man of a woman born, / But, and fortune be my chance, / I dar met him, on man for on" (st. 21). He repeats the words in stanza 35.

9 Manning, *Hunters and Poachers*, 49.

10 An extreme version of this tendency may be seen in the Coburg Hunting Chronicle of the Emperor Maximilian, written in 1499–1500. Images from the Chronicle are reproduced in William A. Baillie-Grohman, *Sport in Art*, 2nd edn. (London: Simpkin, Marshall, Hamilton, Kent and Co., 1919); figure 113, for example, which depicts the weighing of stags, shows about fifteen corpses meticulously lined up according to size in an enclosed field full of dogs, hunters, horses, and carts.

11 The Oxford editor, T. W. Craik, provides a useful survey of these issues in *The Merry Wives of Windsor* (Oxford: Clarendon Press, 1989), 1–13, 48–63. See also Leah Marcus's convincing treatment of the Quarto and Folio as independent texts in "Levelling Shakespeare: Local Customs and Local Texts," *Shakespeare Quarterly* 42 (1991): 168–78, and Barbara Freedman's thoughtful challenge to the conventional arguments surrounding the questions of date and occasion: "Shakespearean Chronology, Ideological Complicity, and Floating Texts: Something is Rotten in Windsor," *Shakespeare Quarterly* 45 (1994): 190–210. Arthur F. Kinney has extended Marcus's approach to the texts of the play; see "Textual Signs in *The Merry Wives of Windsor*," *Yearbook of English Studies* 23 (1993): 206–34. In view of Marcus's argument, I should note that my interpretation is directed primarily to the Folio text, which highlights the locale of Windsor. The edition of the play in *The Riverside Shakespeare*, which I cite parenthetically throughout this study, is based on the Folio.

12 R. S. White, *The Merry Wives of Windsor* (New York: Harvester Wheatsheaf, 1991), 2.

13 Anne Barton, "Falstaff and the Comic Community," in *Shakespeare's "Rough Magic"*, ed. Peter Erickson, and Coppélia Kahn (Newark: University of Delaware Press, 1985), 142.

14 Linda Anderson, *A Kind of Wild Justice* (Newark: University of Delaware Press, 1987), 68.

15 For the generalizations in this paragraph, see Peter Clark, "A Crisis Contained? The Condition of English Towns in the 1590s," *The European Crisis of the 1590s*, ed. Peter Clark (London: Allen and Unwin, 1985), 45; David Underdown, *Revel, Riot, and Rebellion* (Oxford: Clarendon Press, 1985), 33; and Keith Wrightson, *English Society 1580–1680* (London: Hutchinson, 1982), 149–82.

16 Wrightson, *English Society*, 150.

17 Ibid., 157.

18 Keith Wrightson, "Two Concepts of Order: Justices, Constables and Jurymen in Seventeenth-Century England," in *An Ungovernable People*, ed. John Brewer, and John Styles (London: Hutchinson, 1980), 24.

19 Mildred Campbell, *The English Yeoman* (1942; rpt. The Hague: Krips Reprint Company, 1960), 382.

20 Wrightson, *English Society*, 51.

21 Ibid., 51–57.

22 See Martin Ingram, "Ridings, Rough Music and the 'Reform of Popular Culture' in Early Modern England," *Past and Present* 105 (1984): 86, and Susan Dwyer Amussen, *An Ordered Society* (Oxford: Basil Blackwell, 1988), 50.

23 Manning, *Hunters and Poachers*, 68

24 *The Political Works of James I*, ed. Charles H. McIlwain (Cambridge, Mass.: Harvard University Press, 1918), 342.

25 Manning, *Hunters and Poachers*, 160, 164, 167.

26 If Shallow represents Sir Thomas Lucy, as seems to be the case, and if the satire commemorates Shakespeare's own poaching as a youth, then the episode includes an additional kind of symbolic assault, identifying Shakespeare, delightfully, with Falstaff; see above, p. 20.

27 Manning, *Hunters and Poachers*, 188.

28 Resolutions in the Privy Council for 1582 and 1589 attempted rather ineffectually to shift the burden of private complaints to other courts, unless they concerned, as stated in the 1582 resolution, "'the preservacion of her Majesties peace or shalbe of some publicke consequence to touche the government of the Realme'"; see Sir William Holdsworth, *A History of English Law* (London: Methuen, 1903), 1: 498.

29 Wrightson, *English Society*, 61.

30 Rosemary Kegl, "'The Adoption of Abominable Terms': The Insults that Shape Windsor's Middle Class," *ELH* 61 (1994): 265. Kegl also provides a useful account of the ineffectuality of Shallow and Evans as representatives of legal and ecclesiastical authority.

31 Joan Rees, "Shakespeare's Welshmen," in *Literature and Nationalism*, ed. Vincent Newey, and Ann Thompson (Liverpool: Liverpool University Press, 1991), 38.

32 Other critics have noted the relevance of charivari to the play; for especially helpful comments, see François Laroque, "Ovidian Transformations and Folk Festivities in *A Midsummer Night's Dream, The Merry Wives of Windsor*, and

As You Like It," *Cahiers Elisabethains* 25 (1984): 23–36, and C. Gallenca, "Ritual and Folk Custom in *The Merry Wives of Windsor,"* *Cahiers Elisabethains* 27 (1985): 27–41. As far as I am aware, no critic has dealt with the play's reflections upon charivari, or with the tensions created by adapting such a social form to comic ends.

33 Ingram, "Ridings," 86.

34 Ibid., 82.

35 Ibid., 86.

36 E. P. Thompson, *Customs in Common* (New York: New Press, 1991), 480.

37 Natalie Zemon Davis, *Society and Culture in Early Modern France* (Stanford: Stanford University Press, 1975), 140.

38 Ingram, "Ridings," 96.

39 For an insightful treatment of the complex relationship between the two characters, see William C. Carroll, *The Metamorphoses of Shakespearean Comedy* (Princeton: Princeton University Press, 1985), 183–202.

40 In his reproduction of Norden's 1607 map of Windsor Castle, William Green situates Herne's Oak within the Little Park; see *Shakespeare's* The Merry Wives of Windsor (Princeton: Princeton University Press, 1962), fig. 2.

41 Manning, *Hunters and Poachers,* 153; see also 157 and 218–19.

42 See Thompson, *Customs,* 470–71, and Theo Brown, "The 'Stag-Hunt' in Devon," *Folklore* 63 (1952): 104–9. Although probably of ancient origin, this brutal sport is not recorded until well after the Elizabethan period.

43 Jeanne Addison Roberts treats the ambiguity of Falstaff's role in the final scene with particular insight; see *Shakespeare's English Comedy* (Lincoln: University of Nebraska Press, 1979), 110–16.

44 John M. Steadman, "Falstaff as Actaeon: A Dramatic Emblem," *Shakespeare Quarterly* 14 (1963): 231–44.

45 G. R. Hibbard, for example, sees the play as endorsing "the values of the Elizabethan bourgeoisie, the class from which its author came and to which he belonged"; see his edition, *The Merry Wives of Windsor* (Middlesex: Penguin Books, 1973), 14. George K. Hunter takes a similar view, arguing that Shakespeare implicitly endorses the efforts of Windsor to resist social change; see "Bourgeois Comedy: Shakespeare and Dekker," in *Shakespeare and His Contemporaries,* ed. E. A. J. Honigmann (Manchester: University of Manchester Press, 1986), 14. Peter Erickson sees the image of the Garter and the triumph of Fenton as justifying the aristocracy, although he concludes that male anxiety about female rule prevents Shakespeare from endorsing the power of the state; see "The Order of the Garter, the Cult of Elizabeth, and Class-Gender Tension in *The Merry Wives of Windsor,"* in *Shakespeare Reproduced,* ed. Jean E. Howard, and Marion F. O'Connor (New York: Methuen, 1987), 126–34. Rosemary Kegl notes that the restoration of order by the wives reinforces "the play's more general sense that town gentlemen are the ideal custodians of both the town and the nation" ("Adoption," 272).

46 Both the Quarto and Folio texts assign the role of Fairy Queen in act 5 scene

5 to Mistress Quickly. During the preparations for the scene, however, Mistress Page says that "My Nan shall be the queen of all the fairies, / Finely attired in a robe of white"(4.4.71–72). The discrepancy has led some directors to substitute Anne for Quickly in the role; see Peter Evans, "'To the Oak, to the Oak!' The Finale of *The Merry Wives of Windsor*," *Theatre Notebook* 40(1986): 106–14.

6 PASTORAL HUNTING IN *AS YOU LIKE IT*

1 Paul Alpers, *What Is Pastoral?* (Chicago: University of Chicago Press, 1996), 22.

2 I quote from *The Pastoral Poems*, trans. E. V. Rieu (Harmondsworth, Middlesex: Penguin, 1949), 33, 21, 83. For a general discussion of Roman hunting in the time of Virgil, see J. K. Anderson, *Hunting in the Ancient World* (Berkeley: University of California Press, 1985), 83–100; Anderson restricts himself to the hunting of gentlemen and nobles and does not indicate whether there were restrictions placed on the hunting of common people, as there were in the Elizabethan period.

3 *The Works of Edmund Spenser: A Variorum Edition*, ed. Edwin Greenlaw et al., 11 vols. (Baltimore: Johns Hopkins Press, 1943), VII.

4 For the legal position of wild animals among the Romans, see C. M. C. Green, "Did the Romans Hunt?," *Classical Antiquity* 15 (1996): 222–60. See also Robert Pogue Harrison, *Forests: The Shadow of Civilization* (Chicago: University of Chicago Press, 1992), 49. Harrison observes: "The public Roman domain – the domain of its civic jurisdiction – included the sacred city as well as the patricians' rural estates, but it did not extend past the edge of the forests. The forests were in fact commonly referred to as the *locus neminis*, or 'place of no one'(it is probable that even the Latin word *nemus*, or woodlands, comes from *nemo*, meaning 'no one')."

5 Sir Thomas Elyot, *The Book Named the Governor*, ed. S. E. Lehmberg (London: Dent, 1962), 68.

6 William A. Ringler, Jr., ed., *The Poems of Sir Philip Sidney* (Oxford: Clarendon Press, 1962), 25, 103.

7 Sir Philip Sidney, *The Countess of Pembroke's Arcadia (The New Arcadia)*, ed. Victor Skretkowicz (Oxford: Clarendon Press, 1987), 54.

8 Michael Drayton, *The Works of Michael Drayton*, ed. J. William Hebel (Oxford: Basil Blackwell, 1961), III: 294.

9 Edward, Duke of York, *The Master of Game*, ed. Wm. A. and F. Baillie-Grohman (London: Chatto and Windus, 1909), 8–9.

10 [George Gascoigne], *The Noble Arte of Venerie or Hunting* (1575), 90.

11 Edward, Duke of York, *Master of Game*, 10.

12 [Gascoigne], *Arte of Venerie*, 140.

13 Francis James Child, ed., *English and Scottish Popular Ballads*, 5 vols. (Boston: Houghton, Mifflin, 1888), III: 78.

14 Manning, *Hunters and Poachers*, 20–22.

15 Anthony Munday, *The Huntingdon Plays: A Critical Edition of The Downfall and The Death of Robert, Earl of Huntingdon*, ed. John Carney Meagher (New York: Garland Publishing, 1980), 199–200.

16 See, for example, Louis Adrian Montrose, "'Eliza, Queene of shepheardes,' and the Pastoral of Power," *English Literary Renaissance* 10 (1980): 153–82, and Annabel Patterson, *Pastoral and Ideology* (Berkeley: University of California Press, 1987). Patterson's account of Spenser's pastorals allows more room for social and political criticism than Montrose's, but even she finds Spenserian pastoral ambivalent rather than subversive.

17 For social protests in the forests, see Peter Stallybrass, "'Drunk with the Cup of Liberty': Robin Hood, the carnivalesque, and the rhetoric of violence in early modern England," in *The Violence of Representation*, ed. Nancy Armstrong and Leonard Tennenhouse (London: Routledge, 1989).

18 For a useful survey of the forest and pasture settings in the play, see A. Stuart Daley, "Where are the Woods in *As You Like It?*," *Shakespeare Quarterly* 34 (1983): 172–80.

19 Thomas Lodge, *Rosalynde*, ed. Geoffrey Bullough, vol. II, *Narrative and Dramatic Sources of Shakespeare* (London: Routledge and Kegan Paul, 1958), 180, 183.

20 John Manwood, *A Treatise of the Lawes of the Forest* (1615; facs. rpt. Amsterdam: Walter J. Johnson, 1976), 18–18v.

21 J. Charles Cox, *The Royal Forests of England* (London: Methuen, 1905), 229.

22 Lucy Toulmin Smith, ed., *Leland's Itinerary in England and Wales*, 5 vols. (London: Centaur Press, 1964), II: 47.

23 Quoted in William Cooper, *Henley-in-Arden* (Birmingham: Cornish Bros., 1946), xi.

24 Ann Hughes, *Politics, Society and Civil War in Warwickshire, 1620–1660* (Cambridge: Cambridge University Press, 1987), 5.

25 V. Skipp, *Crisis and Development: An Ecological Case Study of the Forest of Arden, 1570–1674* (Cambridge: Cambridge University Press, 1978); see especially 18, 33, 41, 51, 68. For general surveys of conflicts in pastoral and sylvan societies, focusing mainly on the seventeenth century, see Roger B. Manning, *Village Revolts* (Oxford: Clarendon Press, 1988), 255–83; Buchanan Sharp, *In Contempt of All Authority: Rural Artisans and Riot in the West of England, 1586–1660* (Berkeley: University of California Press, 1980); and Andrew Charlesworth, ed., *An Atlas of Rural Protest in Britain 1548–1900* (London: Croom Helm, 1983).

26 Quoted in Joan Thirsk, ed., *The Agrarian History of England and Wales* (Cambridge: Cambridge University Press, 1967), IV: 411.

27 Nigel Nicolson and Alasdair Hawkyard, *The Counties of Britain: A Tudor Atlas by John Speed* (London: Pavilion Books, 1988), 177.

28 Quoted in Manning, *Village Revolts*, 224; see also 220–29.

29 Drayton, *Works*, IV, 276.

30 For a contrary view, see Richard Wilson, "'Like old Robin Hood': *As You Like It* and the Enclosure Riots," *Shakespeare Quarterly* 43 (1992): 1–19. Wilson,

whose article contains much useful information about the social context surrounding the play, argues that "the play is powerfully inflected by narratives of popular resistance"(4) but that its subversive possibilities are contained by a conservative ending. For an illuminating critique of Wilson's argument, and of New Historicist approaches generally, see Andrew Barnaby, "The Political Conscious of Shakespeare's *As You Like It*," *Studies in English Literature* 36 (1996): 373–95. Even Barnaby, whose views I share, finds in the social critique of the play only an endorsement of traditional social ideals. The play's most progressive gestures, I hope to show, are not political but ecological.

31 Henry Howard, Earl of Surrey, *Poems*, ed. Emrys Jones (Oxford: Clarendon Press, 1964), 65, 15. For a brief survey of the literary tradition, see Arthur Sherbo, "Cowper's 'Stricken Deer' and the Literary Tradition," *Bulletin of Research in the Humanities* 85 (1982): 336–340.

32 A. Stuart Daley, "The Idea of Hunting in *As You like It*," *Shakespeare Studies* 21 (1993): 83.

33 The image is reproduced in Matt Cartmill, *A View to a Death in the Morning: Hunting and Nature through History* (Cambridge, Mass.: Harvard University Press, 1993), 81.

34 *The Scythe of Saturn: Shakespeare and Magical Thinking* (Urbana: University of Illinois Press, 1994), 189. I discovered Woodbridge's complementary reading of this episode after formulating my own argument. For an account of the scene against the background of humanist attacks upon hunting, see Claus Uhlig, " 'The Sobbing Deer': *As You Like It*, ii.i.21–66 and the Historical Context," *Renaissance Drama* 3 (1970): 79–109.

35 José Ortega y Gasset, *Meditations on Hunting*, trans. Howard B. Wescott (New York: Charles Scribners, 1972), 102.

36 P. J. Frankis, "The Testament of the Deer in Shakespeare," *Neuphilologische Mitteilungen* 59 (1958): 65–68.

37 Daley, "Idea of Hunting," 88–89.

38 Lodge, *Rosalynde*, 196.

39 Munday, *Huntingdon Plays*, 304–05.

40 William Twiti's directions for the procession homeward are as follows: "Carry the head home before the Lord; and the heart, tail, and gullet should be carried home on a forked branch, and you should blow the menée at the door of the hall" (*The Art of Hunting [1327]*, ed. Broc Danielsson, *Stockholm Studies in English 37* [Stockholm: Almqvist and Wiksell, 1977], 51. For the Horn Dance of Abbots Bromley, in which men dance carrying antlers, see Ronald Hutton, *The Rise and Fall of Merry England: The Ritual Year 1400–1700* (Oxford: Oxford University Press, 1994), 47–48 and Jon Raven, *The Folklore of Staffordshire* (London: B. T. Batsford, 1978), 114–16. The Feast of St. Paul at St. Paul's Cathedral features a procession in which the head of a buck is carried before the cross in procession and then taken outside the West door of the church, where horns blow its death; see John Stow, *A Survey of London*, ed. Charles L. Kingsford, 2 vols. (1603; rpt. Oxford: Clarendon Press, 1971), I: 334–35.

41 Elyot, *Governor*, 67–68.
42 Richard Knowles, "Myth and Type in *As You Like It*," *English Literary History* 33 (1966): 5–6.
43 Michel De Montaigne, *The Essays*, trans. John Florio (1603; facs. rpt. Menston, England: Scolar Press, 1969), 265.
44 Harrison, *Forests*, 26.
45 Montaigne, *Essays*, 249–51. In a later work, "The Hunting of the Hare"(1653), Margaret Cavendish develops a similar critique of hunting; the poem concludes with an attack on the cruelty and arrogance in the hunter's presumption that God made "all *Creatures* for his sake alone . . . to *Tyrannize* upon"(lines 103–06); see *Kissing the Rod: An Anthology of Seventeenth-Century Women's Verse*, ed. Germaine Greer, et al. (London: Virago Press, 1988), 170.
46 See Cartmill, *A View to a Death*, 92–111 and Thomas, *Natural World*, 33–36.

7 POLITICAL HUNTING: PROSPERO AND JAMES I

1 For an illuminating survey of representations of Caliban, see Alden T. Vaughan and Virginia Mason Vaughan, *Shakespeare's Caliban: A Cultural History* (Cambridge: Cambridge University Press, 1991).
2 Desiderius Erasmus, *Chaloner: The Praise of Folie*, ed. Clarence H. Miller, *Early English Text Society* (London: Oxford University Press, 1965), 54.
3 Jean Calvin, *Commentaries on the First Book of Moses Called Genesis*, trans. John King, 2 vols. (Edinburgh: Calvin Translation Society, 1847), I: 317.
4 Sir Philip Sidney, *The Countess of Pembroke's Arcadia (The Old Arcadia)*, ed. Jean Robertson (Oxford: Clarendon Press, 1973), 254–59; Henry Cornelius Agrippa, *Of the Vanitie and Uncertaintie of Artes and Sciences*, ed. Catherine M. Dunn (Northridge: California State University, 1974), 262.
5 Agrippa, *Vanitie*, 262.
6 Ibid., 260.
7 Ibid., 263.
8 Michel De Montaigne, *The Essays*, trans. John Florio (1603; facs. rpt. Menston, England: Scolar Press, 1969), 243; I use Prosser's italics through-out to highlight verbal resemblances. Stephen Orgel follows Prosser in noting the close similarity between the two passages; see his edition of *The Tempest* (Oxford: Clarendon Press, 1987), 189n.27–8.
9 See, for example, Arthur Kirsch, "Montaigne and *The Tempest*," in *Cultural Exchange between European Nations during the Renaissance*, ed. Gunnar Sorelius and Michael Srigley (Uppsala: Uppsala University, 1994), 111–21, and Ben Ross Schneider Jr., "'Are We Being Historical Yet?': Colonialist Interpretations of Shakespeare's *Tempest*," *Shakespeare Studies* 23 (1995): 125–26.
10 Montaigne, *The Essays*, 248.
11 Ibid., 251.
12 Orgel, ed., *The Tempest*, 1–4.

13 For studies that feature the world of the court, see David M. Bergeron, *Shakespeare's Romances and the Royal Family* (Lawrence: University of Kansas Press, 1985), 178–202, Donna B. Hamilton, *Virgil and "The Tempest"* (Columbus: Ohio State University Press, 1990), and Gary Schmidgall, *Shakespeare and the Courtly Aesthetic* (Berkeley: University of California Press, 1981). For studies of treason and colonialism see Curt Breight, "'Treason doth never prosper': *The Tempest* and the Discourse of Treason," *Shakespeare Quarterly* 41 (1990): 1–28, Frances E. Dolan, "The Subordinate('s) Plot: Petty Treason and the Forms of Domestic Rebellion," *Shakespeare Quarterly* 43 (1992): 317–40, Paul Brown, "'This thing of darkness I acknowledge mine': *The Tempest* and the discourse of colonialism," in *Political Shakespeare*, ed. Jonathan Dollimore and Alan Sinfield (Manchester: Manchester University Press, 1994), 48–71, and Meredith Anne Skura, "The Case of Colonialism in *The Tempest*," in *Caliban*, ed. Harold Bloom (New York: Chelsea House, 1992), 221–48; the latter article, which first appeared in *Shakespeare Quarterly* in 1989, contains a useful critique of the vast critical literature devoted to colonialism.

14 I am much indebted to Donna B. Hamilton's thoughtful book, *Virgil and "The Tempest"* (Columbus: Ohio State University Press, 1990), which first drew my attention to this context.

15 Elizabeth Read Foster, ed., *Proceedings in Parliament 1610*, 2 vols. (New Haven: Yale University Press, 1966), I: xv.

16 Quoted in Foster, ed., *Parliament 1610*, vol. I, xx.

17 James I, *The Political Works of James I*, ed. Charles H. McIlwain (Cambridge, Mass.: Harvard University Press, 1918), 307.

18 Foster, ed., *Parliament 1610*, vol. II, 101, 103.

19 For Chamberlain's comments, see Wallace Notestein, *The House of Commons 1604–1610* (New Haven: Yale University Press, 1971), 325.

20 D. Harris Willson, *King James VI and I* (London: Jonathan Cape, 1956), 279.

21 Quoted in Caroline Bingham, *James VI of Scotland* (London: Weidenfeld and Nicolson, 1979), 75–76.

22 Robert Ashton, ed., *James I by his Contemporaries* (London: Hutchinson, 1969), 250.

23 G. P. V. Akrigg, ed., *Letters of King James VI and I* (Berkeley: University of California Press, 1984), 245–49.

24 The letters are quoted in Bergeron, *Shakespeare's Romances*, 39.

25 Ashton, ed., *James I*, 271.

26 Ibid., 232–33; Akrigg dates the letter [July? 1604].

27 Ibid., 294; Akrigg dates the letter [19? October 1607].

28 Ibid., 250; Akrigg dates the letter [Early 1605?].

29 McIlwain, ed., *Political Works of James I*, 307.

30 Ibid., 324.

31 Quoted in Ashton, ed., *James I*, 250.

32 Kirby, "Stuart Game Prerogative," 240.

33 Roger B. Manning, *Hunters and Poachers* (Oxford: Clarendon Press, 1993), 65.

34 Ibid., 208.
35 E. K. Chambers, *The Elizabethan Stage*, 4 vols. (Oxford: Clarendon Press, 1923), II: 53.
36 Annabel Patterson, *Censorship and Interpretation* (Madison: University of Wisconsin Press, 1984); see especially, 3–23.
37 Curt Breight, "Discourse of Treason," 15n.38.
38 Jonathan Bate, "Caliban and Ariel Write Back," *Shakespeare Survey* 48 (1995): 155–62.

8 CONCLUSION: SHAKESPEARE ON THE CULTURE OF THE HUNT

1 D. H. Madden, *The Diary of Master William Silence* (London: Longmans, Green, 1907), ii; Matt Cartmill, *A View to a Death in the Morning: Hunting and Nature through History* (Cambridge, Mass.: Harvard University Press, 1993), 79. Caroline F. E. Spurgeon's study of Shakespeare's imagery of the hunt supports Cartmill's view; see *Shakespeare's Imagery* (Cambridge: Cambridge University Press, 1968), 30–33, 100–05.
2 Robert Greene, *Friar Bacon and Friar Bungay*, ed. Daniel Seltzer (Lincoln: University of Nebraska Press, 1963), I: 3–11.
3 Gervase Markham, *Countrey Contentments* (1615; facs. rpt. Amsterdam: Theatrum Orbis Terrarum, 1973), 7.
4 William Somervile, *The Chase* (London: George Redway, 1896), 6.
5 Ovid, *Metamorphoses*, trans. Mary M. Innes (Baltimore: Penguin Books, 1955), 186–90.
6 David Riggs, *Ben Jonson: A Life* (Cambridge, Mass.: Harvard University Press, 1989), 70.
7 G. A. Wilkes, ed., *The Complete Plays of Ben Jonson*, 4 vols. (Oxford: Clarendon Press, 1981), II: 110, 99, 106.
8 Ibid., vol. I: 185, 312.
9 William B. Hunter, Jr., ed., *The Complete Poetry of Ben Jonson* (Garden City, New York: Anchor Books, 1963), 82. The same point is made of James I in the masque, *The Gypsies Metamorphosed*. The gypsy captain, echoing James's own views as he reads his palm, prophesies that he will love "To hunt the brave stag not so much for the food / As the weal of your body and the health o' your blood"; see Stephen Orgel, ed., *Ben Jonson: The Complete Masques* (New Haven: Yale University Press, 1969), 328.
10 Ibid., 406–08.
11 William Somervile, *The Chase* (London: George Redway, 1896), 2.
12 Spurgeon, *Shakespeare's Imagery*, 101–02.
13 José Ortega y Gasset, *Meditations on Hunting*, trans. Howard B. Wescott (New York: Charles Scribners, 1972), 142.
14 For reproductions of the portraits of Henrietta Maria, see Oliver Millar, *Van Dyck in England* (London: National Portrait Gallery, 1982), 22 (figs. 19 and 20).
15 E. P. Thompson, *Whigs and Hunters: The Origin of the Black Act* (London: Allen Lane, 1975), 56.

Index

Adams, Robert P., 25
Agrippa, Henry Cornelius, 24, 25–26, 27, 196, 216
Allen, Don Cameron, 48
Alpers, Paul, 159
Anderson, J. K., 245 n. 2
Anderson, Linda, 139
As You Like It, 25, 27–28 159–89, 210, 222–23

Barnaby, Andrew, 247 n. 30
Barton, Anne, 99, 138–39, 235 n. 17
Barton, John, 60
Bate, Jonathan, 49, 50, 57, 207
Bath, Michael, 236 n. 26
Bean, John C., 96, 111
Beaver, Dan, 237 n. 34
Berkeley, Henry, 11th Lord, 44, 92–93, 121–32
Berkeley, Katharine, Lady, 31, 122–32
Berkeley, Sir Thomas, 44
Bert, Edmund, 101, 103, 104
Bevington, David, 67
Bible, 26, 51, 61, 68, 97, 104
Blome, Richard, 21–22
boar-hunting, 45–48, 232 n. 20
Boose, Lynda E., 95, 237 n. 2
bow and stable hunting; see park hunting
Breight, Curt, 206
Brown, Paul, 206
Burkert, Walter, 71–72

Calvin, John, 28, 195–96
Camden, William, 168
Campbell, Mildred, 141
Carroll, William C., 61, 244 n. 39
Cartmill, Matt, 15, 28, 48–49, 209
Cavendish, Margaret, Duchess of Newcastle, 27, 248 n. 45
Cecil, Sir Robert, 202–03
Chamberlain, John, 201
Chambers, E. K., 21
charivari, 147–51, 154

Charles I, king of England, 3, 42–43, 204
Charles II, king of England, 3, 43
Chasses de Maximilien, Les, 33, 45, 181, 231 n. 19
Chevy Chase, 135–38
Cockaine, Thomas, 23
Coriolanus, 50, 92, 217–18
Cornish, William, 32
Cummins, John, 45, 228 n. 31
Cymbeline, 47, 219–20

Daley, A. Stuart, 173, 181
deer, 15–18
deer-coursing, 17–18
Devonshire Hunting Tapestries, 32–33
Dolan, Frances E., 110
Dover, Robert, 107
Downame, John, 28
Drayton, Michael, 161, 170–71
Dubrow, Heather, 56, 58
Dürer, Albrecht, 175

Edward, Duke of York, 161–62
Edward VI, king of England, 3
Elizabeth I, queen of England, 3–6, 18, 22–23, 31–33, 52–53, 60–61, 69, 92–93, 181, 214–15
Elizabeth of Bohemia, 51–52, 233 n. 35
Elyot, Sir Thomas, 18, 23–24, 31, 42, 45–47, 53, 160, 182
Erasmus, Desiderius, 24–25, 62, 78–79, 88, 90, 94, 195, 216
Erickson, Peter, 244 n. 45
Evelyn, John, 22

falconry, 97–111
Fineman, Joel, 96
Fletcher, John, 96, 100
Foster, Elizabeth Read, 199–200
fox-hunting, 15–16, 244
Frankis, P. J., 177

Frederick II of Hohenstaufen, 102
Freedman, Barbara, 242 n. 11

Gabriner, P. J., 240 n. 46
Gallenca, C., 244 n. 32
Gascoigne, George, 4, 10–11, 28, 29, 33–34, 45,
    54, 72–75, 90–91, 116–17, 162–63, 175, 181,
    227 n. 9, 230 n. 67, 230 n. 79
Gest of Robyn Hoode, A, 163
Gilbert, Miriam, 60
Girard, René, 88
Greene, Robert, 210–11

Hamilton, Donna B., 206, 249 n. 14
hare-coursing, 53–55
Harrison, Robert Pogue, 187, 245 n. 4
Harrison, William, 15, 30–31, 51, 53, 84, 242 n. 5
Hatto, A. T., 47
Hawkyard, Alasdair, 170
Heilman, Robert, 95
Henry, prince of Wales, 1–3, 24, 45, 73, 226 n.
    1, 233 n. 35
Henry V, 220–21
Henry IV, Part 1, 133–38
Henry IV, Part 2, 134
Henry VI, Part 1, 217–18
Henry VI, Part 2, 217
Henry VI, Part 3, 17–18, 25, 194, 217–18
Henry VIII, king of England, 3, 19
Heywood, Thomas, 107
Hibbard, George R., 238 n. 20, 244 n. 45
History of Titus Andronicus, The, 70–71
Holderness, Graham, 119
hounds (care of), 116–17
Hughes, Ann, 168
Humphreys, Arthur, 236 n. 25
Hunt, Maurice, 234 n. 57
Hunter, George K., 244 n. 45
hunting: topics
    blooding and initiation, 39–48
    humanists, 24–27, 216–17, 219–21
    love, 32–35, 38–39
    Puritans, 22, 28–30, 55, 223–24
    recreation, 21–23, 210–14
    ritual, 71–79, 86–90
    war, 23–25, 91–92, 137–38, 180, 194–95,
        216–21
    women, 31–36, 38–39, 221–23
hunting laws, 9–10, 12–14, 143–44, 160, 203–04

Ingram, Martin, 148

James, Heather, 236 n. 19
James I, king of England, 4, 6, 13, 18–19, 22,
    24–25, 40–41, 42, 47, 53, 90, 143, 191,
    198–208, 215–16, 220
Jewell for Gentrie, A, 76
Jonson, Ben, 11, 14, 214–16, 221–22
Julius Caesar, 25, 70–79, 86–94, 210, 222

Kahn, Coppélia, 119, 231 n. 6
Keach, William, 48, 55, 58
Kegl, Rosemary, 243 n. 30, 244 n. 45
Kehler, Dorothea, 239 n. 34
Kinney, Arthur F., 242 n. 11
Kirby, Chester and Ethyn, 204
Kirschbaum, Leo, 236 n. 27
Knowles, Richard, 186

Laroque, François, 243 n. 32
Lasdun, Susan, 15
Latham, Symon, 101, 106–07, 115
Leland, John, 168
Lewis, C. S., 113
Liebler, Naomi Conn, 235 n. 5
Lodge, Thomas, 167, 172, 180–81
Love's Labor's Lost, 11–12, 15, 18, 22, 23, 34–35,
    59–69, 210, 222–24

Machiavelli, Niccolò, 23
Madden, D. H., x, 14–15, 209
Maguire, Laurie E., 239 n. 23
Manning, Roger B., x, 10, 19–21, 23, 25, 92,
    137, 204, 232 n. 20
Manwood, John, 6, 78, 168, 227 n. 10
Marcus, Leah, 120–21, 242 n. 11
Marienstras, Richard, x, 235 n. 6
Markham, Gervase, 78, 97, 102, 212
Mary I, queen of England, 3
Merry Wives of Windsor, The, 20–21, 25, 35, 66,
    92, 133–58, 210
Midsummer Night's Dream, A, 23, 31, 79, 81, 130,
    210–14
Montaigne, Michel Eyquem de, 24–25, 27,
    54–55, 62, 68, 78, 186–89, 197–98, 208
Montrose, Louis Adrian, 59–60, 66, 233 n. 49,
    246 n. 16
More, Sir Thomas, 24–25, 27, 62, 216
Morris, Brian, 110, 239 n. 30
Munday, Anthony, 164, 182
Murphy, Patrick M., 231 n. 11

Norden, John, 169
Novy, Marianne, 97

Orgel, Stephen, 199
Ortega y Gasset, José, 24, 27, 177, 221
Osborne, Francis, 201, 204

Ovid, 26–27, 41–42, 49–51, 82–84, 187, 196, 213

Paine, Tom, 3
par force hunting
  assembly, 181
  death and dismemberment, 2–3, 73–79, 86–90
  general, 17–18, 72–73
  procession, 74–75, 181–85
park hunting, 15–18, 51–53, 59–61
Parker, Patricia, 63
Patterson, Annabel, 206, 246 n. 16
Phoebus, Gaston, 45
Plato, 229 n. 57
Plutarch, 71
poaching, 19–21, 25, 85, 92–93, 138, 143–44, 153–54, 224–25
Prosser, Eleanor, 197

Ranald, Margaret Loftus, 109–10
Rape of Lucrece, The, 35
Rees, Joan, 147
Roberts, Jeanne Addison, 244 n. 43
Robin Hood, 163–67
Roe, John, 41
Rooney, Anne, 231 n. 7
Roosevelt, Theodore, 18
Russell, Sir Thomas, 130

Saccio, Peter, 95–97
Schoenbaum, S., 20–21
Selwyn, John, 43
Shakespeare, William (biography), 12–15, 20–21, 243 n. 26
Shaw, G. B., 95, 105
Sidney, Sir Philip, 26, 135, 160–61, 196, 219
Skipp, V., 169
Skura, Meredith Anne, 249 n. 13
Slights, Camille Wells, 105–06, 239 n. 29
Smith, Bruce R., 50
Smyth, John, 44–45, 121–22, 240 n. 53
Somervile, William, 213, 216

Speed, John, 15
Spenser, Edmund, 160, 219–20
Spurgeon, Caroline, 15, 216–17
Steadman, John M., 154
Streitberger, W. R., 232 n. 29
Strong, Roy, 32
Stubbes, Philip, 28–29

Taming of the Shrew, The, 23, 35, 59, 95–132, 210, 212, 222
Tempest, The, 27, 29, 190–208, 210
Thiébaux, Marcelle, 232 n. 30
Thomas, Keith, 22, 28, 111, 116
Thompson, Ann, 131, 241 n. 54
Thompson, E. P., 29–30, 149, 224
Titus Andronicus, 20, 21, 23, 25, 31, 35, 70–86, 94, 210, 222–23
Topsell, Edward, 47, 56
Troilus and Cressida, 217
Turbervile, George, 97–98, 104, 227 n. 9
Turner, John, 60
Twelfth Night, 34
Twiti, William, 75, 247 n. 40

Uhlig, Claus, 247 n. 34

van Gennep, Arnold, 72
Venus and Adonis, 35, 38–59, 69, 209–10
Virgil, 82–83, 159–60, 171

Waith, Eugene M. 71
Weiss, Mark, 233 n. 35
White, R. S., 138
White, T. H., 102, 105
William, prince of Wales, 39–40
Wilson, John Dover, 134–35
Wilson, Richard, 246 n. 30
Woodbridge, Linda, 175, 247 n. 34
Woudhuysen, H. R., 241 n. 55
Wrightson, Keith, 141–42, 145
Wriothesley, Henry, 3rd earl of Southampton, 43–44, 49

Xenophon, 24, 47

Printed in the United Kingdom
by Lightning Source UK Ltd.
114292UKS00001B/278